SAGE was founded in 1965 by Sara Miller McCune to support the dissemination of usable knowledge by publishing innovative and high-quality research and teaching content. Today, we publish over 900 journals, including those of more than 400 learned societies, more than 800 new books per year, and a growing range of library products including archives, data, case studies, reports, and video. SAGE remains majority-owned by our founder, and after Sara's lifetime will become owned by a charitable trust that secures our continued independence.

Los Angeles | London | New Delhi | Singapore | Washington DC | Melbourne

Myth of 'FREE MEDIA' and FAKE NEWS in the POST-TRUTH ERA

Thank you for choosing a SAGE product!
If you have any comment, observation or feedback,
I would like to personally hear from you.

Please write to me at **contactceo@sagepub.in**

Vivek Mehra, Managing Director and CEO, SAGE India.

Bulk Sales

SAGE India offers special discounts
for purchase of books in bulk.
We also make available special imprints
and excerpts from our books on demand.

For orders and enquiries, write to us at

Marketing Department
SAGE Publications India Pvt Ltd
B1/I-1, Mohan Cooperative Industrial Area
Mathura Road, Post Bag 7
New Delhi 110044, India

E-mail us at **marketing@sagepub.in**

Subscribe to our mailing list
Write to **marketing@sagepub.in**

This book is also available as an e-book.

Myth of 'FREE MEDIA' and FAKE NEWS in the POST-TRUTH ERA

Kalinga Seneviratne

Los Angeles | London | New Delhi
Singapore | Washington DC | Melbourne

Copyright © Kalinga Seneviratne, 2020

All rights reserved. No part of this book may be reproduced or utilized in any form or by any means, electronic or mechanical, including photocopying, recording or by any information storage or retrieval system, without permission in writing from the publisher.

First published in 2020 by

SAGE Publications India Pvt Ltd
B1/I-1 Mohan Cooperative Industrial Area
Mathura Road, New Delhi 110 044, India
www.sagepub.in

SAGE Publications Inc
2455 Teller Road
Thousand Oaks, California 91320, USA

SAGE Publications Ltd
1 Oliver's Yard, 55 City Road
London EC1Y 1SP, United Kingdom

SAGE Publications Asia-Pacific Pte Ltd
18 Cross Street #10-10/11/12
China Square Central
Singapore 048423

Published by Vivek Mehra for SAGE Publications India Pvt Ltd. Typeset in 10.5/13pt Adobe Caslon Pro by Fidus Design Pvt Ltd, Chandigarh.

Library of Congress Control Number: 2019951352

ISBN: 978-93-532-8674-3 (HB)

SAGE Team: Rajesh Dey, Vandana Gupta, Madhurima Thapa and Rajinder Kaur

Contents

List of Abbreviations	vii
Preface	xi
Acknowledgements	xvii
1 Media Function Theories: Time for a Rethink	1
2 Media in Crisis: Commodification of News	17
3 Did We Ever Have a Truth Era?	49
4 Imbalances in News: Truth Is Subjective	72
5 Dawn of the Post-Truth Era?	106
6 Human Rights: The New Missionary Religion	126
7 Neoliberalism Breeding Inequality: Who Is Telling the Truth?	172
8 Redefining Journalistic Ethics	207
9 Fake News Hysteria: Attempt to Stifle Alternative Views?	223
10 Fighting the Gloom with New Thinking	263
Appendix A: Obama's Final Asian Tour 'Unpivots' US War Crimes in Asia	307
Appendix B: Rounding Up Coca-Colonization: Will the UN Human Rights Council Stand Up for the People?	311
References	314
Index	321
About the Author	326

List of Abbreviations

ABC	Australian Broadcasting Corporation
ACLU	American Civil Liberties Union
ADB	Asian Development Bank
AEC	ASEAN Economic Community
AFP	Agence France Presse
AI	Amnesty International
AJI	Alliance of Independent Journalists Indonesia
AMAN	Indigenous People's Alliance of the Archipelago
AMIC	Asian Media Information and Communication Centre
ANC	African National Congress
ANN	Asia News Network
AP	Associated Press
APEC	Asia-Pacific Economic Cooperation
API	Active pharmaceutical ingredient
ASEAN	Association of Southeast Asian Nations
AU	African Union
AWACS	Airborne Warning and Control System
BIMSTEC	Bay of Bengal Initiative for Multi-Sectoral Technical and Economic Cooperation
BOA	Bank of America
BP	British Petroleum
BRI	Belt and Road Initiative
CBJ	Chequebook journalism
CIA	Central Intelligence Agency
CRI	Commitment to Reducing Inequality
DFID	Department for International Development
EC	Election Commission
EFJ	European Federation of Journalists
EJA	Engaged Journalism Accelerator

ELAM	Latin American Medical School
ETA	Euskadi Ta Askatasuna
EU	European Union
FOE	Freedom of expression
FTA	Free trade agreement
GATT	General Agreement on Tariffs and Trade
GE	General Electric
GFI	Global Financial Integrity
GNH	Gross National Happiness
HRW	Human Rights Watch
IARC	International Agency for Research on Cancer
ICC	International Criminal Court
ICCPR	International Covenant on Civil and Political Rights
ICIJ	International Consortium of Investigative Journalists
IFCN	International Fact-Checking Network
IFJ	International Federation of Journalists
IM	Influencer marketing
IMF	International Monetary Fund
IP	Intellectual property
IPI	International Press Institute
IPS	Inter Press Service
ISDS	Investor-State dispute settlement
ISIL	Islamic State of Iraq and the Levant
ISIS	Islamic State of Iraq and Syria
KEI	Knowledge Ecology International
LDC	Least developed country
LSE	London School of Economics
LTTE	Liberation Tigers of Tamil Eelam
MCR	Mahaweli Community Radio
MEDICC	Medical Education Cooperation with Cuba
MGC	Mekong–Ganga Cooperation
MSF	Medecins Sans Frontières
MSM	Mainstream media
NAFTA	North American Free Trade Agreement
NAM	Non-Aligned Movement
NATO	North Atlantic Treaty Organization
NAVSTAR	Navigation Signal Timing and Ranging

NGO	Non-Governmental organization
NIEO	New International Economic Order
NSA	National Security Agency
NTC	National Transitional Council
NWICO	New World Information and Communication Order
NYT	*New York Times*
OBE	Other business enterprise
OECD	Organisation for Economic Co-operation and Development
OFW	Overseas Filipino worker
PCI	Press Council of India
PCIJ	Philippine Center for Investigative Journalism
PFA	Press Foundation of Asia
PM	Propaganda model
PSTI	Public Service Trust of India
RFA	Radio Free Asia
R2P	Responsibility to Protect
RCEP	Regional Comprehensive Economic Partnership
SAP	Structural Adjustment Programme
SDGs	Sustainable Development Goals
SEAPA	Southeast Asian Press Alliance
SLBC	Sri Lanka Broadcasting Corporation
STAR TV	Satellite Television Asian Region
TNC	Transnational corporation
TWN	Third World Network
TPP	Trans-Pacific Partnership
TRIPS	Trade-Related Aspects of Intellectual Property Rights
UDHR	Universal Declaration of Human Rights
UNCTAD	United Nations Conference on Trade and Development
UNDP	United Nations Development Programme
UNESCAP	United Nations Economic and Social Commission for Asia and the Pacific
UNESCO	United Nations Educational, Scientific and Cultural Organization
UNHRC	United Nations Human Rights Council
USAID	United States Agency for International Development

UTS   University of Technology Sydney
UXO   Unexploded ordnance
WB   World Bank
WEF   World Economic Forum
WHCA   White House Correspondents' Association
WHO   World Health Organization
WMD   Weapons of mass destruction
WSF   World Social Forum
WTO   World Trade Organization
ZANU–PF   Zimbabwe African National Union–Patriotic Front

Preface

When my son Nishan was just eight years old, this was in the early 1990s in Sydney, he brought a video recording his teacher had made during a school excursion to a science centre. The students were asked to sit in a simulated television news studio and read a piece of news. He had put on a jacket and said looking straight into the camera: 'Today in Sri Lanka there was a bomb blast and the army has bashed and killed many people.' Aghast at what he saw as news, both me and my wife Priyani asked: 'How can you say that? You have been to Sri Lanka many times and you haven't seen that there?' He replied, 'The teacher asked me to read news and that is what I did.'

Every evening, both Priyani and I used to watch television news on Channel 9, SBS and ABC, and he used to sit with us and watch it. So he knew, even at that young age, that news was about conflict and violence, but the reality was different. Thus, when President-elect Donald Trump in his first news conference told off a CNN journalist saying 'you are fake news', it reminded me of what Nishan said to us 25 years ago—that news is not about reality.

I can recall interviewing veteran Indian journalist Chakravarti Raghavan in Geneva in the 1980s, when he told me 'exception makes the news'. Few months later when I put this question to Michael Ruepka, the then editor-in-chief of Reuters news agency, he told me: 'No one is interested to know if I went to work safely, but, if you fell under a bus, they will be interested to know how.' News reporting is about exceptional circumstances, not the everyday reality.

At the height of the New World Information and Communication Order (NWICO) debates, UNESCO Radio[1] produced a feature titled

---

[1] Transcript of the programme 'Point of View', no. 19, PI/R/1949, UNESCO Radio, Paris.

'A Plurality of Voices' bringing together viewpoints from Western and non-Western news professionals on the subject of news bias.

Hector Wynter, editor of Jamaica's daily *The Gleaner*, while admitting that the media is criticized in his country for always carrying bad news, defended thus:

> The fact of the matter is that good news is not news. Good news is accepted as, you know, normal. But bad news is the abnormal, at least ought to be, and therefore people get excited by what is abnormal. In other words, that is the news.

Speaking on the same programme, James Halloran, president of the International Association for Mass Communication Research, argued that media does two tasks at the same time—it reflects and conditions public perception. He defended Western media's news values of negativity, conflict and sensationalism with this argument:

> [In] Western societies the products of journalists—their commodities—like others, have to be sold. So the end product is going to be governed in a sense by market or commercial considerations and, over a period of time, not necessarily deliberately or consciously, what is good, what is accepted, what is conventional, comes to be the tenets of the journalistic profession. And, these are governed by market forces. So in a sense it's what sells, that makes what's news, and that's how those values are developed and they will be developed in different ways in different social systems.

This takes me back to 1976 when I was a university student studying engineering in England. I decided to join the British Universities North America Club and obtain a three-month visa to go on a working holiday to the USA. Growing up in Sri Lanka, I have got a rosy picture of the USA. The news we got at the time did not paint the USA in a negative light. So as a young man, I was quite excited to go to the USA for the first time. I expected to see and experience a 'developed' rich country. What I saw on my second day in the USA not only shocked me but also changed my attitude towards the Western media, which still persists.

I was in Chicago and visited the university there and decided to take a shortcut to the railway station close by. I was with a White British student and we walked into a Black ghetto. It was summer, so many people were roaming in the streets. They weren't well dressed, some were dressed in somewhat ragged clothes; they did call me 'brother' and greeted me, but I did not feel comfortable in that environment. The pavements were dirty, buildings were dilapidated, some even with broken glass windows (wonder how they cope with the winter), the walls were brownish or blackened. I immediately started asking myself, 'why I did not know about these communities in the USA before?'

I began to question the reliability of the Western media to give us a balanced picture of the world. It was further exacerbated when I returned to England three months later and elections took place in India, where Prime Minister Indira Gandhi was surprisingly beaten by a large margin and the Congress party lost power for the first time since Independence. As a young man growing up in neighbouring Sri Lanka, I had high regards for Mrs Gandhi as a strong and assertive leader who brought India from the brink of starvation to a self-sufficient country that is among top 10 industrial powers in the world. The BBC reports of her defeat projected her as a 'Third World despot'. I thought it was extremely unfair and lacked clarity. For the next few months, I had a number of heated discussions with fellow British students about the bias of the BBC in reporting about India.

Few years later, when I migrated to Australia to join my family, who had already moved there, I found that the Australian media was reporting Asia as if it is in the backwaters of civilization. Asia was all about poverty, illiteracy, floods, buses falling off cliffs, train crashes in India, corruption and dictators. I grew up in Sri Lanka, which had one of the world's highest human development indexes (this was not a UN development criteria at that time), a model democracy in the world and peace-loving people. If you were to believe the Australian media, countries like Sri Lanka in which I grew up did not exist in Asia.

Though I came to Australia with a degree in engineering and found employment as an engineer there, I was more interested in the media. I thought that I could contribute to the Australian media to have a better picture of its neighbourhood from where increasing numbers of highly qualified professionals were migrating looking for greener pastures. This made me do a graduate diploma course in mass communications at the then NSW Institute of Technology (which later became University of Technology Sydney [UTS]) and get involve in radio broadcasting with the university radio station 2SER-FM. I had been still working as an engineer for seven years to earn a living and when I gave that up to embark on a career in the media, it didn't take me long to realize that the Australian media was a 'White institution' and first-generation migrants like me were not welcomed. In order to enter the system you had to learn to 'communicate to fit in'—in other words, to think and speak like an Anglo-Saxon.

Few years later when I moved to Singapore in search of greener pastures and was teaching mass communications at Ngee Ann Polytechnic and writing regular commentaries on international affairs for *Straits Times*, I used to tell my students that I have more freedom of expression in Singapore than in Australia. Most of my Singapore students did not believe me. Some used to come and ask me privately, 'how come sir, this is an authoritarian government and Australia is a free democracy?' After you read this book, you would find the answer for that.

In August 2018, I attended the first Asian Buddhist Media Conclave in Delhi, where the keynote speaker was Dr S. Gurumurthy, a chartered accounted turned journalist and influencer. 'We are in a world which is driven by conflict', he told the predominantly Buddhist audience. He asked, 'In the context of the media, to which I belong, the media is interested only in hourly news. So in a media which is so conflict driven, how are we going to infuse eternal thought, eternal models, eternal thinking, eternal goals?'

Dr Gurumurthy argued that ideology and philosophy are two different subjects. The former means only, while the latter means also. He noted:

> The idea that I am the only truth, that I only know what the solution is, this applies even to modernity [which is an ideology]. Modernity thinks that it has answers to every issues of the world, whether it is man (and) human, whether it is languages, politics, whether it is economic, living relationship, for everything modernity claims that we see the only solution, any other solution is not even worth having dialogue with. Being part of the media, I have

struggled against it, because to write against an ideology is the worst crime that you can commit in media. Media is a very difficult animal; those who are even the right minded in the media cannot produce right communication, because the ecosystem has been taken over by ideological trolls, including modernity.

With the advent of the social media, the economic model of the media is collapsing all over the so-called 'disruptive world'. Newspapers are going online and publications like London's *Guardian* and America's *Huffington Post*, which have traditionally been local publications, have built substantial audiences globally. Singapore's Channel News Asia is also building a regional audience via its website's text-based news features that are linked to its TV 'podcasts', while Hong Kong's *South China Morning Post* is also expanding outside its base into the Asia-Pacific region via its web presence. If these will help to create a new viable economic model for serious journalism is yet to be seen.

In Europe, a newly formed Engaged Journalism Accelerator (EJA) is trying to innovate a community-engaged journalism culture across Europe. In a study involving five European countries, it found that journalists are struggling to engage with their communities. As one expert has suggested: 'We need to get people in newsrooms to forget for a second about journalism as a public good and think of it like selling tyres.' The survey found that there is no organization in Europe that can help publications on their way to resilience. There is little data from Europe about whether the organizations that focus on community engagement are more sustainable in the long run.

In January 2003, I was part of an Inter Press Service (IPS) reporting team covering the World Social Forum in Porto Alegre in Brazil. Addressing a gathering of over 5,000 people at the local indoor stadium, Ignacio Ramonet, editor of *Le Monde Diplomatique* and communication professor at the Paris University, argued that the media, which has been for a long time the resource of the citizenry to oppose the decisions of the government that would have harmful effects on the people, was no longer playing that role. He pointed out that with the globalization of the international economy, transnational companies have become more powerful than governments and they have taken over the media. He told a gathering of mainly young people from South America, Europe, Africa and Asia:

> Corporation now own and produce not only traditional media but everything which we call culture and communication. These were earlier separated from the media. Now we have fewer differences in what is done in journalism, advertising and mass culture. They are also involved in leisure, pop music, cinema and sports. Key companies like Time Warner, Disney and AOL are key lead actors in globalisation. They have no objective of being the fourth power. They have come together as a power. The fourth power is now exploiting and oppressing the populations [for their own profits]. How can we tackle this power, which has transformed from friends of the citizenry to its enemy? Now we have to find a 'fifth power'.[2]

Few weeks after labelling CNN 'fake news', President Trump went even further in an address to his supporters claiming that the American mainstream media (MSM) is the 'enemy of the people'. It is a phenomenon of our times that a leftist French professor and a rightist American president both believe that the mainstream commercial media is not serving the people.

This is basically the theme of this book, and it has been written more in the style of journalistic writing rather than academic writing, but with referencing that encompasses the world of academia. Though looking at the media from a global context, its Asian focus is designed as a textbook for use in Asia in particular, where there is a dearth of Asian perspectives on communication issues. Most universities in Asia teach mass communication and journalism straight out of textbooks written for American students by mainly American academics.

As the name itself suggests, *Myth of 'Free Media'*, most of the material in this book will be critical of what we often call the 'free media', but that does not mean that I do not believe in a free media. I hope you will enter this book with a mindset of a 'free thinker', where you will not accept liberalism nor conservatism as the gospel truth.

---

[2] Quoted from personal notes of the author, who covered the session for IPS news agency.

Acknowledgements

It has been a long and sometimes arduous journey in changing my career from a professional engineer (in the 1980s) to a journalist. First of all, I must thank my wife Priyani for not objecting to it and in the initial stages facilitating and supporting my transition with valuable intellectual input to pursue my passion. My initial foray into journalism was after I had spent a week in New York with US$25 in the summer of 1976 while studying engineering in the UK. On the suggestion of a friend from Sri Lanka, I put this experience in pen and paper. Then I remembered that my neighbour during my teenage years, Phillip Cooray, was the editor of *The Observer* in Sri Lanka. I posted the copy to him and he published it in the Saturday Youth section of *The Observer* and invited me to write more. During the next few years, while studying and later working as an engineer in Australia, I wrote a number of features on travel, cricket, dating, social issues and even solar power. I would like to pay my gratitude to the late Phillip uncle for planting the seed in my mind that I could have an alternative career to engineering.

My real serious foray into journalism, however, was through community-based university radio 2SER-FM in Sydney, and I should thank station manager John Martin and news director Stafford Sanders for the valuable guidance and support given to me. At the time when I was feeling extremely frustrated with the lack of professional avenue in Australia for first-generation migrants to pursue a career in mainstream journalism, IPS was my lifeline when its Asia-Pacific director Kunda Dixit offered me the position of Australian and South Pacific correspondent. I took it with an evangelical zeal to provide an 'un-Western' perspective on news and Kunda supported me to the hilt, finding funds for me to travel across Australia and to a number of South Pacific countries for reporting assignments. In the 1990s, he also included me in the Terra Viva team covering UN conferences in Cairo, Copenhagen and Istanbul, and WTO conferences in Singapore and Sydney. Kunda was a great inspiration and supporter in developing my international journalism career. Later, his successor Johanna Son also gave me assignments to cover international conferences such as the World Social Forum in Porto Alegre, Commonwealth Summit in Auckland and Non-aligned Summit in Kuala Lumpur. Lately, Ramesh Jaura, director general of IDN-InDepthNews, provided me opportunities to practise international journalism. I wish to thank them all.

I would also like to acknowledge the great support and encouragement given to me to pursue an academic career in journalism and communication field by Professor Andrew Jakubowicz and the late Professor Alan Knight of UTS in Australia by opening the door of the academia for me. I also wish to thank Dr Victor Valbuena, former head of the Film and Media School of Ngee Ann Polytechnic in Singapore, for facilitating my foray into the media academia in Asia. And I also wish to express my gratitude to the late Dr Indrajit Banerjee for giving me the opportunity to work with Asian Media Information and Communication Centre (AMIC) and appointing me as its head of research.

There are many others who, over the past 30 years, have been a great inspiration or encouraged me or supported me in my journalism and academic career. They are too numerous to mention here, but I thank them all. And finally, my thanks to my son Nishan and daughter Amali for the love and support given to me over the years, although at times they were not happy with the father missing from home as he pursued his passion for journalism.

CHAPTER 1

Media Function Theories
Time for a Rethink

At the root of the Western 'free media' model is the Libertarian Media Function Theory that says the media should be the peoples' 'watchdog' of government's abuse of power. This theory forms what is called the *Four Theories of the Press*, which was developed after the Second World War and articulated in 1956 by three American professors of communication: Fred S. Siebert, Theodore Peterson and Wilbur Schramm. This has for more than half a century defined the role of journalism and the media across the world with its all-encompassing media function theories of libertarian, authoritarian, social responsibility and communist models. In this chapter, we will consider the first three models only.

In recent years, the libertarian model has been recommended as an essential prerequisite for good governance and economic development. However, there are also other compelling arguments that challenge this assumption and point out that Asia's economic rise was precipitated by countries—such as China, Singapore, South Korea and Taiwan—that adopted an authoritarian media function model in recruiting the media to promote government policies to the people and guide them in adopting the government's development policies for economic progress. There are some who also point out that the libertarian media function model may hinder development and economic progress since it could create social and political chaos in a country, pointing out to India and the Philippines in the Asian region as such examples.

Libertarian Media Function Model

The major features of the libertarian media function model could be listed as follows:

- There is absolute freedom to media to play the role of a watchdog.
- No censorship of any kind is to be done.
- The government does not own the media and media is a different body in the functioning of the state.
- Media is accountable to the law of the country.
- Media must follow a code of conduct.
- Media encourages pluralist truths like both sides of the same story.
- The theory says people are rational and their rational thoughts lead them to find out what is good and what is bad.

The practicalities of this model could be summarized with the following points:

- People can criticize the government policies and work through social media or any other media such as newspapers, radio and television.
- These opinions cannot be censored unless it is against the rights of an individual.
- A person can file a lawsuit if they are defamed or their privacy is compromised.
- It also prevents the growing effect of corruption by making government as much transparent as possible and keeping people aware of their work.

Thus, the strengths of the libertarian model could be summarized as follows: the media is free to give any information as it likes; there is no censorship by the government; all individuals can express their opinions and thoughts in the media openly without fear and favour; this creates healthy competition in thoughts and ideas that could lead to progress of a society and it encourages checks and balances of the government and helps to reduce or, better, completely eradicate corruption.

The libertarian model also has its weaknesses such as the media will not always act with responsibility; media practitioners may not have good intentions and ethics; people cannot always make rational judgements; peoples' ideas, opinions and judgements can conflict one another; media could misuse its power to harm other peoples' privacy and reputation; it could slander, defame, publish obscenity or cause sedition and also cause national security threats or challenges.

Sevanthi Ninan,[1] founder of India's media watchdog website 'The Hoot', notes that for the libertarian model to function, the media has to have financial independence:

> Independence comes from a viable business model (the media) makes money only if (others) advertise (and) half the problems comes when you have to report on people whom you are dependent for your advertising. If they don't like (what you report) they will pull out advertising. In India there are far too much media. It's ridiculous, there are 800 TV channels—who wants so many? Why are they in existence? (Just) Four or Five TV channels in one language is enough, in some state there are 40 TV channels in the same language ... businessmen everyone owns TV because costs are cheap like Satellite TV. So there is a problem of too much TV, all have viability issue chasing the same advertising and they will all go to the lowest common denominator ... government is not the only one you have to investigate (you need to investigate) business and when you are after their advertising that cannot be done.

At the peak of the 2016 US presidential election primaries, Democratic Party nomination challenge Bernie Sanders gave a very interesting interview to social media channel in the USA called 'Young Turks' in

---

[1] Interview with the author in Delhi, 9 December 2016.

which he pointed out several areas in which there are conflict of interest in the American corporate media:

> We have a corporate media by definition [it] has conflicts of interests ... you have Disney ... paying their workers eight and nine bucks a hour bringing in (cheaper) people from around the world to replace American workers. These are important issues they don't want to discuss. The model for media coverage right now is six second sound bites and an unwillingness to talk about real issues in a serious way. For example climate change. I wrote to presidents of all the TV channels telling them that on their Sunday show they never talk about climate change. Why? Is it got to do with a lot of energy, coal and oil companies running advertising (on their network)? I think it does, they don't talk about it. Income and wealth inequality, they don't talk about it. There needs to be serious discussion on why the middle class is disappearing and people at the top gets all of it. Health care? .... I talk to young people, they don't even know that we are the only rich country with no healthcare insurance for all. They don't know, in Germany, Scandinavia, college is free. Media is not telling them. So media is an arm of the ruling class of this country and they want to talk about everything in the world except the most important issues. If the people get educated on the real issues you know what happens next? They may actually want to bring about change.[2]

Authoritarian Media Function Model

The authoritarian media function model is the opposite of the libertarian model and some of its common features are as follows:

- Media must respect what authorities want and work according to the wishes of the authorities, although not under direct control of the state or ruling classes.
- The press and media cannot work independently and their works are subjected to censorship (by the state).

---

[2] https://www.youtube.com/watch?v=v4EP0PZIsfA (accessed on 28 May 2019).

- The state directs the citizenry which is not considered competent enough to make critical political decisions.

The authoritarian model is seen as a theory used by dictatorial regimes to stifle freedom of speech, but its application can also be seen in democratic nations. Often the media cannot offend or go against the majority or dominant groups. In an authoritarian media model, many forms of information are not available to the media, in some countries not even national economic statistics. It is believed that if state information is distributed, it might put state security at risk and pose a national threat. Democratic governments also use this approach as the only option in these types of conditions, especially when fighting terrorist groups—military or other national security-related information would not be available to the media. To put it simply, in an authoritarian model, the government believes that the role of the media is to support the government to implement its policies and not to criticize it and create social disharmony.

In an authoritarian media model, it is the media licencing regime that is the most powerful tool in controlling the media, especially where media outlets have to apply for annual licencing to continue to publish. Lately, a new tool has entered this arena—using the tax regime to close down troublesome media. In September 2017, *The Cambodia Daily* owned by an American for 24 years was forced to close down when the government's tax authorities slapped a US$6.3 million unpaid tax bill. *The Cambodia Daily* has been accused of biased reporting by the pro-China Cambodian government.

The authoritarian model, however, has its advantages too, especially for countries that are in a nation-building process. It could keep social and cultural conflicts in check, motivate the people to work for the country and the people; it can prevent the media from acting irresponsibly and creating social, economic or political chaos in the country.

After the 9/11 attacks and the subsequent 'war on terror', even in countries where a libertarian model has functioned for a long time, concerns of national security and safety from terrorism has seen certain authoritarian model functions creeping into the way the news media functions.

There has been a rush to adopt anti-terror laws in the aftermath of 9/11, and this has undermined respect for human rights and the rule of law. One worrying aspect of these laws has been the general extension of surveillance powers over citizens, and their personal communications. We are particularly concerned about the shift of power to police and security agencies to monitor and intrude upon the professional activities of journalists and media, which seriously impede their ability to report on matters of public interest. (Seneviratne and Hwee 2011: 1)

The foregoing statement was issued by 40 representatives from the media, legal and civil rights organizations that met in a forum on anti-terror legislation and its impact on freedom of expression (FOE) and information in preparation for the 1st Council of Europe Conference of Ministers responsible for media and new communication services that took place in Reykjavik, Iceland, in May 2009.

McChesney (1997) argues that even in the USA, there is an authoritarian media function model that has developed because of the corporate domination of the media industry and particularly the news production. 'What is tragic—or absurd—is that the dominant perception of the "free press" still regards the government as the sole possible foe of freedom', he says. 'This notion of press freedom has been and is aggressively promoted by the giant media corporations should be no surprise'. McChesney points out that if the government demands that newspapers and broadcast media should cut staff by half, foreign bureaus be closed and news tailored to suit government interests, there will be an outcry, 'yet, when corporate America aggressively pursues the exactly same policies, scarcely a murmur of dissent can be detected in the political culture'. This has dramatically shifted the balance of power to the public relations industry 'that tries to fill the news media with coverage sympathetic to its clients', he argues.

Social Responsibility Media Function Model

Social Responsibility Theory of media function is a relatively new concept that was developed in the mid-20th century and is used mostly by non-Western countries. The model was designed formally in 1956 when *Four Theories of the Press* was presented. It encourages total freedom to the press and no censorship, but it should be regulated according to social responsibilities.

> Freedom of expression under the social responsibility theory is not an absolute right, as under pure libertarian theory. One's right to free expression must be balanced against the private rights of others and against vital society interest. (Siebert, Peterson and Schramm 1956)[3]

The origin of this theory goes back to the Hutchins Commission—whose official name was the Commission on Freedom of the Press—that was formed during the Second World War—headed by Robert Hutchins, president of the University of Chicago. The Commission was established in response to criticism from the public over media ownership. It inquired into the proper function of the media in a modern democracy.

After deliberating for four years, the Commission came to the conclusion in 1947 that the press plays an important role in the development and stability of modern society and, as such, it is imperative that a commitment of social responsibility be imposed on mass media. Social Responsibility Theory was born at a time when large and powerful publishers were unpopular with the public, and when the public had a high degree of suspicions about the motivations and objectives of the press.

Thus, what the social responsibility model of media function does is to argue that unfettered freedom is not real freedom, in that FOE is a moral right that comes with certain aspects of duty (to the society). Thus, the theory differs from the libertarian theory on the nature of the right.

Thus, under the Social Responsibility Theory, one's right to free expression must be balanced against the private rights of others and against vital social interests. The Social Responsibility Theory of mass

---

[3] https://www.businesstopia.net/mass-communication/social-responsibility-theory (accessed on 28 May 2019).

media changed the way press published news from objective reporting to interpretative reporting. Before this theory, facts were presented without any interpretation. The audience interpreted it the way they wanted to and this caused problems as interpretation was not based on reality and it affected the social order. In the Social Responsibility Theory, the media is taken to be for the people and society. The media must be responsible towards the society.

This came into stark reckoning in the aftermath of the 2011 'Arab Spring' uprising, where unfettered freedom was exercised by Arab youth. Many of them were trained by Western-funded media training programmes that promoted the libertarian media model with social media as the tool to practise it. They were made to believe that such tools could assist them to circumvent the authoritative media models that were in existence in the Arab world. They did that thinking they were exercising their freedom of speech—which they did—but it led to widespread social and political chaos right across the Middle East.

Ibrahim Saleh,[4] communications expert from Egypt's Nile University, argues that the term Arab Spring is misleading and it will be more correct to say the 'Arab Autumn' because of the chaos it has led into. 'Media was a tool and initiator but was not the major player (in the uprising)', he argues. 'People who are frustrated, upset come to no return and they felt many things have to change; they couldn't wait any longer. Here came the media to give a face to the agony'.

Saleh says that training was given to Arab youth by outsiders, but he has many misgivings about it. He asks, 'Are you training to give skills or competencies or are you brain washing?' He believes that giving voice to the voiceless or a voice to interest groups are two different propositions. If one is desperate to get their voice heard, they may use social media to highlight their issues, hoping to solve their problems. But the problem is if they are trying to serve the needs of certain political groups or ideologies. This is the question that needs to be asked. Saleh argues:

---

[4] Personal interview with the author recorded in Kuala Lumpur, November 2016.

I'm not going to talk about intentions but intentions can be great. But ABC of reporting is looking at things objectively and reporting with facts what is happening, balancing as much as you can. It cannot be I'm always seeing negative things and reporting what coincide with my agenda. And this is what alternative or NGO media is about...problem is it is making us more and more polarized on this or other side and that should not be the aim of alternative journalism. This kind of citizen journalism, journalists who are supposed to be empowered, who can use new technology to (help) those who does not have a voice...you think you are giving a voice to the voiceless but most of the time you are giving a voice to serve certain interests.

Chapters 5–7 will be explaining this point.

Libertarian and Cultural Freedom Model

The media function theories we have discussed in this chapter are pegged to mainly individual human rights—the right to communicate—but it is political in nature. It does not adequately cover the communication problems that members of migrant communities face, especially those from post-colonial countries that have migrated to 'First World' nations, nor does it address the urban bias of the national media in most Asian countries that keep the voices of the rural populations out of the national media. These problems arise from institutionalized cultural barriers in the media. The same principles would apply to the global media that practise cultural values in interpretation of news that are mainly from a Christian cultural perspective.

In this section, we will look at the cultural authoritarian media structures within countries that hinder access to the media for rural populations, minority members as well as minority voices. For example, when I was working in Australia, the Australian Broadcasting Corporation (ABC) told me a number of times that my radio productions did not fit into their 'style and standards' for broadcast. Though they never spelt it out for me, it was clear that what they meant was that I did not have an 'Australian' accent and my perspective did not fit into the Anglo-Saxon narrative. They deemed it biased, and thus I could not get my programmes broadcast on the network, which also had a bearing on my ability to earn a living.

In the mid-1990s, at the same time I was fighting my battles in Australia. I went to Sri Lanka to research on Mahaweli Community Radio (MCR) there for my master's thesis looking at community radio as a human right. This radio is the third tier of the government-owned Sri Lanka Broadcasting Corporation (SLBC) radio network. It broadcasts to a rural rice farming population living in a 50-km radius from Girandurukotte in north-central Sri Lanka. There I met local volunteer broadcaster, Kalyani Menike, daughter of a local rice farmer and a high school graduate. She asked me to listen to some programmes she had produced in Sinhalese and broadcast on the MCR. I was greatly impressed with the quality of the programmes and asked her if the SLBC national network broadcast these. The programmes were not political, and it covered nutrition, animal welfare and farming topics. She said she has offered these to them, and producers in Colombo have said that her presentation style does not fit into their 'professional' broadcasting framework. Basically, she was given the same excuse the ABC gave me about the 'style and standard'. In her case, she belonged to the majority Sinhala-Buddhist community, and the producers making that decision were also presumably from the same community. Her problem was that her rural Sinhala accent and presentation style was not deemed as 'professional' by the urban producers, who were broadcasting to the nation.

In the 1980s and the 1990s, for over 15 years, I was broadcasting on Sydney's university community radio station 2SER-FM and my listeners were mainly Anglo-Australians, and according to the station my weekly broadcasts—done on a volunteer basis—were very popular. I was one of the first 'ethnic' journalists—if not the first—on that radio station to be given a weekly slot to broadcast in English, programmes that covered international affairs, multiculturalism and the arts.

In 1987, I received a UN Media Peace Award from the UN Association of Australia, beating a number of nominations from ABC Radio. In fact, in the citation they said that my programmes, which the ABC had told me were not up to its 'style and standard', gave a 'refreshingly new perspective on international affairs'. The series for which I received the award was broadcast on the Australian community radio network (in over 15 stations including 2SER-FM)—after the ABC rejected it for broadcast—and it looked at the relationship between the rich and poor countries or what is called the 'North' and the 'South'. Using a grant from the Ministry of Foreign Affairs to mark the 'International Year of Peace', I had travelled to London, Paris, Geneva and Rome to interview Third World[5] experts who were working for international agencies. Among others, I conducted interviews with the then Secretary General of the Commonwealth, Shridath Ramphal, the Head of the United Nations Conference on Trade and Development (UNCTAD) and Sri Lankan economist Gamani Corea. To get the Western voices, I also interviewed senior officials at United Nations Educational, Scientific and Cultural Organization (UNESCO) and Organisation for Economic Co-operation and Development (OECD) in Brussels. I used a formula where the 'Two-Thirds World' voices were used first and the 'First World' voices followed, usually responding to the views of the Two-Thirds World experts. The ABC uses a reverse method, often not even having a Two-Thirds World expert voice. That is why they found my radio documentaries not up to their 'style and standard', and they also had another problem in that my accent as the presenter/narrator did not fit into their view of being 'professional'. However, they did not have a problem in broadcasting interview grabs of a diversity of people who did not have Anglo-Saxon accent.

In 1993, I received another award for my community radio broadcasting, the Educational Award from the Community Broadcasting Association of Australia for services to the community radio sector in Australia. But, a few years later, I had to move to Asia in search of greener pastures to pursue my media career. I have often been asked by Asians why I moved to Asia to pursue a media career. That is because they think Australia is an open society with a 'free media'. In fact, I have had more freedom in Asia to express my views in the media

---

[5] I will be using the term 'Two-Thirds World' rather than 'Third World' hereafter in this book, as the 'Third World' Western media refers to is composed of over two-thirds of the world's population.

and I often wonder with regard to the cultural censorship I faced in Australia, what model of media function theory Australia belongs to—should we invent a new model to facilitate countries that have large ethnic migrant groups whose voices are marginalized? The media function theories focus on political censorship by governments but are inadequate in analysing the Australian media model that practises a cultural censorship model.

The freedom—which Asians think existed in Australia—is a façade. In the 1980s and the 1990s, it largely existed in the so-called 'ethnic media' where you could broadcast for a limited time per week in your own language to your own ethnic community. But what I wanted was to broadcast in English to the wider Australian community. At the time, with Australia trying to open up to neighbouring Asia to tap into new economic opportunities opening up in the region, I thought with my intimate knowledge of Asian society and my Asian cultural roots, I could contribute to that push. At that time, Australian media was reporting about Asia as if Asia was in the backwaters of civilization and it is the European races that 'civilized' the world and we must be thankful for it. That was of course based on ignorance of Asian history, philosophy, culture and Asia's great contributions to humanity for centuries before the Europeans colonized the region using two Chinese inventions—gunpowder and the compass. I thought I can help to fill that vacuum in Australia, but the Anglo-Saxons who control the Australian media did not see it that way.

Fast forward 20 years, in July 2017, when Australia's Race Discrimination Commissioner Tim Soutphommasane said that there were too many Anglo-Saxon people in the media and they controlled, he faced a barrage of attacks both from within the media and outside, some claiming that he was attempting to 'reopen ideological cultural wars' (Balogh 2017). 'A lack of diversity in leadership and in the media could conceivably lead to a perception of what it is to be "Australian" that does not reflect our multicultural character', the Commissioner had told a Senate inquiry examining ways to strengthen multiculturalism by creating ethnically diverse employment targets for corporate Australia.

Soutphommasane, who was born in France to Laotian parents who fled Laos at the end of the Indo-China war and migrated to Australia as a child, was even asked by one Murdoch-owned Sky TV anchor to 'hop on a plane and go back to Laos'. Balogh's article in *The Australian*, another Murdoch-owned media outlet, garnered over 400 comments, most of them critical of Soutphommasane and some openly hostile. For example, one reader complained:

> The trouble with multiculturalism is that most of us don't want it ... but to say so labels you as racist. I don't want a messy mélange of cultures or festering ethnic enclaves of dysfunction and disadvantage ... these things breed animosity and mistrust. I want to remain a single culture, with the same cultural ideals, aims and laws.

Another asked: 'Too many Anglo-Celts running Australia? That's like saying there are too many Japanese people running Japan or too many Arabs running Saudi Arabia'. Many complained that the Commissioner is able to get away with his criticism of Australian society, but if they criticize multiculturalism they are labelled 'racist' and they attribute it to leftist ideology.

Today, such views are also reflected in the US and many European media discourses that oppose the integration of refugees from Two-Thirds World countries into their society. Often it is argued that such integration will undermine or dilute the Christian identity of these societies. Husband (1994) argues that citizenship and ethnicity are 'problematically related' when it comes to the construction of national agendas in contemporary nation-states. Thus, in contemporary multi-ethnic European societies, this by itself challenges the old construction of citizenship within countries. 'The "glorious past" has to be resituated in relation to contemporary political realities', he argues pointing out that the 'other' in European discourse that defined the European as 'superior' had to be renegotiated because the 'geographically distant and culturally exotic' labour no longer play that role. 'In the postcolonial later part of the 20th century such self-serving strategies are no longer so easily sustained'.

While we examine the Western societies' media function model vis-à-vis its minorities, it is also interesting to compare it with Eastern societies such as India, Singapore, Malaysia and Sri Lanka. In all these countries, the diverse ethnic communities are served by media that broadcast in their own languages. It is really ethnic broadcasting rather than multicultural broadcasting. When it comes to national language broadcasting, there is another barrier that comes up, the urban–rural divide, which I pointed out earlier with an example from MCR.

In India, the issue of caste plays a similar role to the issue of race in Australia. In December 2016, I met Jeyarani, lifestyle editor of a popular newspaper in Tamil Nadu, who is a Dalit.[6] When interviewing her, what I was listening to reminded me of my experience in Australia trying to build a career as a professional journalist. She explained many battles she had to fight with fellow women journalists, who were her editors, to get her stories published; often she was asked to stick to cooking and fashion stories and not to touch political or human rights issues. She told me one such story that ended very tragically.

> I did a story on Oorapakkam Panchayat[7] leader Maneka—she is a Dalit Panchayat president. She came up with a lot of stories of how she was treated by panchayat, not allowed to take independent decisions, not able to sit in chairs in the office allocated for the president. She complained to police many times that she was threatened by people but no action by police. She was murdered in 2001 after police did not take any actions on the complaints. After the murder I was very upset. This paper was not giving me the right to write the facts. After coming back to Chennai I spoke to the editor of an investigative magazine published by the same group and he agreed to publish Menaka's interview. After all, it was her last interview before being murdered. It had news value now. When I said (to my editor) I did the story on her earlier and they did not publish; now she's killed. The editor said stick to cooking, fashions.[8]

Jeyarani says that she is still writing on fashion, food and travel.

[6] Dalits, formerly known as 'Untouchables', are members of the lowest social status group in the Hindu caste system.
[7] Panchayat—meaning assembly of five—is the oldest system of local government in India. Some argue it is the oldest system of democracy in the world.
[8] Personal interview with the author recorded in Chennai on 5 December 2016.

I have worked for many reputed news agencies. I have challenged, repeatedly, the reality of women and Dalits. The fact is, because they don't publish (thus) people can't understand what is going on in society. People wait for sensation to happen and then report on caste discrimination. But once the sensation dies there is no reporting.

She says, now as the editor of a lifestyle magazine, she can write on Dalit issues occasionally, but not to the extent she does in alternative Dalit media.

Jeyarani argues that the mainstream media (MSM) is not for the poor, not for the oppressed. It has carved its kingdom out of loyalty to the powers, to bureaucracy, to domination. She points out that about 70 to 80 per cent of the top positions are occupied by dominant caste men. 'Dalits don't even constitute 1 per cent when it comes to deciding power in the country's media', she claims.

According to the libertarian theory, a journalist was to be a voice for the voiceless, especially to challenge abuse of power by the ruling class. But 'if and when a Dalit journalist writes on Dalit issues or even speaks about it, their colleagues call it caste affinity or caste pride', Jeyarani says.

A journalist Ajaz Ashraf has done research on Dalit journalists for media watchdog website 'The Hoot'. He has found that a lot of Dalit journalists quit jobs that neither offer them security nor development and they look for government jobs that give them economic security but not professional pride.

'When Ajaz was doing this research, he got in touch with me. I was then with a lifestyle magazine as its editor. Something he refused to believe', Jeyarani recalls.

> He kept asking me how can a Dalit journalist be an editor of a lifestyle magazine. ... For me it was easy to become an editor of a lifestyle magazine. But despite my fieldwork of 15 years as a socio-political journalist, I can't think of becoming an editor for a socio-political news magazine or paper. I don't see that happening.[9]

---

[9] See Jeyrani's article, available at https://thewire.in/media/caste-bias-mainstream-media (accessed on 28 May 2019).

Interestingly, this was exactly the situation I was in, in Australia. Thus, a Dalit journalist in India and a migrant journalist in Australia face the same barriers.

What media function model we need to place this in? We should have a new theory called the 'cultural authoritarian media function model'.

CHAPTER 2

Media in Crisis
Commodification of News

After paying some half a billion dollars in 1993 to take control of Asia's first satellite broadcasting venture, Satellite Television Asian Region (Star TV), based in Hong Kong with a mainland 'footprint', News Corporation's Chairman Rupert Murdoch presented himself as the great White Knight, a man of conscience, who will help to bring freedom to long repressed people of Asia.

Three months after acquiring Star TV, Murdoch delivered in London the celebrated speech, which suggested his satellites would soon eliminate totalitarian regimes throughout the world.

> Advances in the technology of communications have proved an unambiguous threat to totalitarian regimes: Fax machines enable dissidents to bypass state-controlled print media; direct-dial telephone makes it difficult for a state to control interpersonal voice communication; and satellite broadcasting makes it possible for information-hungry residents of many closed societies to bypass state-controlled television channels.[1]

---

[1] https://www.theguardian.com/media/2003/aug/24/chinathemedia.rupertmurdoch (accessed on 28 May 2019).

It positioned Western media values and its technology as liberators of Asia, just four decades after Asia liberated itself from repressive European colonial rule. Star TV was the new frontier, and the rulers in Beijing were quick to sense the challenge it posed to them. It did not take them long to act. Chinese government almost immediately banned the sale of satellite dishes in the mainland, a device Murdoch would be dependent on for taking Star TV to Chinese homes.

As Jack Shafer (2008) notes in reviewing the book *Rupert's Adventures in China* by his former close associate Bruce Dover, Murdock quickly set about to allay the fears of the Chinese. Just a few months after his London speech, when he found out that the Chinese were not happy with the way BBC reported their affairs, he quickly took the BBC off their North Asian beam. In 1995, his publishing arm HarperCollins even bought the rights to publish a biography of the then Chinese leader Deng Xiaoping written by Deng's youngest daughter, and in 1998 he scrapped an agreement to publish the memoirs of Hong Kong's last British Governor Chris Patten since it was deemed offensive to the Chinese regime. Also, in 1996, he underwrote the website development of Chinese Communist Party's official mouthpiece *People's Daily*. Dover has said in his book, according to Shafer, that he and Murdoch plotted to nullify the effects of the London speech in order to penetrate the Chinese market for which he invested over US$2 billion.

Kahn (2007) of *New York Times* (*NYT*), in a comprehensive analysis of Murdoch's dealings with the Chinese government over a decade, pointed out how Murdoch and News Corporation were willing to go as far as assisting the Chinese government-owned media to get its point of view across to the world in return for business deals by cultivating personal relationships with people closely connected to the Chinese regime. But, as Bruce Dover, a former China manager for Murdoch's business interests, told Kahn: 'Our thinking was that we would show off our technology and they would contract News Corporation to do the same for them (but) their thinking was "We want this for ourselves" (and) it ended being more of a giveaway.'

American Media 'Enemy of the People'

Fast forward to 16 February 2017, President Donald Trump—whose rise to power was hugely aided by Murdoch's Fox News channel in the USA—giving his first solo press conference at the White House said:

> Unfortunately, much of the media in Washington DC along with New York, Los Angeles, speaks not for the people, but for the special interests and for those profiting off a very, very broken system. The press has become so dishonest that if we don't talk about it, we are doing a tremendous disservice to the American people.[2]

In an extraordinary outburst, President Trump tweeted on 18 February 2017[3] that the nation's news media is the 'enemy of the American people'. He said: 'The FAKE NEWS media (failing @nytimes, @NBCNews, @ABC, @CBC, @CNN) is not my enemy, it is the enemy of the American people'.

President Trump, in fact, started tweeting about the 'Fake News' American MSM even before his inauguration on 20 January 2017. Christopher Rosen of the Entertainment news site listed over 70 tweets the president transmitted between 20 December 2016 and 24 July 2017 that used the word 'fake news'.[4]

In the tweets, he accused the media of a 'total political witch-hunt' with regard to Russian interference in the elections and argued that 'crooked opponents try to belittle our victory with FAKE NEWS' (11 January 2017). He called upon someone to buy the 'FAKE NEWS and failing @nytimes and either run it correctly or let it fold with dignity' (29 January 2017). On 8 February, he listed 16 'fake news' stories the media had run since he won the presidency and on

---

[2] https://www.youtube.com/watch?v=SYRYHsnNvf4 (accessed on 28 May 2019).

[3] https://twitter.com/realDonaldTrump/status/832708293516632065?ref_src =twsrc%5Etfw%7Ctwcamp%5Etweetembed%7Ctwterm%5E832708293516632 065&ref_url=https%3A%2F%2Few.com%2Ftv%2F2017%2F06%2F27%2Fdon ald-trump-fake-news-twitter%2F (accessed on 28 May 2019).

[4] https://ew.com/tv/2017/06/27/donald-trump-fake-news-twitter/ (accessed on 28 May 2019).

10 February, he accused *NYT* of telling lies about his relationship with the Chinese leader Xi Jinping. He also accused the 'Fake News' media of being driven by conspiracy theories and blind hatred (of him). In another tweet, he told the American people: 'Don't believe the main stream (fake news) media. The White House is running VERY WELL. I inherited a MESS and am in the process of fixing it' (18 February 2017).

He basically labelled the American MSM (except Fox News) as the 'opposition party'. Trump's criticism could be contrived as reflecting the 'watchdog' role of the media in a libertarian media system. Yet, as we will discuss later, that may be far from the truth.

As *NYT* commented, 'the language that Mr Trump deployed is more typically used by leaders to refer to hostile foreign governments or subversive organizations. It also echoed the language of autocrats who seek to minimize dissent'. But as it notes, Trump and his top advisers strongly believe that an elitist news media lost its credibility by failing to anticipate his political rise and Trump's tactic of pitting the press against the public was mirrored in a survey distributed by the president's team the day before his comments, which urged Trump supporters 'to do your part to fight back against the media's attacks and deceptions' (Grynbaum 2017).

An American president may call the media in his own country the 'enemy of the people', while the media would defend itself claiming to represent the peoples' interests against a president with authoritative tendencies. The question, however, is how far could the media go in claiming to represent the peoples' interest? When information is becoming a commodity and the public service role of the media is usurped by business interests, does the media really subscribe to the 'watchdog' principles enshrined in the Libertarian Media Function Theory that underpins the 'free media' ideology of the West?

'Davos Class' Lying to the People

Naomi Klein (2017) argues in her book *No Is Not Enough* that for the past eight decades, large-scale shocks to societies have been exploited by politicians and corporations, when the media creates a disoriented population. It has created the space for expanding the power of private wealth over the political system. This should also bring into the question the tenets of the Libertarian Media Function Theory where the private media is given the role to be the watchdog to protect the population from the abuse of power by the powerful. In such a system, are we being told the truth about the function of our economies?

> The divide between the Davos class and everyone else have been widening since the 1980s. But for a lot of people, the breaking point came in 2008 financial crisis.
> After forcing decades of grinding austerity on people, Treasury secretaries and finance ministers and chancellors of the exchequer suddenly found trillions of dollars to rescue the banks; people witnessed their governments printing vast sums of money. They had given up so much—pensions, wages, descent schools—when in fact, contrary to what Margaret Thatcher claimed, there were alternatives. All of a sudden it turned out that governments can do all kinds of things to interfere in the market, and have seemingly unlimited resources with which to help you out, if only you are rich enough. At that moment, everyone on earth found out that they have been lied to.
> The implications of this unmasking are still reverberating. The anger that is roiling electorates, on both the right and left side of the political spectrum, is not only about what's been lost. It's also about the injustices of it all, knowing that the wrenching losses of our era are not being shared, that the Davos class were never really looking after those at the bottom of the mountain. (Klein 2017: 119)

To examine that, we need to first understand the principles and application of neoliberal economics that have greatly influenced media development across the world in the past three decades.

Neoliberalism and the Media

Neoliberalism has its origins in the 1980s with the rise of right-wing politics in the West, particularly with the economic policies promoted by the regimes of Ronald Reagan in the USA and Margaret Thatcher in Britain. It laid emphasis on economic growth spearheaded by free-market economics.

As Encyclopaedia Britannica[5] describes:

> neoliberalism is often characterized in terms of its belief in sustained economic growth as the means to achieve human progress, its confidence in free markets as the most-efficient allocation of resources, its emphasis on minimal state intervention in economic and social affairs, and its commitment to the freedom of trade and capital.

These philosophies were also reflected in the wave of media liberalism and globalization of media in the 1990s and the 2000s that led to the commercialization of the media and the undermining of the public service role of the media.

With corporations that benefit from neoliberalization owning much of what we call the MSM today, the Libertarian Media Function Theory that underpins the 'free media' model has come into question in the very countries that have been espousing it. What constitutes a 'free media', and if the commercialized Western media epitomize it, has become a debatable issue.

As pointed out in the Preface, French Professor Ignacio Ramonet argued in an address to the World Social Forum (WSF) in 2003 that the media, which was for a long time has been the resource of the citizenry to oppose the decisions of the government that would have harmful effects on the people, was no longer playing that role, and we need to invent a 'Fifth Estate' now.

It is a search for such a fifth power that is the focus of this book, where we explore the 'myth of the free media' theories.

Commercialization and the Truth

The Pew Research Center's Journalism Project[6] after spending three years talking to journalists in America came up with nine points that defines journalism, and the top three points emphasized that

---

[5] https://www.britannica.com/topic/neoliberalism (accessed on 28 May 2019).
[6] http://www.journalism.org (accessed on 28 May 2019).

journalism's first obligation is to the truth, its first loyalty is to the citizen and its essence is a discipline of verification. It is worthwhile asking the question in this context whether reporting the news of exception, though the truth of the event is verified, is really being loyal to the citizen.

When I sat down to write this book in late 2016, the USA was in the midst of an acrimonious presidential campaign. Often I wondered if the wide coverage the Republican candidate Donald Trump was getting in the media was because of its entertainment value rather than its news quality. What provided me the most entertainment in this whole saga of observing the coverage of the 2016 US Presidential campaign and the aftermath was when President-elect Trump during his first press conference shouted down a CNN journalist while he was shouting a question back at him. It was sheer entertainment. But it was also providing some news value because an incoming US president was accusing its MSM of fabricating news.

Perhaps he may have a point here. While the coverage given to Trump during his campaign focused almost exclusively on his rhetoric that sounded racist and xenophobic, there was hardly any serious coverage about why people in their thousands were flocking to his rallies. What is driving them to support him? Is it just pure racism and fear? What the mainstream commercial media largely missed out was the damage neo-liberal economics have done to grass-roots communities across the USA and their supposedly racist or xenophobic fear had much to do with it.

The media campaign against President Trump that followed his election victory reminded me about an editorial in the *South* magazine of February 1984 (a copy of which I still hold) written by its editor, London-based Pakistani journalist Altaf Gauhar. He wrote this in response to the campaign unleashed against UNESCO and its then Director General Amadou-Mahtar M'Bow from Senegal, after the UN body called for a New World Information and Communication Order (NWICO) accusing the Anglo-American Western media of misrepresenting two-thirds of the world—what was then called the 'Third World'. He wrote:

> The power of the press attains awesome heights when it acts in unison, particularly in defense of some perceived threats to its own

interest. A campaign is unleashed and a mighty roar goes up, drowning every note of dissent. Prejudice turns into judgment and suspicion into conviction while facts and evidence are swept aside by the volubility of the media. (Gauhar 1984: 9)

In 1984, M'Bow was the villain for consistently implying that the Western media reporting of Africa and Asia in particular was basically disinformation ('fake news' had not come into the media discourse then) designed to distract attention from the unjust global economic system that favour the West. Fast forward to 2017 and it is interesting that such a campaign was launched by the American media against its own president, whose grass-roots supporters were unfavourable or even hostile to corporate interests.

Later in this book, we will be discussing about fake news, alternative facts, bias and disinformation in news. The communication theories that we have examined in Chapter 1 have been used in training journalists for the past 50 years and we may need to question whether some of it is still relevant. At a time when some American universities are renaming mass communication departments as strategic communication departments, it is the time we question the very nature of news and the role it plays in the overall context of mass (or strategic) communications.

Media in Crisis in the World's Biggest Democracy

In the world biggest democracy India, media has been a powerhouse for generations, but it is yet to develop a socially responsible model. Some argue that in recent years with the proliferation of commercial television and economic liberalization, the country has taken a backward step in terms of acting as the fourth estate.[7]

Magazine editor and communication lecturer Milind Kokje argues that the problem is that two of the other three estates are corrupt

---

[7] The four pillars on which a nation stands are known as the four estates—the legislature, the armed forces, the judiciary and the media.

(except judiciary) and personality cults have developed around institutions like parliament with the 'Modi wave' that brought Prime Minister Narendra Modi to power in 2014 (a good example). This has also extended to the media.

> Our generation failed to understand the changes that is taking place in the media. We didn't keep basic ideologies intact (and) we allowed management to take control and force change upon us ... if you take the younger generation ... I teach at colleges—90 per cent of students come to study only because of the celebrity (status) the anchors have got. They are fascinated by that (but) they don't realize the work that you have to put and also they don't do any reading ... they don't know a lot of things but they get into the profession and companies want this type of people ... some of them come because of good faces. When that happens there is no resistance everybody is accepting what the management is doing (and the) new generation is not resisting this.[8]

This is also a trend that I have noted in young undergraduates I have been teaching in Singapore and Thailand in recent years. I have been alarmed by their lack of knowledge, especially of the history, culture, philosophy and the socio-economic conditions of their own societies. Their knowledge seems to come from what they access now more and more via their mobile phones to which they are addicted. Even during lectures, they cannot resist the temptation to go online. It's a real worrying preposition that we are letting them go into the media (with a degree) without the proper skills to act as socially responsible communicators (journalists).

Beginning in the 1990s, Kokje says that there has been a basic change in the Indian media houses, in that they have become corporate houses more interested in their market share and profit share, and this has undermined the important role the editorial department used to play. 'When I joined journalism in 1980, editors were strong', he recalls.

---

[8] Personal interview of Milind Kokje with the author in Mumbai, 8 December 2016.

Post-1990s editors power slowly started diminishing. Now it has come to a level people don't know the editor (and) many editors today do not write. They are the production managers more than the editors. They are not known for their intellectual or ideological capacities but they are paid very heavily ... like CEOs.

Veteran Singaporean journalist and newspaper editor B. N. Balji[9] believes that it is a tough task today for independent media to be established, because newspaper editors have to be CEOs at the same time.

For independent media to be established you need philanthropy journalism. Identify people who are willing to spend money because they think this is good for the future of the country. And let the journalist handle the job ... in America businessmen invest in papers through Trusts. Profits in media business is declining everywhere, very few makes profits, journalists have to think business ... they have to think like businessmen.

The Straits Times group for which Balji used to work for over 30 years is beginning to do exactly that he says. Journalists have created a new unit to go out and get revenue for the newspaper, which never happened 10 or 15 years ago. When he was appointed as the founding editor of a new daily, a free circulation tabloid called *Today*, he was also appointed as the CEO of the newspaper's publishing business. Balji explained,

Which mean I was responsible for the business. I had to go out and get the revenue. I had to talk to advertisers and sometimes shape stories not sacrificing the journalism ideals to do stories. It creates a conducive environment for advertising and we succeeded.

When asked if the media has to be a business, how can you create a watchdog? Balji argues:

If you just play the watchdog role don't worry about the business. Then how are you going to pay the journalist? How are you going to survive? I don't say there is no fourth estate there is a model somewhere in between. You can play the role you are expected to

[9] Interview with the author in Singapore, 14 January 2017.

play ... in different countries there are different ways to do it (but) let make it a business first and once you are entrenched in society you can do journalism.

With television news becoming more popular with multiple news bulletins late at night, the role of the newspapers as news providers has changed. Thus, Kokje notes that newspaper reporting has become more interpretation of news. He argues:

> Every TV watcher gets the news by 10.30 at night so why should he read the news next morning? So interpretative analytical news were allowed on a large scale. It looked very attractive to have this kind of news ... but it also gives rise to corruption. As an individual reporter I can take money from somebody and while interpreting the news I will put it in such a way that will favour the person who has given me the money ... you can't blame me because that is my interpretation if you like it or not.

Aidan White, director of the Ethical Journalism Network, laments the fact that the traditional market for fact-based journalism has collapsed because of the draining of advertising revenue to digital markets. This has led to dramatic falls in funding of journalism that would serve the social responsibility role of the media. While the traditional press is still vibrant in the Middle East and Asia, he believes that the level of corruption within the media has increased around the world due to shortage of funds in the industry.

'The notion of journalism as a cornerstone of democracy is weakened these days because it is no longer able to provide the scope and intensity of public interest information people need at all levels in society', argues White (George 2014: 7). 'In all countries less money is spent on investigative journalism. Less money is spent on training. Less money is spent on people who work in journalism.'

'Watchdog' to 'Manufacturing Consent'

> Everyone knows that authoritarian regimes, regardless of their ideology, use the mass media for propaganda. But, what about democratically elected regimes in the 'free world'? Today, thanks

> to Noam Chomsky and his fellow media analysts, it is almost axiomatic for thousands, possibly millions, of us that public opinion in 'free market' democracies is manufactured just like any other mass market product—soap, switches or sliced bread. We know that while, legally and constitutionally, speech may be free, the space in which that freedom can be exercised has been snatched from us and auctioned to the highest bidder. (Roy 2004: 43–44)

As pointed out by Indian novelist and Booker Prize-winner Arundhati Roy, we live in an age of 'manufactured' public opinion. Noam Chomsky has been credited with having coined the term 'manufacturing of consent' and for almost three decades he has been passionately arguing that the so-called 'free media' is nothing but a factory churning out a 'manufactured' product called 'freedom' that does not match the meaning of the word.

Though his theory seems as much valid to most of the rest of the world's media like it is to that of the USA, this theory is hardly known to many mass communication students around the world because it is rarely included in American communication textbooks that are also used in universities across the globe. Perhaps it is because 'manufacturing consent' theory challenges the very roots of Libertarian Media Function Theory that underpins the 'free media' model. Mass communication teachers have been drilling the latter into young peoples' minds as the yardstick of 'freedom'. So how does manufacturing of consent occur in a 'free media' model?

In a 1996 documentary 'Riding the Storm: How to Tell Lies and Win Wars', British journalist Maggie O'Kane[10] documented how multinational PR company Hill and Knowlton was hired by the Kuwaiti government for a fee of US$11 million to create stories for television to persuade Congress to vote for President George W. Bush to go to war against Iraq.

One defining example of this propaganda (PR) campaign was how they created the 'dead baby story', coaching Nayirah, the daughter of

---

[10] http://www.worldcat.org/title/riding-the-storm-how-to-tell-lies-and-win-wars/oclc/221846217 (accessed on 4 June 2019).

Kuwaiti ambassador in Washington, to pose as a nurse in front of cameras in 'evidence' given to a Congress hearing at Capitol Hill claiming that she was a nurse at a children's hospital in Kuwait when Iraqi soldiers invaded and pulled the babies out of incubators and left them to die. She cried during the presentation to Congress, and TV cameras even showed her father, the Kuwaiti ambassador, wiping away tears while listening to it. It was later revealed that she never worked at the hospital and had lived in the USA with her father. Hill and Knowlton coached her to tell a lie for the TV cameras, which broadcast the hearing via satellite, without investigating and fact-checking.

When O'Kane asked a Hill and Knowlton executive, who coached her, if what they did was unethical, he said: 'It is always difficult to get the public support heavily behind a commitment to go to war, the administration has made the commitment and it was our job to help the American public (understand) the advantages to it (going to war)'. When he was pressed on, he added, 'if we erred I would definitely apologize to anyone I mislead, but I hope they will understand that it was very unintentional misleading'.

So 'unintentional misleading' has provided the American television networks and President George W. Bush the necessary media package to transmit to the American people and 'manufacture consent' for America to go to war against Iraq. It was instrumental in convincing a few wavering Congressmen to vote for Bush to go to war and he got his war against Saddam Hussein in 1991.

In 1932, American journalist Walter Lippmann warned us about manufacturing consent in his book *Public Opinion*. As a journalist, Lippmann suggested that the 'news' and the 'truth' are not synonymous. The news, according to him, functions as a way of signifying how an event happened. In this sense, the subjective interpretation of the writer is a factor (see Chapter 4). The truth, he argued, could be in concealed facts.

While the *Four Theories of the Press* (Siebert et al. 1956, cited in Nordenstreng 1997) has for more than half a century defined the role of journalism and the media across the world, US academics Noam Chomsky, Robert McChesney and Edward Herman have been arguing—for over two decades—that the 'fourth estate' model of the media is dead and what we have is a propaganda model (PM) that is 'manufacturing consent' for whoever owns the media to serve their economic and political interests. Thus, lately, with the MSM across the world becoming excessively commercial, the PM and manufacturing consent of the news media theories have been gathering traction. They argue:

> It is much more difficult to see a propaganda system at work where the media are private and formal censorship is absent. This is especially true where the media actively compete, periodically attack and expose corporate and governmental malfeasance, and aggressively portray themselves as spokesmen for free speech and the general community interest. What is not evident (and remains undiscussed in the media) is the limited nature of such critiques, as well as the huge inequality in command of resources, and its effect both on access to a private media system and on its behaviour and performance.[11]

In the introduction to their book *Manufacturing Consent: The Political Economy of the Mass Media*, Herman and Chomsky (1988) explain how this PM functions.

> Structural factors are those such as ownership and control, dependence on other major funding sources (notably, advertisers), and mutual interests and relationships between the media and those who make the news and have the power to define it and explain what it means. The propaganda model also incorporates other closely related factors such as the ability to complain about the media's treatment of news (that is, produce 'flak'), to provide 'experts' to confirm the official slant on the news, and to fix the basic principles and ideologies that are taken for granted by media personnel and the elite, but are often resisted by the general population. In our view, the same underlying power sources that own the media and fund them as advertisers, that serve as primary definers of the news, and that produce flak and proper-thinking

---

[11] http://www.thirdworldtraveler.com/Herman%20/Manufac_Consent_Prop_Model.html (accessed on 4 June 2019).

experts, also, play a key role in fixing basic principles and the dominant ideologies.

What Herman and Chomsky (1988) did was revisiting Lippman's theory and applying it to the multitude of media we have today, which is supposed to give us freedom of choice, but they argued it only massage us into political apathy. Herman (2003) argued that what they did was to take Lippman's argument forward and look at structural factors of the mass media to study how the media 'depends heavily and uncritically on elite information sources and participate in propaganda campaigns helpful to elite interests'.

The filters that are used work mainly by the independent action of many individuals and organizations; and these frequently, but not always, have a common view of issues and similar interests. In short, the PM describes a decentralized and non-conspiratorial market system of control and processing, although at times the government or one or more private actors may take initiatives and mobilize coordinated elite handling of an issue. Propaganda campaigns can occur only when they are consistent with the interests of those controlling and managing the filters (Herman, 2003).

Propaganda Model and News Filters

Propaganda is to democracy what violence is to a dictatorship.
—Noam Chomsky (1991)

The PM, which sought to explain the behaviour of the mass media in the USA, was developed by Edward Herman and Noam Chomsky with their book *Manufacturing Consent: The Political Economy of the Mass Media* published in 1988.

The essential ingredient of the PM is a set of news 'filters' that fall under the following categories:

- the size, concentrated ownership, owner wealth and profit orientation of the dominant mass media firms;
- advertising as the primary income source of the mass media;

- the reliance of the media on information provided by government, business and 'experts', funded and approved by these primary sources and agents of power;
- 'flak' as a means of disciplining the media; and
- 'anti-communism' as a national religion and control mechanism.

Herman and Chomsky argue that these elements interact with and reinforce one another. The raw material of news must pass through successive filters, leaving only the cleansed residue fit to print. They fix the premises of discourse and interpretation, and the definition of what is newsworthy in the first place, and they explain the basis and operations of what amount to propaganda campaigns.

Since the communist filter is problematic in an era where communist governments have adopted a market economy, we will look at only the other four filters.

Ownership Filter

> Media is free in the sense that you can talk about the president who is not doing well, or criticise any government official, if that government official is not related to or does not own the commercial media. You are free to say anything, except against the owners or controllers of media enterprises who are protected. It happens that there is always a link between politicians and business people—Louie Tabing, founder Tambuli Community Radio, Philippines.[12]

When media ownership gets concentrated, so also does its power. The Herman–Chomsky PM concentrates on the media industry where there are relatively few, large companies that dominate many of the news channels. Even with the advent of the Internet, the control is gradually being regained, for example, through ownership of key hubs and influencing control-oriented legislation.

---

[12] Interview with the author in Manila, October 2004.

Every year, the US-based Freedom House publishes a global media freedom map[13] and report. In it, it gives every country a colour—green for 'free', yellow for 'partly free' and purple for 'not free'. The green countries include mainly North America, Europe and Australia. But in most of these countries, the media ownership is heavily concentrated in a few powerful corporations or individuals. By applying a filter of mainly government control, it creates a flawed map of what constitutes a 'free media'.

As media watchdog 'FAIR'[14] points out, the US military–industrial complex extends to much of corporate media with NBC as a classic example. In the 1991 Gulf War, NBC's owner General Electric (GE) designed, manufactured or supplied parts or maintenance for nearly every major weapon system used by the USA during the Gulf War—including the Patriot and Tomahawk Cruise missiles, the Stealth bomber, the B-52 bomber, the AWACS (Airborne Warning and Control System) plane and the NAVSTAR (Navigation Signal Timing and Ranging) spy satellite system. 'When correspondents and paid consultants on NBC television praised the performance of US weapons, they were extolling equipment made by GE, the corporation that pays their salaries', points out Norman Solomon, an associate of FAIR. 'During just one year, 1989, General Electric had received close to USD two billion in military contracts related to systems that ended up being utilized for the Gulf War.'

Thus, one would ask if the 'smart bombs' we saw on television news footage during the war taken from 'high-tech' cameras installed on the bombs were actually advertisements for GE targeted at policymakers and defence ministers worldwide. Also, we should question the 'free media' tag of such mainstream Anglo-American media that was slanting news without fact-checking to assist the USA and its allies to go to war (Box 2.1).

---

[13] https://freedomhouse.org/report-types/freedom-press (accessed on 4 June 2019).
[14] http://fair.org/extra/the-military-industrial-media-complex/7/?issue_area_id=6 (accessed on 4 June 2019).

> **Box 2.1: When Arms Manufacturers Sponsor the News**
>
> Over two decades ago, just after the first Gulf War, Herman and McChesney (1997) through their book and accompanying research at Wisconsin University exposed that many of the American global media networks that provided news on the Gulf War to global audiences had as its major shareholders the largest arms manufacturers in the world—GE and Westinghouse—and thus their news reports about 'smart bombs' hitting 'precision targets' in Iraq shown through video cameras installed on the bombs which show no images of human casualties on the ground were nothing more than advertisements for these products for war masquerading as news.
>
> In April 2018, after the USA, UK and France fired missiles at Syria using news reports from Western media sources alleging chemical attacks by Assad's forces on civilians, RT channel transmitted a report that pointed out major arms manufacturers and oil companies' funding of 'think tanks' that provide the sources and 'expert' opinion for such news stories.[15] Meanwhile, Global Research, a Canada-based organization providing alternative perspectives to global audiences via the Internet, alleged in an article that the British Prime Minister Theresa May's husband Philip May is a senior executive of Capital Group, an investment firm which buys shares in all sorts of companies across the globe—including thousands of shares in the world's biggest defence firm, Lockheed Martin, whose share price went up after it was revealed that missiles used by UK to bomb Syria on 14 April 2018 were new cruise missiles produced by Lockheed Martin.[16]

The conflict between media ownership and conflicts of interests cannot be starker than what happened in Sydney on 10 October 1999, when Ian Heads, one of Australia's most respected sports journalists who has worked in newspapers for 36 years, resigned as sports editor of Rupert Murdoch-owned News Corporation's *Daily Telegraph* when a story he wrote about an impending mass protest against the closure

---

[15] https://www.rt.com/usa/424414-why-think-tanks-lobby-war/ (accessed on 4 June 2019).

[16] https://www.globalresearch.ca/disgusting-conflict-of-interest-theresa-mays-husbands-investment-firm-made-a-financial-killing-from-the-bombing-of-syria/5636632 (accessed on 4 June 2019).

of a rugby club which is also owned by the Murdoch clan was not published by the newspaper.

News Corporation was developing a major national rugby league, which was to be a money-spinner for the tycoon's business empire, and the working class-supported South Sydney Rabbitohs—one of the oldest rugby clubs in Australia—was not going to be part of it. The day the newspaper article was to appear, over 40,000 people demonstrated in Sydney on a Sunday evening against the closure of the club and Murdoch's business empire. It was front-page news in most of Sydney's newspapers and on TV and radio channels across Australia, but Australia's largest circulation newspaper *Daily Telegraph* completely ignored it, though this was perhaps the biggest protest march seen in Sydney since the Vietnam War protest days. 'When the right to know rubs up against the commercial stakes of a mogul, you know which cause will win the day', said Richard Ackland, presenter of ABC TV's 'Media Watch' programme soon after.[17]

Advertising Filter

The business model developed for the news media can be either a subscription model or an advertising one. Many newspapers and magazines use a combination model, with both a cover price and advertising that helps to reduce the price to consumers. However, when advertising is a key source of funds, all will be viewed with regard to what advertising revenues may be gained from them. This then leads to caution on the part of editors and media managers not to rock the boat by airing issues that may upset their major advertisers (who will not be shy in withdrawing their funds if they feel they are being slighted in any way). Further, advertisers may deliberately support items which offer biased views that help them and which mislead the reading/viewing public.

The PM theory argues that:

- Advertisers acquired a de facto licensing authority since, without their support, media ceased to be economically viable.

[17] http://davidleser.com/wp-content/uploads/2016/03/skinned.pdf (accessed on 4 June 2019).

- Advertiser's choice influences media prosperity and survival.
- Mass media are interested in attracting audiences with buying power, not audiences per se—it is affluent audiences that spark advertiser interest.
- It discriminates against political ideas which oppose capitalism.
- Large corporate advertisers on television will rarely sponsor programmes that engage in serious criticisms of corporate activities, such as the problem of environmental degradation, the workings of the military–industrial complex or corporate support of and benefits from authoritarian regimes.

Childhood obesity has become a global epidemic as children are increasingly becoming overweight and less physically active, and media use has been identified as a major contributory factor, such as time spent watching television, playing video games and using a computer. But what about the role the news media could play in making both children and parents aware about the bad diets they are getting hooked onto because of the proliferation of fast-food chains globally that promote a high fat diet assisted by media advertising? With the global fast-food industry, a major advertiser in the media, can we expect a commercially driven media to be partners in confronting this health threat?

Use of 'cheap' labour or even child labour in the international supply chain for global supermarket chains or fashion labels is an issue that comes up in the media, often in non-commercial media and social media, but the practice continues unabated. In 2012, when the Dhaka garment factory fire occurred and a journalist found global fashion labels among the ruins of the burnt-out factory that created an international news story, it was hardly followed up by global news networks questioning the ethics and morality of fashion labels that charge huge prices for their products at the supply end but basically use 'slave labour' to stitch them working in unhealthy and unsafe factory buildings half way across the world.

Advertising lever could also be used by governments to control independent newspapers that are critical of the government or are trying to ferment political or social problems. There are many examples of such government actions from around the world. For example, in

October 2016, chief minister of the South Indian state of Kerala told the legislative assembly that a local Malayali language daily *Thejas*, run by a Muslim management, has been denied government ads because its stories and editorials 'encourage extremism, promote religious hatred and destroy communal harmony'. The newspaper denied the charges and claimed they are victimized because the paper's funding agency is a trust linked to an opposition party.[18]

Sourcing Filter

When news stories appear, where do they come from? With relatively few key sources for news, this also becomes a filter point. Smaller (and even larger) news organizations often source their news items from what is available via easy channels rather than sending reporters out on every street. The pressure to publish at minimum cost also means that very little time is spent in checking out how true these stories are.

It is very much in the interests of those in power to control the news. Companies and governments have large marketing and PR departments, which create press releases that news organizations accept with little challenge. Organizations may also offer experts for interview who of course will support their employers' or sponsors' goals. This is where the PR machines and journalism come into interplay. Thus, the source filter could be summarized as the mass media being drawn into a symbiotic relationship with powerful sources of information by economic necessity and reciprocity of interest, as the media needs a steady, reliable flow of the raw material of news. Government and corporate sources arrange news conferences—they also have the great merit of being recognizable and credible by their status and prestige. Corporations have large budgets for 'public information' and many of the jobs available for mass communication graduates are in these 'PR' units.

For journalists, the most important asset is your sources. News media could be controlled with two contrasting strategies by manipulating your

---

[18] http://www.thehoot.org/mediawatch/regionalmedia/nogovtadsforextremistkeralapaper9762 (accessed on 4 June 2019).

sources. Governments, businesses, non-governmental organizations (NGOs), religious groups and you name it, anyone would try to provide their point of view to influence a news story; at the same time, these very same people could deny you information, refuse to speak to you or deny you access to news sources to control what you could report.

News media itself could be influenced by the type of sources you use, and whom you think are credible and who are not. Often business or economic reporters see economic 'experts', government officials or business leaders as credible sources for your story and not union officers, market or street vendors or small business owners. Thus, your stories will be biased towards big business and will not reflect the daily struggle of the 'informal' sector to make a living. You may quote a mayor or a government official about why the streets of Bangkok need to be cleared up of street food vendors because pavements are there for pedestrians and Bangkok should reflect the image of a modern city. But if you speak to the street vendors, they would tell you a story of their daily struggle with corrupt officers, police or whoever to make a meagre living to feed their families.

Flak Filter

Sometimes information does leak out that those in power do not like. Protecting one's sources is an important element of journalistic ethics. There was a saying in journalism some time ago that if you use some information leaked to you, especially from a government official, you say that the documents 'fell off a truck' and in a Libertarian Media model that was usually acceptable. Today, documents are supposed to come to you via hackers. But the flak filter says that these defences are no longer possible. 'Flak' refers to negative responses to a media news report or programme.

Corporate lawyers have become a number one flak filter for the media, who threaten and perhaps sue those who 'defame' their clients, even to the point of causing financial ruin or imprisonment. In some countries, like Indonesia, a defamation conviction is a criminal conviction. Journalists have been campaigning for it to be lifted for a while.

After President Suharto was overthrown by a people's revolt in 1998, media in Indonesia was relieved of many government controls, but when the media started to expose corruption of its business tycoons, they found that there was a limit to the new-found freedom. The flak factor came in and it could have a devastating effect.

> The step taken for those who feel grieved by the reports was court, so at the beginning there were a lot of libel and defamation even though we have the press law and the freedom of expression. There is a clause in criminal code that makes libel and deformation a crime. So this is how they got to us with libel and defamation, which is difficult to prove or defend because this is a characterization. This is something that we have to grapple with, it could be a big drain on a publication's finances. Defamation is the tool that is used by every one and the penalties are harsh. If the judge finds out against you, then you have to pay a lot of money or it is a lot of money when the media concerned has to publish an apology for a whole page. For example, businessmen or any politician usually who is grieved by your reporting would demand like 'I demand an one page apology for seven days'. You can easily imagine what this does to our business. (Yuli Ismartono, Editor, *Tempo English*)[19]

There are also many other forms of flak, such as phone calls and other methods of buying off, wearing down or punishing those who would oppose or otherwise create a nuisance. Today, journalists could also be killed by some religious fanatics, who feel defamed (or offended), and criminal syndicates are also well known to threaten or even kill journalists.

Public Relations Journalism

McChesney (1997: 15) observed that the emergence of professional journalism was quickly followed by the establishment of public relations as an industry 'whose primary function was to generate favourable coverage in the press without public awareness of its activities'. Public

---

[19] Interview with the author, June 2010.

relations journalism is well funded and attracts many of the brightest mass communication graduates today.

With funds drying up for investigative reporting, the power in the information age is now shifting to the public relations industry with ever-increasing intensity. The Reuters Institute in a study (Llyod and Toogood 2015) on the relationship between journalism and public relations (PR) found that there is a diminution of public relations' dependence on journalism, and the growth of journalism's dependence on PR. While PR still needs journalism, which has always acted as a 'third-party endorsement' of its claims, but now it has other, often more powerful allies.

> Public relations and journalism have had a difficult relationship for over a century, characterized by mutual dependence and—often—mutual distrust. In recent years, developments in corporate PR, and in political communications means that the news media outlets are less and less important to the persuaders. The communications business is often able to bypass the gatekeepers. The internet, especially the social media, has made reputations more precarious—but it has also given companies, governments and public figures channels of communication of their own. The need to proclaim and protect the brand—personal, corporate or political—means that public relations is now a top-table profession ... whilst journalism struggles for survival.[20]

In their report, Reuters Institute argues that a large new area has opened up for public relations in protecting and burnishing the reputation of companies, institutions and individuals. Though always part of PR, reputation is now seen to be more fragile, more open to attack, especially on social media. New techniques of guarding reputation on the Internet have been developed, with corporations taking part in the debates that concern them, including issues in the political and social spheres.

---

[20] http://reutersinstitute.politics.ox.ac.uk/our-research/journalism-and-pr (accessed on 4 June 2019).

As I'm about to finish this book, I got a job advertisement via my LinkedIn account (see box on the right). These are the jobs commonly available, especially for new journalism/mass communication students these days. A journalist is today more a PR person than an 'independent' reporter trying to protect the citizen from abuse of power by the powerful, including governments. They are supposed to work with 'corporate and technology clients' in crafting storytelling for different media and communication platforms to 'create, manage and execute' marketing and/or communication campaigns for their clients. Thus, if you come to learn journalism or mass communication in order to make a lot of money, this may be the training you need to have. What Noam Chomsky theorizes as 'manufacturing consent' and this is what 'watchdog' journalism has ended up with—as a 'propaganda lapdog'.

> **Job Advertisement**
>
> You will be working collaboratively with your teammates to create, manage and execute marketing and/or communications campaigns for our corporate and technology clients.
> Duties include but not limited to:
>
> - *Storytelling* through content development: Content management of all types of material including executive Q&As, key messages, media support documents, web contents, etc.
> - *Campaign support:* Collaborate in a team to execute on multichannel and integrated marketing communications campaigns.
> - *Media relations:* Responsible for all components from start to finish—identifying the story/news angle creating the release, pitching to local/regional/international media and bloggers, complete management of executive interview/media briefings, etc.
> - *Social media:* Operations including content development and editorial calendar planning and scheduling to drive fan base growth, engagement and awareness of brand.

The Libertarian Media Function Theory of the 'free media' model which is the subject of this book says that there is absolute freedom to media, where it plays the role of a watchdog. So there should be no censorship of any kind, because the theory says people are rational and

> **About Us**
>
> Established in June 2012, we serve as a hub for strategy, content and marketing communications. Our client portfolio covers diverse areas including personal and enterprise technology, hospitality, travel and retail.
>
> We believe that marketing and communications can be used as a catalyst and lever to help brands and their audiences to connect in a positive relationship.
>
> Our team has both local and international experience in communications, targeting and influencing a brand's audience such as end customers, traditional media, social media and trade channels.

their rational thoughts lead them to find out what is good and what is bad.

The box on the left is part of the introduction to the company, which is an Asian company. The same skills their new recruit is supposed to have are to 'cover diverse areas including personal and enterprise technology, hospitality, travel and retail' and to synergize marketing and communication as a 'catalyst and lever to help brands and their audiences connect in a positive relationship' is also what would be discussed in Chapter 10 as human-centric mindful journalism. But instead of brands and clients, this is talking of people and communities. The challenge is that the companies that are recruiting these new graduates have the funds to employ them and guide them to achieve what they want. But communities and public service media need funds. How to fund the latter media should also be part of the communication teaching curriculum and subject of discussion in academic forums.

In 1997, McChesney warned about how such PR blitz on journalism by big business mounting sophisticated multi-million dollar PR campaigns would obfuscate issues, confuse the public and weaken any opposition to the activities of these powerful corporations. At that time, large transnational corporations (TNCs) were almost unanimous and aggressive in their support of 'free trade' such as the General Agreement on Tariffs and Trade (GATT) and North American Free Trade Agreement (NAFTA) deals. But there wasn't the same unanimous support in the business community for affordable health care with the insurance industry having an enormous stake in maintaining control of the health sector.

Today, one could argue that journalism has failed in exposing the injustices and inhumanities of the activities of the global pharmaceutical industry in resisting efforts to make life-saving drugs affordable to everyone and also the obesity epidemic around the world fuelled by unhealthy diets for children promoted by powerful global food chains using media platforms.

Hobsbawm (2003) argued that, however, much the 'members of the fourth estate' hate PR, without it they will not survive in today's entertainment-driven world. Pointing out that conservative estimates have shown that 75 per cent of entertainment stories and 50–80 per cent of business stories emanate from public relations, 'it is understandable that journalists resent their dependence on us'.

For the journalist who has to cover a story in half an hour (and often in less time than that), the communications expert can be a lifeline for facts and figures and basic information-gathering, argues Hobsbawm (2003). 'Yes, publicists brief people but briefings are based, in the vast majority of cases, on facts alone and reflect the often stringent regulatory frameworks of the profession involved', she notes. 'The reality is that the balance of information has shifted, from being news-based to being entertainment or opinion-based. Journalists need PR not just to give information, but also to provide access to sexy spokespeople to fill columns, host programmes and give soundbites'.

This umbilical cord between journalism and PR is reflected in the way royal families brand themselves in an age that this institution is largely seen as ceremonial and waste of public funds. Reuters Institute report highlighted how the British royal family manages its PR campaign to garner public support for the succession, indicating the changing role of journalism and PR campaigns in the 21st century. The British royal family has been a central element for public relations in the UK for much of the present monarch's reign, and this is likely to become more crucial for her successor. The way Prince Harry and Meghan Markle's marriage was reported hiding her Black mother is a classic example of the palace PR machine influencing the media. 'I suspect she will be strongly advised by royal advisers to avoid discussing her ethnicity', Ellis Cashmore, a British sociologist and cultural critic, told *Newsweek* (Gill 2017) when the royal wedding was announced.

That is what happened and the British media faithfully followed almost en masse.

'The media sophistication of Britain's royal family is a barometer of how clients for all types of reputation management are now changing their approach to media-engagement', argue Lloyd and Toogood (2015). 'Reputations are no longer won or lost in a daily dialogue between PR agents and their media counterparts.'

In Thailand, when the 70-year reign of the revered King Bhumibol Adulyadej ended with his death at the age of 89 in October 2016, the Royal Palace faced a formidable task in public relations to make his successor Prince Maha Vajiralongkorn acceptable and respected by the Thai people, because for a long time he has had a bad image in the minds of the people in the kingdom. Many have much love and respect for his sister Princess Maha Chakri Sirindhorn, who is unmarried and in her 60s. She is unable to take the throne due to constitutional restrictions on succession. Repressive laws that carry long jail terms for those criticizing the royal family are designed to protect the reputation of the monarchy. But, in the social media age, these measures by itself are not enough and it could backfire on the institution. Most Thais see the continuity of the monarchy as crucial to the protection of Buddhism in the country at a time when it is facing many threats from within and outside. Thus, the palace PR machine would need to use this fact to brand the monarch as the protector of the precious Thai Buddhist identity. Thais are a proud race as it is the only Asian country not to have been colonized by European powers. Like in Britain, media and the palace PR machine would need to work collaboratively in coming years to protect the institution of the monarchy.

Creating a Propaganda Blitz

Since the fall of the Berlin Wall, we have lived in a time when state-corporate interests have cooperated to produce propaganda blitzes intended to raise public support for the demonization and destruction of establishment enemies. And since the 'war on terror' started after the 9/11 attacks, this model has expanded beyond Western democracies to many countries around the world.

Britain's media watchdog Media Lens in 2016 examined[21] the process of how an effective propaganda blitz is crafted to demonize the enemy before attacking them. One may call it propaganda and yet others will say it is public relations.

Dramatic New Evidence

A propaganda blitz is often launched on the back of 'dramatic new evidence' signifying that an establishment enemy should be viewed as uniquely despicable and targeted with 'action'.

The Blair government's infamous September 2002 dossier on Iraqi WMD (Weapons of Mass Destruction) contained four mentions of the claim that Iraq was able to deploy WMD against British citizens within 45 minutes of an order being given. But the original intelligence said nothing about whether Iraq possessed the chemical or biological weapons to use in these weapons. The government had turned a purely hypothetical danger into an immediate and deadly threat.

In 2011, it was claimed that the Libyan government was planning a massacre in Benghazi, exactly the kind of action that Gaddafi knew could trigger Western 'intervention'. As investigative journalist Gareth Porter[22] noted: 'When the Obama administration began its effort to overthrow Gaddafi, it did not call publicly for regime change and instead asserted that it was merely seeking to avert mass killings that administration officials had suggested might approach genocidal levels' (media propaganda role in the overthrow of Gaddafi will be discussed in Chapter 6).

Emotional Tone and Intensity

A crucial component of the propaganda blitz is the tone of political and corporate commentary, which is always vehement, even hysterical.

---

[21] http://medialens.org/index.php/alerts/alert-archive/2016/818-anatomy-of-a-propaganda-blitz-part-1.html (accessed on 4 June 2019).
[22] http://www.middleeasteye.net/columns/us-military-leadership-s-resistance-regime-change-1343405723 (accessed on 4 June 2019).

High emotion is used to suggest a level of deep conviction fuelling intense moral outrage. The Kuwait 'dead baby story' discussed earlier is a good example.

Manufacturing Consensus

A third component of a propaganda blitz is the appearance of informed consensus. The dramatic claim, delivered with certainty and outrage, is typically repeated right across the political and media 'spectrum'. This cross-spectrum 'consensus' generates the impression that 'everyone knows' that the propaganda claim is rooted in reality. This is why the myth of a media 'spectrum' is so vital.

In late 2017, it looks as if the American media is held-bend in providing President Trump and his generals the American public consensus needed to start a war in Asia. There has been a barrage of propaganda demonizing the North Korean leader Kim Jong-un, Trump even calling him the 'rocket man' in a speech to the UN General Assembly. But what is ignored is South Korean President Moon's passionate belief that only negotiations with the North Korean regime will solve the problem. Fortunately, in a dramatic public relations coup, in a new year message, President Kim offered to send a North Korean team to the Winter Olympics in South Korea and this set in motion a chain of events that eventually led to the diffusion of tension in the Korean peninsula and a face-to-face meeting between the two Korean leaders in April 2018 and a Trump–Kim summit in Singapore in June 2018.

Demonizing Dissent

In 2012, after WikiLeaks founder Julian Assange requested asylum in the Ecuadorian embassy in London, the corporate media rose up as one to denounce him as a 'hacker', a security threat and a 'sex maniac'. 'To challenge a propaganda blitz is to risk becoming a target of the blitz', argues Media Lens, who can be smeared as 'useful idiots', 'apologists', 'genocide deniers', etc. Anyone who even questioned the campaigns targeting Julian Assange risked being labelled a 'sexist', a 'misogynist' and a 'rape apologist'. The Swedes who accuse him of sex charges later dropped the case (see Chapter 3 for more discussion).

Timing and Strange Coincidences

The 'dramatic new evidence' fuelling a propaganda blitz often seems to surface at the worst possible time for the establishment target. On one level, this might seem absurdly coincidental—why, time after time, would the official enemy do *the one thing* most likely to trigger invasion, bombing, electoral disaster, and so on, at exactly the wrong time?

In November 2002, before the UN vote on Resolution 1441, which 'set the clock ticking' for war, the Blair regime began issuing almost daily warnings of imminent terror threats against UK ferries, the underground rail system and major public events. In 2003, Blair actually surrounded Heathrow Airport with tanks—an action said to be in response to increased terrorist 'chatter' warning of a 'missile threat', of which nothing more was subsequently heard (Media Lens 2016).

In November 2016, when the Assad regime in Syria with Russian air support was about to liberate Aleppo from Western-supported Islamic terrorists, it was widely reported in the Western media that the Syrian regime has used chemical weapons in the campaign with dubious pictures of children effected by these chemicals being circulated (this will be discussed in Chapter 5). In January 2017, Iran's Press TV reported that Syrian forces engaged in mop-up operation in Aleppo have discovered Saudi-produced chemical weapons agents left behind by foreign-backed terrorists in the city.[23] In August, Press TV reported that more than 600,000 Syrian refugees who fled the war have returned to Aleppo since January, a fact confirmed by the International Organization of Migration.[24] One is then entitled to ask if President Assad is such an 'evil' person as the Western media projected him to be, why are these people returning? The response from

---

[23] http://www.presstv.ir/Detail/2017/01/11/505784/Syria-Aleppo-Saudi-Arabia-chemical-weapons (accessed on 4 June 2019).

[24] http://www.presstv.ir/Detail/2017/08/13/531575/Syria-Aleppo-Province-International-Organization-for-Migration-OPCW (accessed on 4 June 2019).

the Western media is likely to be that this is Iranian propaganda (fake news).

Propaganda blitzes that paints leaders who are perceived in the West as being their 'enemies' and 'perverted mega maniacs' has now become a useful asset for human traffickers who work in concert with asylum lawyers and a consortium of human rights activists and international human rights organization. It could be Afghans fleeing from the Taliban, Syrians from Assad's regime, Iraqis from the ISIS or Libyans from the warlords—asylum seeking has become a good business. While the media in the West has been reporting widely about opposition to these asylum seekers in Europe in particular, this same media never asks the question how and why these refugee flows have originated. If they do so, they will be left with addressing an issue their own people should not be encouraged to think about, that is, the West (or its allies) have been involved in war crimes of their own in those countries, which makes these people to flee their homelands. Sometimes 'manufacturing consent' by the media could be a double-edged sword.

In Chapter 3, we will focus on if we ever had a truth era and what do we mean by a 'post-truth' era?

CHAPTER 3

Did We Ever Have a Truth Era?

If you look at the communication trends in Asia and the West today, there seems to be little difference in the way the MSM operates. On one hand, in Asia, particularly in India, excessive commercialization of the news media beginning around the mid-1990s has introduced what Daya Thussu (2007b) calls the 'Murdochization of the Media' that has its roots in the rise of infotainment-driven television news, especially led by Rupert Murdoch-owned Fox News in the USA and executed brilliantly in India by Arnab Goswami (see discussion later in this chapter). On the other hand, the latest fad in the West, especially in the USA, is mindfulness, a system of human communications that originated in India over 25 centuries ago and was taught by Gautama Buddha as Vipassana Bhavana (meditation). This development could bring Asian and Western thinking on communications much closer together. But it will take time, because it needs an understanding of so-called eastern 'mythology' as modern wisdom, by the West in particular (read Chapter 10).

The Role of Journalism

The role of journalism today is an adversarial one that finds solace in digging out conflicts and fuelling them in order to get the eyeballs to attract advertising revenue. This adversarial model was developed in the West. What is news are confrontations, arguments, combativeness, antagonistic attitudes, accusations and dissent—all relating to conflicts. The media is driven by conflict reporting, and the objectivity is giving at least two sides of the story. That often turns a story into a conflict—one view against another. Unfortunately, this tradition of journalism has led to the news media painting the society with a negative brush and makes you feel pessimistic of the future. Because of that, many people do not want to watch news programmes anymore.

Mass communication courses taught in universities, including across Asia, are usually based on Eurocentric concepts of communication with a heavy focus on individual rights, FOE and dissent—the so-called 'fourth estate' principle. This again focuses perhaps too much on confrontation and too little on accommodation, compromise and harmony. In the Asian region where the protection and promotion of community and social harmony play an important role in political and social discourse, media practitioners' focusing on individual rights over community harmony sometimes creates unnecessary conflicts that could be avoided by more sensitive and mindful communication strategies (see Chapter 10) that would have the same result of opening up public and community space for more FOE, although it may need some patience. It could also create a more positive outlook of society so that people would look for win-win situations.

In September 2016, Singapore's Deputy Prime Minister Tharman Shanmugaratnam[1] speaking at the Singapore Summit told delegates from 36 countries that the gloomy narrative on the global economy has been overplayed and overstated. 'Future depends on us and what we do', he argued. 'The world economy looks very different when you sit in Asia. There is growth and business is being done in the region, jobs are being created and incomes are rising'.

He said this in reference to stories on Asia that are often transmitted by Western news agencies that look for conflict in the South China Sea, or in North Korea or in the Indian subcontinent. Even the

---

[1] http://www.todayonline.com/singapore/asias-eyes-world-economy-not-funk-says-tharman (accessed on 6 June 2019).

journalists in Asia are following this adversarial model (Box 3.1), where they are looking for conflicts, be it in the North Korean nuclear issue or in China's rise as a global economic power rather than looking at its benevolent side, such as helping to build Asian infrastructure and create new trading routes across Asia and into Central Asia and Europe.

> **Box 3.1: July 2017: North Korea's Firing of an Intercontinental Ballistic Missile**
>
> On 4 July 2017, when North Korea announced the firing of its first Intercontinental Ballistic Missile (ICBM), the Korean Herald reported it with a headline 'S. Korea, US hold missile drills as NK claims key ICBM technology',[2] and it went on to report about how South Korea and the USA staged a 'massive combined ballistic missile exercise' to 'send a warning to North Korea'. It described the advanced technology used and quoted the US military as saying that they mobilized the assets to 'counter North Korea's destabilizing and unlawful actions'.
>
> CNN followed suit with a similar report focusing on US Secretary of State Rex Tillerson's call for 'global action to stop a global threat'. The CNN also showed footage[3] of the missile tests and talked at length about the technology and how it could strike South Korea. CNN said the joint exercises between the two allies are a 'clear signal' that the Pentagon has no intention to stop these exercises as demanded by North Korea to stop its missile testing programme.
>
> Al Jazeera in contrast focused on a joint statement made by President Xi Jinping of China and Vladimir Putin of Russia during their meeting in Moscow calling for restraint on all sides.[4] It reported that although the two leaders said the missile tests were 'unacceptable', they have called for a simultaneous freeze on North Korean nuclear and missile tests, and military exercises by the USA and South Korea. It also said that the statement has called for the start of negotiations by both sides for a 'comprehensive resolution of the problems of the Korean peninsula for a lasting peace'.

(Continued)

[2] http://www.koreaherald.com/view.php?ud=20170705000054 (accessed on 6 June 2019).

[3] http://edition.cnn.com/2017/07/04/politics/us-officials-meet-north-korea-missile-launch/index.html (accessed on 6 June 2019).

[4] http://www.aljazeera.com/news/2017/07/russia-china-korea-missile-test-unacceptable-170704145934120.html (accessed on 6 June 2019).

(Continued)

Al Jazeera also carried an opinion piece by Professor of Korean Studies Andrei Lankov[5] at Kookmin University in Seoul who pointed out the seemingly uncompromising stance of both sides. For North Korean leaders, their nuclear status is seen as the only guarantee against a Western attack or instigation of a regime change internal plot like what happened to Saddam Hussein in Iraq and Muammar Gaddafi in Libya. On the other hand, the USA cannot accept any compromise that will allow North Korea to become a nuclear power. But Lankov points out that although the USA has the capacity to make a precision attack on North Korea's nuclear facilities, it will not be welcomed in both South Korea and China.

The Korean dilemma provides a good opportunity, especially for the media in Asia, particularly in East Asia, to play a peacemaker role rather than an adversarial role. They should see that a confrontation in the area, especially a nuclear one, would have a devastating effect on the whole region and derail the great economic advances made by all countries in the region.

Interestingly, President Trump's rhetorical speech at the UN in September 2017 where he called the North Korean leader 'Rocket Man' and threatened to nuke the whole of North Korea, possibly killing millions of people, was a wake-up call for the world, especially for Asia. In commentaries and reporting in Asia, there was subtle rethinking of the US role in the region as a 'peacekeeper'. President Kim grabbed the opportunity and made peace overtones to South Korea offering to take part in the Winter Olympics in South Korea. President Moon quickly accepted the offer and this set in motion a highly visible 'romantic' relationship between the two leaders that has dramatically reduced tension in the region. It also led to the landmark Trump-Kim summit in Singapore in June 2018.

The image of Kim has also changed dramatically across Asia, where he is seen as a chubby smiling leader who is not threatening anyone. While there is a growing perspective in Asia that denuclearization of North Korea is going to be a gradual process that needs building of mutual trust and compromises—which is supported by statements and actions of South Korean leadership—reports in the Western media—particularly American—reflect an uncompromising view that North Korea would have to first denuclearize completely before the USA reciprocates in any form. It is as stupid a view as asking the government to withdraw a president's bodyguards while he is threatened by armed terror groups.

The solution to a permanent peace in the Korean peninsula and the possible reunification of the country involve a gradual process where the state of war that still exists between North and South Korea,

---

[5] http://www.aljazeera.com/indepth/opinion/2016/11/korean-war-trump-presidency-161126124759694.html (accessed on 6 June 2019).

> more than half a century after the war ended, has to cease. For this to happen, the USA and China have to sign such a declaration as they were signatories to the armistice that ended the war. That would be followed by the USA dismantling its bases in South Korea. At the post-summit press conference in Singapore, Trump gave a hint of such an eventuality, when he gave a figure of the costs to the USA of maintaining the bases, an important news focus that the Western media has ignored. They have been harping on the long-held view if Kim and his regime could be trusted. It is important that the Asian media divorces itself from such thinking and give the two Korean leaders the coverage they deserve for their step-by-step peace moves.
>
> Interestingly, a week after the second summit in February 2019 between Kim and Trump in Hanoi—which the American (and international) media described as a 'failure'—Trump announced that the annual war games between the USA and South Korea will not take place in future. This is what Xi and Putin called for when the rhetoric were heating up in 2017. Their call for the halting of North Korean nuclear and missile tests have already become a reality.

If it is okay for the American media to harp on their security, it is equally necessary for the Asian media to focus on the security of their region. A war in Korea, especially a nuclear war, will destroy what Asia has painstakingly built since the fall of European colonialism in the region since the mid-20th century. A war will not only benefit America and its arms industry. It will also help the West to re-establish its hegemony in the East. At this stage, such critical thinking is essential among Asian media practitioners.

Thus, there is a need to train journalists to be mindful of what is happening around them and not blindly follow a news agenda that is borrowed from the West that always looks for conflicts and problems. A news paradigm needs to be developed that will find solutions to the problems and harmony in the societies they live in.

The Death of the 'Fourth Estate' and the Crisis in Democracy

At the root of the Western 'free media' model, as discussed in the previous chapters, is the Libertarian Media Function Theory that says the media should be the peoples' 'watchdog' of government's abuse of power. Also, such media should be privately owned to play that role—the 'Fourth Estate' model—where the media forms the fourth pillar of a democracy.

Well, it worked okay as long as media companies only owned media. But today, in both Asia and the West, media is owned by large corporations that are often more powerful than governments. They often use the media to protect and promote their vested interests. Rupert Murdoch's News Corporation is a good example.

Looking at the concentration of media ownership in the hands of a few powerful corporations in the USA, McChesney and Herman (1998) argue:

> Such concentration of media power on organisations dependent on advertiser support and responsible primarily to shareholders is a clear and present danger to citizens participation in public affairs, understanding of public issues, and thus to the effective working of democracy.

In his book *News as Entertainment: The Rise of Global Infotainment*, Thussu (2007a: 41) maps the development of the American-inspired infotainment to reach a global audience. He argues that it is crucially important to understand the creation of the global infotainment infrastructure, which began with the fundamental ideological changes that took place during the 1990s after the end of the Cold War, when the triumph of the free market liberalism was routinely bandied about in media and policy discourses. He noted:

> This led to a process of deregulation and privatization in the communication and media industries combined with new digital communication technologies that resulted in a quantum leap in television news channels. The convergence of the telecommunications, computer and media industries enabled the instantaneous delivery of infotainment across a digitally linked globe.

Across Asia, in the past two decades, we have had a lot of 'media liberalization' and 'democratization' of the political systems, India, the

Philippines and Indonesia are prime examples, but many other countries have gone through this process in different ways. This process has been accompanied by media liberalization policies starting in the 1990s that have specially created private electronic media channels and networks. These private media are often owned by business cronies of ruling parties and are unable to play the 'watchdog' role or are excessively entertainment driven.

Tabloidization of Indian Television News

With Star TV and Murdoch's entry into the Indian market and liberalization of Indian media regulations, there has been a rapid growth of Indian television, and along with it has come the growth of television news industry. The newspapers have to compete with television that has adopted a tabloid form of journalism the News Corporation is good at. Also, the news is now provided by the evening news bulletins on TV, and newspapers had to invent a new role for themselves.

'Traditional style of 5W, 1H is no more', says Mumbai-based journalist Milind Kokje.[6] 'Writing style changing was a good thing but allowing for interpretation in news (opened the door) for either corruption or putting your own ideology into the news ... earlier you were not allowed to put your ideology into the news.'

Accepting a Lifetime Achievement Award from the Mumbai Press Club in May 2015, founder of NDTV Prannoy Roy[7] lamented that Indian television news has gone tabloid, which he saw as the biggest threat to the news industry in India. Why has every news channel (English, Hindi or regional) turned tabloid? Why are we trying to emulate Fox News? He asked. Going on to explain the problem faced by Indian news media, he noted:

> Tabloidization is the death of good journalism. But I don't blame our anchors or journalists for this tsunami of tabloid news. I also

---

[6] Interview with the author in Mumbai, 8 December 2016.
[7] https://www.ndtv.com/opinion/prannoy-roy-on-the-tabloidization-of-indian-news-760247 (accessed on 6 June 2019).

strongly disagree with the widely held hypothesis that blames the Indian viewer—Indians love tabloid sensationalism ... Indians have base, tabloid tastes. So if our anchors are not to blame, and it's not about viewer preferences—why is India becoming 'no country for honest journalism'?

Many feel that the advertising fraternity must carry part of the blame. The advertising pie is distributed based entirely on numbers—many in the advertising fraternity tell me that our media buyers are essentially eyeball-chasers (the media equivalent of ambulance-chasers). While our advertisers and media buyers are as skilled as those in the West in their media modeling skills, for some reason they have not created methods that enable them to evaluate news on factors others than just numbers of eyeballs. ... Unless we model quality and credibility into our advertising rates, and not go just by the eyeball count, we shall go headlong into tabloidization—with no place for news that is at the serious end of the spectrum.

Arnab Revolution—News as Panel Discussion

Television, as we know it, may not be dead after all. Television anchor and media proprietor Arnab Goswami has given a new dimension to news that has been hailed by some as 'revolutionizing' the news industry and by others as 'corrupting' it. His moderator-centred shouting opinionated brand of television news where four to five panellists may speak over each other may be more entertainment than news, but he and his many supporters in India believe he is turning news into a crusading industry which the 'watchdog' model of the free media was supposed to do in the first place. His news programmes on Times Now and lately on his own channel Republic TV have been top-rated programmes on Indian TV.

Goswami has been often criticized for not giving focus to the problems that continue to infect India such as poverty, hunger, illiteracy and caste discrimination. Instead he focuses on terrorism, national security and nationalism. Many have lamented that this TV-driven journalism will not address such serious socio-economic and cultural issues like how the newspapers used to do.

Outlook's Anuradha Raman (2015) argues that this style of television journalism is 'wrecking news' and raising many question about the industry itself.

> Make no mistake, Arnab kills boredom big time, with his amazing drive, energy and articulation. His larynx-popping dialogue delivery has reduced his peers on rival channels like NDTV, CNN-IBN and Headlines Today to purring kittens. And Arnab—a pleasant, courteous man sans the suit and pencil—knows what he is doing. The ratings show that he is getting more people to watch his channel and he has essentially made all the other channels irrelevant by boldly taking up the kind of issues he does and by raising the pitch in the style and manner he does.

As former TV reporter Sandeep Bhushan (Raman 2015) notes, Goswami came at the right time when after 2008 financial crisis Indian television industry was feeling the pinch of reduced advertising revenue and was shedding reporting staff because reporters meant money. 'This was when anchors defined news', he says and the shouting screaming, finger-wagging, table-thumping brand of news made a comeback. TV channels started to match each other with such programming.

Publisher Anurag Batra[8] argues that the Goswami brand of journalism needs to be given more credit than what he gets. It is not fair just to brand it as entertainment.

> It's fashionable to call it entertainment. It is news and it is done in a way that it gets your attention. You must see how much that man contributes to news (media)—depending on what side you are, you can see it as positive or negative. I see it as positive. He brought up issues like Commonwealth Games scam, I think the way he went after things and issues is commendable. Journalists tend to over simplify … Donald Trump won because white male overwhelmingly voted for him. Don't simplify Goswami and his news. Keep an open mind (and) you will be surprised to see how there are so

---

[8] Interview with the author in Delhi, 12 December 2016.

many Indian journalists out there to promote honesty, integrity and make a real difference to common man. At the end what matters is viewers and there is 70% of viewership.

Mahesh Vijapurkar,[9] a former news editor, has an interesting take on Arnab the man and his 'Newshour' on 'Times Now' comparing it to another popular news programme on rival station NDTV.

> Arnab set up a different model of TV not seen by people 24/7.... Prime time is 9 pm... you come switch on TV and see people fighting on screen without knowing what the issue they are fighting about. I come and see people arguing but how do I make sense of it. No one seems to bother at TV stations anymore. There is an assumption that each and every viewer has been monitoring the TV during the day—it's not the case. If its purpose is to inform, it's not doing it.
> NDTV's Ravish Kumar spends 15 minutes of his one hour show detailing the issue, such as telling what has happened in parliament today, this is the background, and he explains all the nuances to it. Sometime he says you better Google and find out more... then he introduce two or three people to explain the issues and don't allow them to fight with each other... this is not the case in other stations ... Arnab is opposite ... people have a lot of respect for Ravish Kumar. People abuse Arnab but like to watch him.
> Arnab has developed this model because Indian law–abiding tax-paying poor are left helpless after elections and whole establishment abandons them totally. So who is going to deliver broadsides at this establishment? I hate politicians I know they are into black illegal money, I know they stack money at home, so what can I do? I'm a helpless citizen. So Arnab gets on TV delivers punches after punches on their nose, so by proxy he appeals to them. In India today, politicians walk with hangers-on who does not let anyone approach them. He is the person, who approach them, he is useful to the politician and vice versa and that is where the patronage is provided.

---

[9] Interview with the author recorded in Mumbai, 7 December 2016.

In a speech at an 'IMPACT' conference in Singapore in December 2016, Arnab Goswami[10] spoke passionately about how he is giving meaning to the 'watchdog' model of journalism. This is some of what he said in his 20-minute presentation:

> I wanted to quit journalism, I was completely frustrated with the way journalism was being done in India principally the way that journalism was being done from New Delhi. I developed a distaste for many things ... so I simply wanted to flee the national capital ... (when I got the opportunity) what we did in our own style—which people like or dislike, agree or disagree—is upset the existing system in Indian journalism ... we needed to change the way in which things were happening because of five principal reasons.
> One, journalism was not confrontational it had become submissive, we're contented with the status quo journalism, was contented with being neutral—so you wanted to be dispassionate in the name of balance and not take a position on issues around you. Journalism had become like the gazetteer of India was in the 18th century merely a source of information, not ensuring any social impact.
> Journalism was also significantly detached from people's issues, the day-to-day challenges that millions of Indians face. I can tell you New Delhi was not caring about it, but most importantly journalism missed the strong element of activism and dissent. That significantly drives the profession today and I see that activism and dissent everywhere and we see ourselves as force multipliers for that activism and dissent.
> So let me ask you a couple of questions. We had a journalism of 2010 and let's say 2000 and a journalism of 2015. If I take away a few things from what we reported at 'Times Now' would we be a better country or would we be a worse country? Would we be a better country or would we be a worst country had we not uncovered (he names some cases) if we'd not ask those questions about those scams in the period between June 2010 and January 2011, would we be a better country or worst country? Would we be a better country or a worse country if we had not made a big deal

---

[10] https://www.youtube.com/watch?v=drxc1crtIwY (accessed on 6 June 2019).

about the Muzaffarnagar riots?[11] Would we be a better country or a worse country if for one month non-stop we had not asked questions about a person who is a fugitive in London called Lalit Modi and his dealings with the Indian establishment? Would we be a better country or a worse country if we had not questioned why celebrating a grand festival graced by Bollywood's biggest stars in Uttar Pradesh at a time when Muzaffarnagar riot victims were dying in the bitter cold two years back. Would we be a better country or a worse country if with absolute neutrality, we had not questioned why women are not allowed inside the Haji Ali shrine? These questions I put to you today.

So many people ask us well it's a good thing that you are doing but why do you do it this way? They're not a different way of doing things, you speak normally, ask the legitimate question, I can speak normally, can be nice and polite. Preface questions but then you know all these stories that I narrated to you ladies and gentlemen have been reported for decades, it's not the first time that we've done it ... but they've been reported in single-column page 11 of a newspaper. So if I were the editor of a newspaper today, I would put it as an 8- or possibly a 12-column headline on the front page, followed by wallpaper coverage in every page. But that doesn't happen in our media industry, because we don't want to say things assertively; when we say things assertively we know that we are going to upset some people, and there are a lot of people in Delhi who don't have the courage or the guts to say things assertively. Because they can't say things assertively, they say that we shout.

Arnab went on to argue that his profession sees themselves as 'agents of social change and there is a domino effect of what we are doing today will be felt one generation from now'. He argues that why the impact is not happening now is 'because of an overestimated commodity called neutrality', and he doesn't believe in that form of neutrality, because 'neutrality becomes a weakness when it perpetuates the status quo'. Thus, journalism becomes an 'exercise in futility in the

---

[11] The clashes between the Hindu and Muslim communities in Muzaffarnagar district of Uttar Pradesh, India, in August–September 2013, resulted in at least 62 deaths including 42 Muslims and 20 Hindus and injured 93 and left more than 50,000 displaced (Source: Wikipedia).

absence of impact', when 'facts stare you in the face' (such as the story of a 16-year-old girl who was raped by police), he argues, you cannot be neutral. 'Because we were determined to ensure there was an impact that the MLA (member of parliament) who raped a young girl and then booked her for theft in 2011 was arrested and brought to book himself'. Thus, he argued that is what 'watchdog' journalism should be in today's corrupted society.

Media watchdog Sevanti Ninan[12] of the Hoot tends to agree. 'TV has gone from reporting to discussion, and agenda setting has moved from newspaper to TV', she argues.

> As the media viability model has been squeezed TV has gone for discussion. There are many roles these TV debates perform for consumers of media.... If you are a TV presenter grilling politicians on TV, who develop a taste for it, because you feel politicians are not accountable to you [that will make them] accountable to some obnoxious TV anchor. That is the reason for the popularity of TV anchor … what the TV anchor says is the sealable topic of the day (and) that is the agenda that is being set.

Did We Ever Have a Truth Era?

The 2016 US Presidential campaign triggered much soul-searching in America about the meaning of democracy and how it has become hostage to big corporate interests, billionaires and corruption. In July 2015, at the beginning of the election campaign when Donald Trump started talking about making 'America great again', former President Jimmy Carter speaking on the Thom Hartmann Program said:

> The essence of what made America a great country is its political system. Now it is an oligarchy with unlimited political bribery being the essence of getting nomination for president or elected a president, the same applies to governors, US senators and congress members. Now we have seen a complete subversion of our political system as a pay off to major contributors who sometimes wants

---

[12] Interview with the author in Delhi, 9 December 2016.

favours for themselves ... it will take a horrible disgraceful series of acts in our country that will turn the public against it and eventually may be the Congress and Supreme Court. But at the same time, the incumbents, Democrats and Republicans look at this unlimited money as a great benefit to themselves.[13]

Carter may sound like a pro-democracy activist in a Two-Thirds World country, but the Trump presidency has opened a can of worms and focused attention on the shortcomings in the American system. The first few months of the Trump Presidency saw the much admired American media landscape breaking down (as noted in the Preface and Chapter 2). In April 2017, speaking at a college leadership seminar in Atlanta, *New York Post*'s Michael Goodman (2017) lamented this fact and made some revealing 'insider' observation regarding the state of the 'free media' which should be compulsory reading for any journalism student. This is some of what he said:

> I've been a journalist for a long time. Long enough to know that it wasn't always like this. There was a time not so long ago when journalists were trusted and admired. We were generally seen as trying to report the news in a fair and straight forward manner. Today, all that has changed. For that, we can blame the 2016 election or, more accurately how some news organizations chose to cover it. Among the many firsts, last year's election gave us the gobsmacking revelation that most of the mainstream media puts both thumbs on the scale—that most of what you read, watch and listen to is distorted by intentional bias and hostility. I have never seen anything like it.

He went on to argue that bias is not a new thing and it grew out of the social revolutions of the 1960s and the 1970s, fuelled by the Civil Rights and anti-Vietnam War movements, where the media jumped on an anti-authority bandwagon. And lately, they have given sympathetic coverage to 'Occupy Wall Street' and 'Black Lives Matter' movements. He said that he knew all of this about the media mindset

---

[13] https://www.youtube.com/watch?v=hDsPWmioSHg (accessed on 6 June 2019).

going into the 2016 presidential campaign. But he was still shocked at what happened.

This was not naïve liberalism run amok. This was a whole new approach to politics. No one in modern times had seen anything like it. As with grief, there were several stages. In the beginning, Donald Trump's candidacy was treated as an outlandish publicity stunt, as though he wasn't a serious candidate and should be treated as a circus act. But television executives quickly made a surprising discovery: The more they put Trump on the air, the higher their ratings climbed. Ratings are money. So news shows started devoting hours and hours simply to pointing the cameras at Trump and letting them run. As his rallies grew, the coverage grew, which made for an odd dynamic. The candidate nobody in the media took seriously was attracting the most people to his events and getting the most news coverage. Newspapers got in on the game too. Trump, unlike most of his opponents, was always available to the press, and could be counted on to say something outrageous or controversial that made a headline. He made news by being a spectacle.

Goodman notes that once the media realized that they had only two candidates now for the presidency and one of them is Trump, their coverage 'grew so vicious and one-sided' with every story 'becoming an opinion masquerading as news, and every opinion ran in the same direction—towards Clinton and away from Trump'. Goodman despises the fact that the media continues to call Trump a liar, while they never called previous presidents liars, even when they blatantly lied.

As we know now, most of the media totally missed Trump's appeal to millions upon millions of Americans. The prejudice against him blinded those news organizations to what was happening in the country. Even more incredibly, I believe the bias and hostility directed at Trump backfired. The feeling that the election was, in part, a referendum on the media gave some voters an extra incentive to vote for Trump. A vote for him was a vote against the media and against Washington. Not incidentally, Trump used that sentiment to his advantage, often revving up his crowds with attacks on reporters.

These attacks on the US MSM, particularly the CNN, continue under the Trump presidency, with the president often calling upon what he calls the 'fake media' to account for negative coverage about him. In October 2018, after a series of postal bombs were discovered addressed to Democratic Party leaders and the media reported about allegations that this is the work of Republican supporters of President Trump, he claimed that a large part of the 'anger' in the American society was caused by the media. He tweeted[14]:

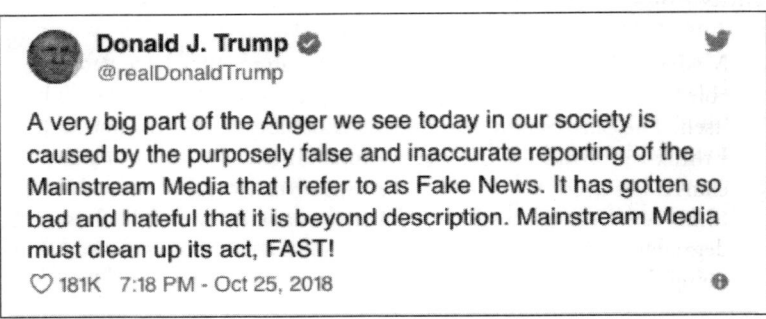

Echoing the principles of the Social Responsibility Media Function Theory (discussed in Chapter 1), President Trump told a rally crowd in Wisconsin that the media has a responsibility to set a civil tone and to stop the endless hostility and constant negative and oftentimes false attacks and stories. He added, 'they've gotta stop. Bring people together'.

Almost every country in Asia, which has democratized and liberalized its media systems in the past two to three decades, faces similar problems. Media is more interested in ratings and this dramatization has led voters to electing people who may not be fit to govern. Many countries are also grappling with a crisis in democracy because the system has been corrupted at its roots.[15]

The 'fourth estate' has become a business. They are there to protect their business interests and journalists seem to be pawns in this

---

[14] https://www.thedailybeast.com/trump-gives-media-some-of-the-blame-for-the-bomb-sent-to-the-media (accessed on 6 June 2019).

[15] http://www.straitstimes.com/opinion/money-politics-rotting-the-roots-of-democracy (accessed on 6 June 2019).

industry. Rather than 'independent' journalists, they have become public relations officers (as noted in Chapter 2).

Indian publisher and Chairman of BW BusinessWorld Anurag Batra (2016)[16] rejects the notion that the media has become commercialized only recently. He argues that media had been a commercial entity from its beginnings. He asks:

> Media has to be sustainable ... you use commercial I use sustainable ... in any business or institution or NGO it need to sustain itself. The cause is important but sustainability is equally important. I think the world has become more commercial—even for politicians it has become a business—even church, temple or gurudwara (Sikh temple) is a business. What is not a business? If there is degradation in media it is a symptom of what the society is undergoing. You cannot isolate media and blame it.

In the Philippines, the Philippine Center for Investigative Journalism (PCIJ) produced an investigative report as far back as 2004 under the title 'News for Sale' that investigated the corruption in the media during the presidential elections that year. They pointed out three developments that led to the corruption of the media. First was the emergence of television as the most important medium for influencing voters; the second was the lifting of the ban on political advertising resulting in a meteoric rise in campaign expenses, especially for those contesting for national office; and the third was the unprecedented use of celebrities for political endorsement that opened the entry into political coverage of the entertainment press. 'These factors combined to produce an environment that saw the emergence of new pressures on journalists and novel forms of influencing election coverage and corrupting the media', stated the report in its introduction (Florentino-Hofilena 2004: 1).

The PCIJ report pointed out that in the both 1998 and 2004 elections, the power of celebrity was too obvious to ignore. In 2004, top three positions for the Congress were occupied by top TV anchors and news personalities, while two more were elected in the top 10.

[16] Interview with the author in New Delhi, 12 December 2016.

It was the first time that TV personalities and movie stars were seriously challenging the traditional monopoly held by political families and big business personalities. The main opposition candidate for the presidency was action star Fernando Poe, while incumbent President Gloria Macapagal Arroyo had as her running mate TV and radio star Noli de Castro an incumbent senator. Arroyo and Castro won a close-fought election. Poe has even lifted lines from his movie scripts in election speeches. These candidacies, the PCIJ report argues, reflected the recognition of the political establishment of the 'importance of showbiz press and signaled the irrelevance of a high level, issue oriented campaign'.

While celebrities contesting and winning congressional and local governorships have not waned in the May 2016 elections yet, the presidential campaign by the former mayor of Davao (Duterte) in the southernmost island of Mindanao dealt a telling blow to the power of celebrity politics at least for the presidency. The tough talking anti-crime mayor, with an impressive record of cleaning up his corruption-ridden and crime-infested city over a 23-year reign as mayor, blunted the MSM's celebrity-ridden campaigning with smart use of old-fashioned electioneering and the use of new media spearheaded by his tech-savvy 'cyber army' of young supporters. As BBC's Southeast Asia Correspondent Jonathan Head[17] noted on the eve of the elections:

> As the long-serving mayor of the southern city of Davao, he is an outsider in the cozy world of Manila political families. And his campaign style and language are certainly something very new. Mr Duterte has scarcely been able to make a campaign speech without threatening to kill someone. In fact he says openly that you need to be willing to kill to be president. He has talked about filling Manila Bay with the 100,000 criminals he says he will kill if he wins the top job, which opinion polls suggest is likely.

In June 2016, the Philippines' President-elect Rodrigo Duterte told a packed press conference[18]:

---

[17] http://www.bbc.com/news/world-asia-36223755 (accessed on 6 June 2019).
[18] www.youtube.com/watch?v=XXRTdljXljA (accessed on 6 June 2019).

> The problem is every son of a bitch who claims to be journalist makes money out of it, milking money, extorting money from the people ... and (when) he is killed and he is glorified because he is a journalist. There is always a paid hack. It is not only in other professions. Do not ever think that you are in a field of purity.

Filipino journalist and Executive Director of the Southeast Asian Press Alliance (SEAPA) Edgardo Legaspi (2017)[19] argues that Duterte was able to tap into a deep distrust of the media among people of the Philippines, especially the rural people.

> Because of the perception that some media, the louder section of journalists in rural areas, tend to throw their weight around, and even use the position to extort… that's common observation in Philippines … Duterte's campaign used that to put down the media and win the election with a unique communication strategy.

He argues adding, 'he did not need to do any convincing, his campaign captured what is wrong with the media. That many media are corrupt, many journalists are misbehaving (and) he used that leverage to attack the mainstream media in general.'

Assange and WikiLeaks Journalism

At this stage, it is appropriate that we address the issue of whether the WikiLeaks model of journalism is putting into practice the fundamental principles of the Libertarian media function model of being the 'watchdog' of governments' abuse of power.

> The two most consequential pieces of journalism of our time came cheap to the newspapers that published them. The release of 720,000 secret documents from the US State and Defense Departments by WikiLeaks and the steady carefully curated series of revelations from Edward Snowden about the massive reach of surveillance conducted by the NSA (National Security Agency) and CIA (Central Intelligence Agency) were published by *The*

---

[19] Interview with the author in Bangkok, 19 January 2017.

Guardian, *The New York Times* and *The Washington Post*, but were not initiated by them and required no investigative efforts by them—editors devoted resources to sifting checking and assessing what to print, but that was it. (Irving 2014)

The aforementioned quote came from a *British Journalism Review* article which discussed the dilemma of declining newspaper budgets and hence the lack of funds to encourage investigative journalism. As Irving (2014) notes, 'the best pieces have a factual density that comes only from months of work. There is little use in setting notional deadlines to control the costs. The story is only ready when it is ready.'

Referring to the WikiLeaks method of 'investigative' journalism, Irving notes:

> There was no way that any journalist could have gained access to and mined these vast troves of state secrets. Only insiders like Snowden and Bradley (now Chelsea) Manning who decided to become whistleblowers could unbury this treasure. This should remind us that modern Western states have widespread powers to conceal their policies and actions. These powers are fortified by intimidating legal barriers. Against them the countervailing force of the press is puny. Even in the US where the First Amendment and Freedom of Information Act together allow far more insubordinate vigilance than British journalism enjoys, the really bad stuff can remain out of view for generations—we still do not know for example how the Bush administration's decision to invade Iraq was influenced by its interest in Iraq's oil fields.

In April 2017, Central Intelligence Agency (CIA) Director Mike Pompeo speaking at the Center for Strategic and International Studies in Washington accused WikiLeaks Founder Julian Assange and Edward Snowden, a former contractor who leaked National Security Agency (NSA) documents to journalists, of disseminating classified information to 'make a name for themselves'. As CNN reported,[20] Pompeo has in the past called for Snowden to receive the death

---

[20] http://edition.cnn.com/2017/04/13/politics/mike-pompeo-wikileaks-csis/ (accessed on 6 June 2019).

penalty. He argued in the speech that 'they care nothing about the lives they put at risk or the damage they cause to national security' and described WikiLeaks as 'a non-state hostile intelligence service often abetted by state actors, like Russia'.

Since the secret cables were revealed in 2010, Department of Justice has investigated the WikiLeaks issue a number of times and prosecutors have struggled with whether the First Amendment precluded the prosecution of Assange. Thus, Department of Justice has determined it would be difficult to bring charges against Assange because WikiLeaks wasn't alone in publishing documents stolen by Manning. Several newspapers, including the *NYT*, did as well. The investigation continued, but any possible charges were put on hold, according to US officials involved in the process then.[21] But these attempts still continue under President Trump's administration though it is widely believed that WikiLeaks revelations about Hillary Clinton's secret e-mail accounts helped tip the scales in Trump's favour during the presidential campaign.

Ever since WikiLeaks exposed US and UK governments' 'dirty deals' through evidence from leaked diplomatic cables, both countries along with its allies have been after Assange trying to nail him on various charges, though none of it relates directly to publishing because in that case *NYT*, *The Guardian* and *The Washington Post* would also have to be in the docks, which would make the West's commitment to 'free speech' a mockery. The Australian-born Assange was originally arrested in London in 2010 under a European arrest warrant issued by Sweden over rape and sexual assault allegations.

Two years later, while on bail, he claimed asylum inside the Ecuadorian embassy in Knightsbridge in London, where he is still living under virtual house arrest (like what Myanmar's Aung San Suu Kyi did during those long years of her pro-democracy struggle with the country's military). In late 2015, the Swedes dropped the rape case against him for lack of evidence but not withdrawn the extradition

---

[21] http://edition.cnn.com/2017/04/20/politics/julian-assange-wikileaks-us-charges/index.html (accessed on 6 June 2019).

request. Assange believes that if he is extradited to Sweden, they will hand him over to the US authorities.

In February 2016, a UN panel gave a verdict that Julian Assange's three-and-a-half years in the Ecuadorian embassy amount to 'arbitrary detention', leading his lawyers to call for the Swedish extradition request to be dropped immediately. The UN Working Group on Arbitrary Detention said that Assange's detention 'should be brought to an end, that his physical integrity and freedom of movement be respected'. The WikiLeaks founder had been subjected to 'different forms of deprivation of liberty', it said, initially while he was held in isolation at London's Wandsworth Prison for 10 days in 2010. The deprivation had been 'continuous' since he was initially arrested in the UK on 7 December 2010. 'Mr Assange should be afforded the right to compensation', it added. The UK Foreign Secretary Philip Hammond branded the UN decision as 'ridiculous' and refused to let Assange go free, for which Snowden tweeted: 'This writes a pass for every dictatorship to reject UN rulings. Dangerous precedent for UK/Sweden to set.'[22]

In an interview on RT,[23] fellow Australian journalist John Pilger pointed out the hypocrisy of the UK government in their response to the UN decision:

> The British government would say to the regime in Myanmar that the UN working group tribunal finding against the junta that they had unlawfully detained Aung San Suu Kyi was binding. In fact the British government has agreed with every judgment that the tribunal has made (you see it with) Egypt, Anwar Ibrahim in Malaysia and others. The only problem with this one for them is that it's an Australian political refugee right in the heart of London next to Harrods and the finger is being pointed at the British government, the Swedish government and of course back in the shadows the US government ... now most of these salient facts have been brought together for this Tribunal and have been

---

[22] http://www.bbc.com/news/uk-35504237 (accessed on 6 June 2019).
[23] https://www.youtube.com/watch?v=RqzZDJrUit0 (accessed on 6 June 2019).

examined by clearly distinguished jurists who don't sit all that often, they've looked at all the pack and they said the rule of law should apply here in Britain and Sweden. (They) are unlawfully detaining Julian Assange.

The case of Assange is a clear case of hypocrisy of the West vis-à-vis human rights and freedom of speech. In Chapter 4, we explore why truth is subjective and how monopolistic news networks create news imbalances as a result.

CHAPTER 4

Imbalances in News
Truth Is Subjective

> Journalists are right to argue that what they print and broadcast is not motivated by ill will. But they are wrong if they believe that ill will is the only cause of distorted information. Many well-intentioned reports from abroad slavishly reflect the values that are acceptable to the editors and readers of the organization the correspondent represents. Yet, these values may be totally repugnant to the people of the country in question. Characterizing Shiite leaders as 'mad mullahs' may be salable copy in secular societies, but it is gross and insulting to many Muslims whose faith is founded on Koranic principles. It is also difficult for such people to understand why a bikini should be considered a more appropriate symbol of civilization than a sari or a chador. Moreover, Muslims are angered when Western press becomes so agitated by public manifestations of belief in Islamic values. The press describes this derogatorily as 'fundamentalism'—connoting a throwback to a dead past—at the same time that they refer with respect to Pope's consistent reiteration of such fundamental Catholic principles as the ban on admitting women into the priesthood.
> —Tarzie Vittachi, Founder of the Asian Press Union
> (*Newsweek*, 11 February 1980)

Tarzie Vittachi, a Sri Lankan journalist, wrote the above in a commentary that was published by the *Newsweek* magazine at a time the Iranian revolution was ringing alarm bells in the West. He is believed to be the first journalist from the Two-Thirds World to become a contributing editor (i.e., a regular columnist) to a major Western news magazine. This was also written just after the release of the *MacBride Report* on the international news media by the UNESCO. This report will be discussed later in this chapter.

In the commentary written under the heading 'Are Journalists News Vultures?' Vittachi (1980) said that he was more concerned with the professional obligation of journalists than with their rights. Referring to the expulsion of Western journalists from Iran and Afghanistan (which was then under Soviet Union occupation), he argued that it is the right time to take stock of the performance of the press and not look at it as yet another proof that Two-Thirds World countries are 'incorrigibly hostile' to Western journalists. Referring to the economically poor nations' suspicion of foreign journalists, he argued that 'it would be a mistake to suppose that this distrust is always motivated by malice'.

'The complaint of many governments of developing nations is not that foreign journalists report the truth', noted Vittachi, 'but, that their reporting is superficial, erratic and distorted. This charge is at the core of the conflict between the Western press and Third World governments'. The main point of the charges he argues 'is that we journalists too often ignore the causes of a troubled human situation. But, when the worst happened, we swarm like vultures to pick up the scraps. It is an ugly allegation but a serious one.'

More than 35 years later, nothing much seems to have changed. Throughout the last four decades, the Western media (because of their monopoly on setting the global news agenda) has been accused from time to time of the same weakness Vittachi has pointed out earlier.

As I write this (in November 2018), I'm following with intrigue how the international media is reporting a brewing political conflict in Vittachi's homeland (as well as mine) Sri Lanka. President Maithripala Sirisena has sacked a pro-Western Prime Minister Ranil Wickremesinghe and appointed the former President Mahinda Rajapaksa known for his pro-China leanings as the new prime minister. A major reason the president gave for his sacking of the PM was his lack of empathy with the common man in the country and his attempts to draw up a new constitution with the aid of his Western supporters, especially US-funded NGOs, to make it easier for foreigners to buy land and do business in the country. Critics across the country have described it as paving the way for recolonization of the country by Western powers without using gunboats. When the president dissolved the parliament two weeks later and declared a national election in January 2019, as Rajapaksa didn't seem to command a majority in parliament, Wickremesinghe opposed it, but most people in Sri Lanka seemed to welcome it. However, the Western media reported the small groups of Wickremesinghe supporters, aided by Western-funded urban NGOs, mounting protests as 'pro-democracy' groups opposing an 'authoritative' president, when these protestors were, in fact, agitating against the holding of a general election! Most of the Asian media blindly took the Western news agency copy and republished it in their newspapers or based their broadcast reports on these.[1]

The News Vultures

Lack of attention given to the views of the masses that don't speak English, and the focus given to the English-speaking urban elites, gives a lopsided view of the world. In this age of neoliberal globalization, the latter provides the fodder for the corporate media to justify their narratives. The 'news vultures' Vittachi referred to almost four decades ago are very much alive today, still descending on the world's troubled spots to report the event but fail to grasp the process that led to it and would lead to many more such events in the future. The aftermath of the Arab Spring of 2011 is one example, the 2004 Asian Tsunami is another, just to mention two major events of the 21st century. If the Sri Lankan political conflict boils over to street clashes, they will be there to report about yet another 'failed state' and calling for Western military intervention under the 'R2P' (Responsibility to Protect) formula the West has devised at the dawn of the 21st century to justify a new era of colonialism. This will be discussed further in Chapter 6.

---

[1] https://www.scmp.com/news/asia/south-asia/article/2171830/west-upset-about-sri-lankas-sacked-pm-its-not-about-democracy (accessed on 6 June 2019).

In an interview with Thai television reporter Pipope Panitchpakdi, Sri Lankan television producer and communicator Nalaka Gunawardene[2] described what happened when Western televisions crews descended on his country during the aftermath of the 2004 Asian Tsunami.

As the tsunami happened on a lean news day (December 26th), the media took some time to ultimately get into the multiple scenes of devastation. Because the scale of the disaster and the magnitude of the impact are not something the journalists and the camera crews were used to in the typical normal working lives. So they took time and I think they did a commendable job in coping with very hard working conditions that prevailed in all the tsunami-hit countries and locations. But, as the days passed we realized there was a certain superficial nature, the coverage was largely looking at death, destruction, and devastation. Yes there was that element in the tsunami, in any major crisis or disaster there would be that element. But also there was an important aspect that we felt the mainstream media did not cover, that was how the affected people, the individuals and the communities coped with the enormous problems that prevailed immediately after.

On one hand, the search and rescue operations that took place in the first few days, and then disposal of bodies, the missing locations of friends and relatives, and a whole range of these stressful and very problematic issues that prevailed, and how there was human ingenuity, there was resourcefulness, and there was resilience, and these stories which were unfolding in many tsunami towns, villages and locations, these were not picked up enough of the times in the media. Media had two or three headlines topics, how much aid was being pledged around the world, which was very good, but that was not the only story and then the media had particular preoccupation with Western tourists who have been unfortunately effected by the disaster, again I would say that was legitimate news coverage but sometimes one wonder whether the Western media news coverage was disproportionately focused on the Western tourists that were affected by the tsunami. So, while

---

[2] https://nalakagunawardene.com/2009/12/25/looking-back-at-asian-tsunami-of-2004-and-media-response/ (accessed on 6 June 2019).

we watched the coverage over time, over a few days and weeks, we felt there was more to this disaster and more to the recovery from the disaster. We wanted to look at some of those unfolding stories of human survival and human resilience.

Gunawardene's team went on to produce a series of television features on 'The Children of Tsunami'[3] to report on the process of recovery from the disaster. This, one would describe as reporting a process as opposed to an event (which was the tsunami waves hitting the communities).

Landmark Debate—New World Information and Communication Order

It is such news values, that Gunawardene described earlier, which were at the core of the call by the Two-Thirds World and the Soviet Union and its allies for a NWICO in the 1970s.

The concept of NWICO was born in an aggressive wave of decolonization spearheaded by the Non-Aligned Movement (NAM)[4] in the first part of the 1970s. It was consolidated during an information war, with a counter-attack by western powers in the mid-1970s, followed by a diplomatic truce in the late 1970s; then it was shunned by another western corporate offensive in the 1980s. Yet, it is an idea carried over to the new millennium, no longer as a

---

[3] https://www.youtube.com/playlist?list=PLE3CAC0F15EC7C0C2 (accessed on 6 June 2019).

[4] The NAM was created and founded during the collapse of the colonial system and the independence struggles of the peoples of Africa, Asia, Latin America and other regions of the world and at the height of the Cold War. The birth of NAM goes back to the Asian-African Conference held in Bandung, Indonesia, on 18–24 April 1955 which gathered 29 heads of state belonging to the first post-colonial generation of leaders from the two continents. The principles that would govern relations among large and small nations, known as the 'Ten Principles of Bandung', were proclaimed at that Conference. Such principles were adopted later as the main goals and objectives of the policy of non-alignment (http://mea.gov.in/in-focus-article.htm?20349/History+and+Evolution+of+Non Aligned+Movement [accessed on 6 June 2019]).

controversial concept, but embedded in a number of key issues in global media policy and study. (Nordenstreng 1997, cited in Frau-Meigs et al. 2012: 31)

In 1973, the heads of state of Non-Aligned Movement (NAM) declared at the summit in Algiers that 'developing countries must undertake concerted action in the field of communication'. Many of the member countries from Africa, Asia and Latin America were newly independent from European colonial rule and they needed international finance and a fairer trading system to develop their economies. Many of their ministers found that when they went to international institutions seeking assistance, the first questions they were asked were about corruption, inefficiency and lack of freedom in their countries. It was clear to them that the Western media's focus on these issues in the coverage of their countries had an impact on the way officials in these institutions—usually Westerners—looked at them. Thus, they were convinced that a New International Economic Order (NIEO), which is fairer to the Two-Thirds World, cannot be established without first reforming and restructuring the international information order.

As Herman and McChesney (1997) note, the Western nations naturally opposed such an order that would disturb the global media status quo. But, for NAM members, the state was the only body that could effectively represent the will of the people and counter the power of global corporations and institutions. However, the USA saw the state as the enemy of a free press; therefore, only a market-driven, profit-based system could legitimately claim democratic credentials.

At the NAM heads of state meeting in Colombo in 1976, Indian Prime Minister Indira Gandhi labelled the West's response to a NWICO as 'apathetic' and made a strong plea for a NWICO and offered India's assistance to set up a Non-Aligned News Agencies Pool. She said:

> The response of advanced countries to the compulsions of a new world economic order has so far been apathetic. Patchwork remedies are no substitute for genuine reform. We need a global perspective plan, which will relate resources to human needs and

provide a system of early warnings of imbalances and disasters. Improved terms of trade and credit, easier access to markets and better value for raw materials and industrial goods are all essential, to secure greater equity in the distribution of benefits. Cooperation between and among our fraternity will enhance our strengths in the dialogue with the economically stronger.[5]

In response, UNESCO set up the 'International Commission for the Study of Communication Problems' in December 1977 and its report was completed and released in the early 1980s under the title *Many Voices One World*. It was headed by Ireland's Sean MacBride—who is both a Nobel and a Lenin Peace laureate—it was known as the *MacBride Report*.

Juan Somavia from Chile was a member of that commission and in a commentary written for the same *Newsweek* issue which carried Vittachi's article, under the heading 'Can We Understand Each Other?', he argued that the perspective about communication has to change.

> Communication is not just news. The well-travelled subject of government control versus freedom of the press, fundamental as it is, is only a part of the problem. The basic question is the relationship between communicators and the whole of society—something that effects the daily life of people everywhere…. People and societies are vastly different. The failure to acknowledge this cultural reality makes dialogue and international understanding impossible. We end up distorting what we see by not knowing how to look. This is why there cannot be a single set of news values to judge reality. (Somavia 1980)

MacBride Report—Challenging International News Norms

> The information media can contribute to commanding respect in all quarters for human beings as individuals, with all the manifold

---

[5] Transcript of Indira Gandhi's speech at the NAM summit in 1976 provided by the Ministry of External Affairs, India.

differences they display, and to winning acceptance of the aspirations common to all peoples in places of self-centred nationalism. They can also foster uninterrupted dialogue between communities, cultures and individuals, in a bid to promote equality of opportunities and two-way exchanges. This presupposes, first, that information in all fields should go unfettered. But we shall never cease to affirm that such freedom cannot be fully effective until it becomes a reality for everybody.

—Dr. Amadou-Mahtar M'Bow, Director General of UNESCO in a Foreword to *Many Voices One World* (MacBride 1980: xiv)

In the 1970s, international debate on communication issues had stridently reached points of confrontation in many areas. Third World protests against the dominant flow of news from industrialized countries were often construed as attacks on the free flow of information, defenders of journalistic freedom were labelled as intruders on national sovereignty. Varying concepts of news values and the role, rights and responsibilities of journalists were widely contended, as was the potential contribution of the mass media to the solution of major world problems.

—Sean MacBride, President of the UNESCO International Commission for the Study of Communication Problems in a Preface to *Many Voices One World* (MacBride 1980: xvii)

The West's argument about free flow of information has always been couched with 'free' trade. They understand the crucial role communication plays in opening up markets for trade—with or without justification. Going back to the 19th century when European mercantile power was expanding, the press played a major role in shaping policy and as a weapon of opening up markets. The European news agencies at the time, Reuters, Havas and Wolff, owned by the three European powers Britain, France and Germany, respectively, manipulated news to do propaganda against each other which led to wars in the continent. The general manager of the Associated Press (AP) accused Reuters of dominating international news and that this monopoly accompanied with prejudice and deception has developed international attitudes and impressions that are unfavourable to American interests (Mankekar 1979). Britain controlled the cable lines around the world at the time and held the key to international communications and

Reuter's supremacy in international news. The chairman of the Coordinating Committee of the NAM News Agencies Pool D. R. Mankekar (1979) noted that:

> In the 19th century, Britain, a nation of shopkeepers who lived on exports, peddled the doctrine of free trade all over the world and reaped all the benefits from it. In this electronic era, America's over-insistence on free flow of information is looked upon by developing countries as of a piece with the British doctrine of free trade.

Quoting from a passage in a Congress Committee report on 'Wining the Cold War', Mankekar (1979) notes that the US policy on free flow of information is very revealing as it advocates opening up the information sector for the USA to pursue its foreign policy goals by going direct to the people of foreign countries rather than through their government. It has argued that using modern communication technology, they could reach large or influential segments of a population 'to inform them, to influence their attitudes, and at times perhaps even to motivate them to a particular course of action'.

Today's 'regime change' campaigns mounted through the use of social media and other communication tools, and the use of 'donor' funding to create NGOs to promote democracy and human rights, could be seen as an application of this policy (see Chapter 6 for more discussion).

The report of the MacBride Commission—which included distinguished communication experts from many parts of the world—is credited to have brought information and communication issues to the global agenda and occupies an important place in the discourse on international communication flows in the past four decades.

The *MacBride Report* linked freedom of the press and expression to the rights to communicate and receive information, as well as the socio-economic and cultural rights contained in the 1976 UN International Covenant on Economic, Social and Cultural Rights.[6]

---

[6] http://www.ohchr.org/EN/ProfessionalInterest/Pages/CESCR.aspx (accessed on 6 June 2019).

It was also critical of the constraints imposed by commercialization and the concentration of media ownership and linked the growth of TNCs to a 'one-way' flow and 'market domination' of media products and messages.

Because of its pluralistic membership, *MacBride Report* (1980) had a plurality of viewpoints on the history and development of the mass media. It challenged the notion popularly thought in mass communications programmes today that mass media started in Germany in the 14th century with the Gutenberg press. It pointed out that books were printed in China in the 1st century AD and in the Arab World in the 8th century (MacBride 1980: 6). It also discussed how press freedom was won in Europe in the 18th century when people rose up against authorities that wanted to control the 'chief medium for the spreading of ideas' (MacBride 1980: 8). It also argued that if the media is dominated by political and cultural elites, it could run into conflict with other cultural, ethnic and religious groups/minorities. While espousing FOE, the report also pointed out that if the media demands total freedom for themselves, while rejecting any degree of responsibility, this could clash with accountability. Thus, it pointed out that there is always a political dimension to the problem of communication and the means of it. 'The best weapon against abuses of freedom is the responsibility exercised by those who enjoy freedom in their action and their conduct' (MacBride 1980: 22).

MacBride (1980) report argued that obstacles to 'free flow' of information are not always set up by public institutions, they also arise due to private monopolies, concentration of media ownership and formation of conglomerates. The report stated:

> When the public has only a single source of news, or where various sources have the same general orientation, it is the monopolist who is in a position to decide what facts will or will not be presented, what opinions will or will not be conveyed. Even if the owner of a monopoly does not abuse his power, no single outlet can present the amount and range of news that multiple sources make possible. Concentration of ownership can produce the same obstructions and tend to standardization of reporting, editing and presentation that is a limiting factor on the type of news that reaches the public.

> Moreover, the financial, commercial or industrial concerns that are involved in the corporate ownership may prevent the publication of facts that can cause an unfavourable light on their activities. (MacBride 1980: 140)

The West, led by the USA, saw the proposed NWICO as 'Soviet-inspired' Two-Thirds World attempt to muzzle the 'free media' of the West through state regulations. They saw it as conflict with the liberal Western values and principles of the 'free flow of information'.

Gauhar (1979) argues that though the Western press is liberal, it does not make it free from all cultural or ideological constraints. 'The word "liberal" is not synonymous with freedom. Liberalism is an ideology, which had had a historical affinity and compatibility with imperialism. There is a certain crusading quality in liberalism, which impels its devotees to carry its benefits to others, even against their will.' This was also stated by Gurumurthy (2018), as quoted in the preface to this book.

The practice of liberalism is also intertwined with its locations. As Gauhar (1979) reflects, when, for example, *The Economist*, one of the world's most influential liberal journals, claims that the Western press is free to gather, report and analyse facts as it chooses, yet the choice is not made in a cultural vacuum but within the liberal tradition.

> Western journalists do not descend from the heavens, nor do they float like bees, free to pollinate truth wherever they find it. They are given specific assignments, which they fulfill according to specific editorial directions. (Gauhar 1979)

He notes the liberal bias in *The Economist*'s coverage of the fall of Shah of Iran and the success of the Islamic Revolution in 1978–1979. Their hostility to ideologies such as political Islam was abundantly clear in the way the revolutionary process was analysed and reported to the world.

Today, we see this bias on reporting about China's peaceful rise as an economic powerhouse. The trade war between the USA and China that began with the election of President Trump is a 21st-century replay of information wars to promote liberalism and free trade according to your own perspective. In 2018, when a trade war between the USA and China gathered steam, the American and Chinese media had different perspectives on the conflict. This fact also reflects why *MacBride Report* called for a balanced two-way flow that will allow the reader (or news consumer) to decide who is right. Though much of the American MSM did not like President Trump, they tend to agree with his argument that China manipulates currency and other trade avenues that has led to a huge trade surplus with the USA. The Chinese media meanwhile focuses on President Xi's speeches at international forums promoting the value of multilateralism and rules-based trade regimes (Box 4.1).

What both media are not addressing is whether the USA is living beyond its means by importing more than what it can sell (or pay for) and if China is exploiting its people by continuing to pay low wages to sell its products cheaply in the world markets. What is a reasonable wage for Chinese workers should be part of the trade discussions, which in turn would also lead to discussion on the global supply chains, outsourcing and sweatshop economics.

Box 4.1: Whom to Trust When Xi and Trump Declared 'Trade Truce' at G20?

At the G20 Summit in the Argentinian capital at the end of November 2018, the main focus of the media worldwide was about how China's President Xi Jinping and the US President Donald Trump would handle the concerns of fellow members on the trade war between the two countries.

Two reports—one in *China Daily* and the other in *NYT*—give a good indication of two contrasting views on the dispute between China and the USA. The former promotes China's credentials as a responsible global trading nation promoting multilateralism, while the latter questions China's sincerity in trade promises.

China Daily (3 December 2018)[7]: Writing under the heading 'President's G20 Speech Wins Praise Worldwide', *China Daily*'s Chen Weihua says that international experts have applauded President Xi

(Continued)

---

[7] http://www.chinadaily.com.cn/a/201812/03/WS5c046648a310eff30328e89d.html (accessed on 6 June 2019).

(Continued)

Jinping's speech at the G20 Leaders' Summit for 'promoting multilateralism, global cooperation and free trade at a time when the world is facing a surge in unilateralism and protectionism'. It said that Xi called on G20 member states to stay committed to openness and cooperation, uphold the multilateral trading system, forge strong partnerships and step up macro policy coordination.

The report quotes 'independent' analysts saying that Xi's speech sends a 'clear and firm message' that China will continue to support the multilateral system and global cooperation. David Gosset, founder of the Europe-China Forum, is even quoted as saying that China's 'openness and predictability' has become a key stabilizing factor in a world of risks and uncertainties—an obvious dig at President Trump's attitude to trade issues.

NYT (3 December 2018)[8]: Writing under the heading 'Trump Says China Will Curtail Fentanyl: The US Has Heard That Before', *NYT*'s Sui-Lee Wee says while China has vowed to target exports of fentanyl-related substances bound for the USA that are prohibited there, 'such promises, echoed in the recent meeting between the countries' presidents, ring familiar'. The report pointed out that this issue first emerged in September 2016, when the Obama administration said China and the USA had agreed on 'enhanced measures' meant to keep fentanyl from coming into the USA. But in its official statements or state media reports made at the time, the Chinese government never specified the steps it intended to take and its follow-up has been patchy at best.

So when the Trump administration said after a bilateral meeting between Xi and Trump that the former had agreed to designate fentanyl as a controlled substance as 'a wonderful humanitarian gesture', *NYT* noted that analysts say there was little to cheer about. The report further said that Trump has repeatedly cited China as the main source of illicit fentanyl in the USA, where it helped drive total overdose deaths last year to more than 70,000—a record. 'Cracking down on the manufacturing and distribution of fentanyl in China is no easy task', *NYT* quoted an American source as saying.

NYT noted that the USA has long pushed China to systemically control all fentanyl substances. 'China controls the majority of global fentanyl sales, so it is a thriving industry there', Jeffrey Higgins, a retired special supervisory agent with the Drug Enforcement Administration was quoted as saying. He added that there are economic incentives for the Chinese to let opioid production flourish and fewer incentives to restrict their economy to cooperate with foreign law enforcement, ironically echoing the Opium War of the 19th century when Britain forced China to buy opium from the British.

[8] https://www.nytimes.com/2018/12/03/business/fentanyl-china-trump.html (accessed on 6 June 2019).

Dangers of Liberalism

In his 2005 Nobel Literature Prize acceptance speech, British author Harold Pinter made a scathing attack on American liberal values that have been exercised in a 'brutal, scornful and ruthless' fashion. He described modern society as a 'vast tapestry of lies, upon which we feed' (Pinter 2005). He gave this as an example:

> As every single person here knows, the justification for the invasion of Iraq was that Saddam Hussein possessed a highly dangerous body of weapons of mass destruction, some of which could be fired in 45 minutes, bringing about appalling devastation. We were assured that was true. It was not true. We were told that Iraq had a relationship with Al Qaeda and shared responsibility for the atrocity in New York of September 11th 2001. We were assured that this was true, it was not true. We were told that Iraq threatened the security of the world. We were assured that it was true. It was not true.

He went on to point out that the Soviet Union's atrocities during the post-war period were fully documented and verified, but the US crimes in the same period were not documented, acknowledged or recognized as crimes. Pinter pointed out another example, that of Nicaragua in the 1980s, which President Reagan has often described as a 'totalitarian dungeon' which the US media gladly subscribed to.

> The Sandanistas weren't perfect (but) they were intelligent, rational and civilized. They set out to establish a stable, decent, pluralistic society. The death penalty was abolished. Hundreds of thousands of poverty-stricken peasants were brought back from the dead. Over 100,000 families were given titled to land. Two thousand schools were built. Quite a remarkable literacy campaign reduced illiteracy in the country to less than one seventh. Free education was established and a free health service. Infant mortality was reduced by a third. Polio was eradicated. The United States denounced these as Marxist/Lenninst subversion. (Pinter 2005)

What the 'liberal media' does not report is more important than what they report with their cultural biases. One such story is the greatest war crime in history, the US bombing of Laos during the Indo-China war.

When President Obama visited Laos in 2016 and announced a grant of US$90 million to help clear unexploded bombs from this bombing campaign, the Western media hailed it as an altruistic gesture but ignored the war crime aspect of it (Appendix A). This perspective is picked up and relayed by media of neighbouring Thailand or Malaysia, for example. All they have to do is take a coach across the border to Laos and speak to the people in rural areas or just observe the damage done without depending on Western news agency copy that has been edited in New York, London or Paris, for Western readers.

Asian governments have to take the blame for not encouraging their media to think critically. Gauhar (1979) notes that suppression of the news media by many Two-Thirds World government has given the green light for the Western 'liberal' media to claim the moral high ground. He argues that they have invited foreign cultural infiltration; though he made these comments four decades ago, it is still relevant (Appendix A).

> By suppressing the national press the governments do not suppress news. They only make it easier for foreign news agencies to report news to their people with much greater impact. In a controlled area everything becomes news. The External Services of the BBC have built up a large audience in the Third World. How? Not by acquiring some special insight into the problems of developing countries, but by just reporting news, which is not allowed to be published or broadcast nationally. By suppressing the national press Third World governments have made their people easier targets of domination by the Western mass media. When Western media report anything positive about a Third World country, the home audience threat it with cynicism. But when they report anything critical it is accepted with enthusiasm. Western reporters can become authoritative interpreters of events in the Third World in a two-week sojourn. Opposition elements lionize them.

Subjectivity and News Values

The heroes of journalism are reporters. What they do is find things out. They go in first, amid the chaos of now, battering at close doors, sometimes taking risks, and capture the beginnings of the truth. And if they do not do that, who will? Editors? Commentators? There is only one alternative to reporters: accepting the authorized version, the one the businesses, bureaucrats and politicians choose to give us. After all, without reporters, what would commentators know? Reporters are, like most all heroes, flawed. As a group, they have a more soiled reputation than most; for enough of them routinely exaggerate, simplify and contort the truth to have made parts of the trade a by-word for calculated dishonesty. (David Randall 2011: 1)

The aforementioned quote was taken from David Randall's book *The Universal Journalist* that reflects very well the universality of the dilemma of good journalism.

In 1999, after the Malaysian Prime Minister Mahathir Mohamad blasted the Western media about their bias in reporting the Asian Financial Crisis, American-owned network CNBC Asia invited me to be on a panel of journalists and media scholars to discuss the issue. Taking part in the panel was Urban Lehner, editor of the *Asian Wall Street Journal*, an American-owned publication operating out of Hong Kong. When the moderator asked him whether the media could always be objective, cannot a position be taken even in the process of selection of stories, he said:

Words I like to stress are accurate and fair. If we are accurate and fair we are doing what we need to do for our readers. Objectivity in the sense of no view, I don't think it is possible. A completely objective story or a completely objective publication will be a boring one to read. What we try to do is to the extent that we have in the story some sort of a subjective viewpoint, but be very careful that it grows out of facts as reported and not out of some pre-conceptual ideology. I think the key word is accurate and fair, rather than objective.[9]

In news reporting, especially of international affairs, it is not difficult to observe how facts (and figures or data as well) could be presented from a subjective viewpoint as Lehner indicated. It is a trade in which you are expected to be objective and honest, but at the same time,

---

[9] Transcribed from the author's personal video copy of the discussion.

people tend to overlook the fact that objectivity would be subjective and this subjectivity could rely on many factors with one of the major ones being your cultural upbringing. A major point of contestation during the NWICO debate was the Two-Thirds World argument that there are no universal journalistic values and cultural perspectives and interpretations play a major part in international reporting. When the international flow of news is dominated by the Anglo-American news agencies and their agenda, what we usually call 'universal' is their cultural perspective and bias towards it. The Anglo-American media's use of the word 'international community' is a classic example. They usually use that term to describe a standpoint expressed—usually in UN forums—by the US, European Union (EU) members and a few of its allies such as Japan, Canada, Saudi Arabia and Australia. They ignore the fact that NAM represents a larger international community.

At an Asia Media Summit in Bangkok a few years ago, I was witness to an absorbing panel discussion moderated by an anchor from China's CCTV English language channel and the panel included senior news executives from BBC, CNN and a Russian news agency. One of the first questions the Chinese moderator raised was that the CNN and the BBC would often refer to Russian President Vladimir Putin as the former head of the KGB, he asked the BBC, do you refer to President George W. Bush (during his presidency) as the former CIA head when you mention him in your newscasts? BBC's reply was that most of their audience knows that anyway. Then the Chinese moderator asked, 'by now most of your audience know that Putin was a KGB agent as well. Why keep repeating it?' When the Russian was asked whether his news agency refers to Putin as former KGB head, his answer was that since he is president, it is not relevant to what we report about him now. The discussion went into looking at how 'unnecessary' reference like this could sway peoples' interpretation of a news story.

In the early 1990s when I was the Australian and South Pacific correspondent for Inter Press Service (IPS) news agency, on the eve of the Australian Prime Minister Paul Keating flying to Bangkok to join the king of Thailand and the prime minster of Laos to open an Australian-built 'Friendship Bridge' across the mighty Mekong River that will link Thailand to Laos by road for the first time, I received an interesting press released faxed to me by the office of the Australian Minister for Overseas Aid. In it, he pointed out that the 100 million Australian dollars spent in building that bridge from Australia's foreign 'aid' budget has generated some five times worth of projects for the Australian construction company that built it in Indo-China. These will be paid for by UN agencies, the Indo-China governments via international loans. At a time when the Australian government was considering cutting the foreign aid budget, the minister was making a case that his ministry was in fact generating business for Australian companies. The press release was meant for the Australian media to make this point to the Australian public. And that is what the Australian media did. But, for me, reporting for an international audience—and with IPS's mission to give an 'un-Western' perspective on news—I saw a great story in it for Asia.

Australia was subsiding its businesses to break into Asian markets, claiming it to be 'aid' to those countries. Thus, I did a critical assessment under the heading of 'Aid is good business for Australia' and even got a local NGO critical of Australia's aid programme to tell me that this was 'boomerang aid' (an Australian aboriginal term where an object you throw at someone comes back to you). My report was published in the front page of *The Nation* newspaper in Thailand on the day of the ceremony, which has greatly embarrassed the Australian embassy that prompted them to write a letter to the newspaper claiming that my report was based on wrong data. If that is true, then it is the minister who has fed me the wrong data via his press release! However, the point here is how subjective interpretation of data could generate stories with different focus.

Subjectivity and Interpretation—Cairo and Baghdad, 1994

In September 1994, I was part of an IPS reporting team that covered the UN International Conference on Population and Development in Cairo over a two-week period and produced a conference daily called 'Terra Viva'. It was my first up-close experience of how international news agencies operate. There were some 4,000 journalists representing news agencies as well as various national and regional news organizations and broadcasters. IPS's brief to us was to present an alternative to the major Western news outlets. As the days unfolded, I found that it was quite easy to find the alternative, as those news organizations were chasing after basically one issue—abortion and the battle, led by the Vatican to stop the UN including abortion as an acceptable family planning measure. Even there, they missed a story about the alliance between Iran's Islamic regime and the Vatican. IPS did the story focusing on this angle because we were on the lookout for news behind the news.

Cartoon depicting the international (Western) news media priorities during the UN Conference on Population and Development in Cairo in September 1994
Source: Terra Viva, IPS.

True, there was a lot of debate on the abortion issue at the conference, but it was not the only issue. There were stories IPS did which covered the other issues. Even as Christians and Muslims argued about 'family values', IPS carried a story about the UN High Commissioner for Refugees and the International Committee of the Red Cross raising the issue of missing children as the Civil War in Yugoslavia intensified. One of our reporters wrote a story about 'Asia's Population Role Models' (Terra Viva 1994: 17)—how Asia's emerging economies led by China, Thailand and Singapore along with Sri Lanka, Bangladesh and Indonesia have controlled their fertility rates without resorting to encouraging abortion or forced sterilization. The report carried quotes from delegates from these countries. The message here is why we are not concerned about rights and a better deal for the living. Instead we are talking about the rights of the unborn, an ideological position taken by some well-funded delegations and lobbyists, particularly from the USA—who were well represented within the US delegations to both the main conference and the parallel NGO forum.

Towards the end of the two-week assignment, I read in the local English language newspaper *Al-Ahram* a one-paragraph story sourced from a Western news agency (cannot remember if it was AFP or Reuters) about how Saddam Hussein was wooing Islamic fundamentalists as he had just banned the sale of alcoholic beverage and closed nightclubs in Baghdad. But Saddam's Ba'ath Party was well known to be a socialist party opposed to Islamic fundamentalism.

This example is a classic case of the 'subjective viewpoint' interacting with international news transmission—something I have been talking about ever since. Few days later, I was in Baghdad on a 10-day visit to report for IPS on the impact of UN economic sanctions on the people of Iraq. When I arrived in Baghdad, I inquired about the bans and found that the fact of it was correct, but the reason given by the international media reports that he was wooing Islamic fundamentalists was wrong. It was a subjective interpretation of facts.

What was really happening was that because of UN-approved economic sanctions, there were no soft drinks available in Iraq (these used to be imported or ingredients needed to make these could not be imported). Thus, a local drinks manufacturer developed a slightly alcoholic drink which was popular in the country, especially among teenagers. The government did not want their young to get hooked up on an alcoholic drink. That is why any drink with alcoholic contents was banned. About the nightclub ban, I was told that Iraq's middle-class women, who were well educated and many used to work in professional jobs, had lost their jobs as the economy was devastated by the 1991 Gulf War and the economic sanctions that followed. With rising inflation, to feed their families or to get ends to meet, they were getting into prostitution via the nightclubs in Baghdad. The government did not want their educated middle-class women to be corrupted and psychologically scarred. That is why the nightclubs were closed.

When I went to Baghdad, I found that there were no Western journalists based there. Iraqi government does not trust the Western media and no visas were given to foreign journalists. Now that the war was over, even the CNN was gone. I was lucky to get a visa (on my Australian passport) mainly because I was reporting for IPS, which Iraqi government probably thought was not hostile to them. How did this story about 'Saddam wooing Islamic fundamentalists' get out? It is very likely, it was picked up by Western journalists based in Beirut, Cairo, Cyprus or even in London through an Iraqi government broadcast and then applying a subjective viewpoint interpret it to report the way they did.

At the time I went to Iraq, the international media narrative on the country was very much focused on how Saddam is trying to break the UN embargo and who or what countries are assisting him on this. But what about the human costs of these sanctions? Having got the visa to enter Iraq, this was the brief given to me by IPS. I also had the advantage of being a non-White journalist because I felt the Iraqis in the street were not afraid to talk to me and some were very frank in their comments such as the Baghdad taxi driver, with whom I was caught in a traffic jam, with smoke belting out of cars all around. He started cursing the Americans for the sanctions, which deprives car spare parts coming into the country to repair these cars. Some even expressed misgivings about Saddam's iron-clad ruling style, even though they did not support American sanctions nor an invasion. One Iraqi public servant told me that the problem with America is that they see the Iraqis through the prism of uneducated 'Bedouin' (nomadic desert people) they often see in American movies and news broadcasts, and when they have to deal with educated Arabs, they are not equipped for it.

The real eye-opener for me was a visit to Saddam Central Teaching Hospital for Children in Baghdad, which used to be a showpiece children's hospital in the region. But since the UN-sponsored economic embargo took effect after the 1991 Gulf War, the hospital was a skeleton of what it was. There was hardly a nurse to be seen because the nurses who used to work there came mainly from Cuba and Asia, and they had fled Iraq before the war. The children who were very sick even to cry were fanned and comforted by caring but helpless grandmothers, mothers and aunts. Let me quote from the first few paragraphs of a story I did for *The Australian* newspaper in Australia. A similar story was done for IPS from Baghdad.

> A three-month-old boy with a bloated, yellow belly breathes uneasily while his young mother watches over him. 'This boy has prolong jaundice', says Dr Jasim Al-Marzoki. 'We can't do the investigations to find out the cause because the drugs are not available'.
> In another bed, a three-year-old girl breathes with the help of a respirator while her mother strokes her head, perhaps hoping to keep her daughter alive for a little longer. She's suffering from heart problems, is partially paralyzed and in urgent need of surgery. 'But, we can't do it here', says the doctor. 'The facility is not operating for open-heart surgery and the drugs are not available'.
> In another ward is a 10-year-old boy with almost total hair loss. He has been cured of leukemia by the hospital a few years ago but has relapsed because the Methotrexate tablets needed to treat him are no longer available.
> 'It is really frustrating to see patients like this', says Al-Marzoki. 'We know how to treat them but can't help them. It's really devastating for a doctor to work under these conditions'.

The doctor who took me around the wards explained the situation with tears in his eyes. As a journalist, I was determined to tell this story to the outside world. We have been bombarded with too many subjective reports that assume Saddam Hussein is a terrible man and he needs to be overthrown at any cost. In the process, the media loses the bigger story of human suffering caused by Western-inspired economic sanctions. From what I saw, I could easily describe such impacts of the UN sanctions as a 'crime against humanity'.

It is interesting how I got the story in—only time I was able to get a story into this Rupert Murdoch-owned newspaper in Australia. When I returned to Sydney from Iraq, the Australian media was full of stories of how Saddam was amassing his troops on the southern border with Saudi Arabia. Just a few days earlier, I had travelled by bus over 20 hours across the Iraqi desert in the south-west parts to Jordon and did not see any Iraqi tanks on the way. Thus, I contacted *The Australian*'s office and said I can give you a good eyewitness story from Iraq and, to my surprise, they bought the story.

Let us fast-forward 23 years to March 2017 and look at a story filled by Reuters news agency from Damascus titled 'Syria Sanctions Indirectly Hit Children's Cancer Treatment'.[10] The story is remarkably similar to the one I filled from Baghdad. Here are the first three paragraphs from the story:

> In the cancer ward at Damascus Children's Hospital, doctors are struggling with a critical shortage of specialist drugs to treat their young patients—and it's not just due to the general chaos of the Syrian civil war.
>
> Local and World Health Organization (WHO) officials also blame Western sanctions for severely restricting pharmaceutical imports, even though medical supplies are largely exempt from measures imposed by the United States and European Union.
>
> Six years of conflict have brought the Syrian health service, once one of the best in the Middle East, close to collapse. Fewer than half of the country's hospitals are fully functioning and numbers of doctors have dived.

When such inhumanity goes largely unreported in the international media, the vicious cycle continues with the media not holding the

---

[10] http://www.reuters.com/article/us-mideast-crisis-syria-sanctions/syria-sanctions-indirectly-hit-childrens-cancer-treatment-idUSKBN16M1UW (accessed on 7 June 2019).

powers (Western governments and the UN) accountable for the misery they create by imposing short-sighted sanctions. The 'watchdog' role of the 'free media' is supposed to do that, but the fact that what I reported from Baghdad is still happening almost 25 years later is the reflection of the dysfunctionality of the 'fourth estate' model.

We need to ask the question what role subjectivity plays in constructing our news agenda. The fact is there are sanctions imposed by the UN—against Iraq in 1994 and against Syria in 2017—but the media narrative supports these sanction because they see the bigger evil as the two rulers Saddam Hussein of Iraq and Bashar al-Assad of Syria, and not the impact of these sanctions on the people of these countries, especially on its health services. Western media is fond of describing countries that impose such barbarity on people as 'crimes against humanity'. Why cannot a non-Western media describe such economic sanction imposed by Western countries similarly?

Global Media and Lack of Respect for the 'Other'

What passes for Global Media in the West is really the media of the West, which raises interesting questions. It is despite, or because the world has grown smaller, a large part of today's intercultural conflicts are as a result of perceived cultural humiliation? Does the media do the best job it can to give a voice and a face to the world's marginalized? Who makes the cut to earn screen time in this brave new world? Yes, there is the occasional Third World voice, but it speaks a First World language…. What passes from my world on TV screens in the West is often a Western perception of my world. Are those speaking for their cultures in the globalised media authentic representatives of them?

—Dr Shashi Tharoor[11]

Dr Shashi Tharoor, who was then the head of public information at the UN, made the aforementioned comments at a conference in Beijing in July 2005. At that time, he was campaigning to succeed

---

[11] Keynote speech at the AMIC annual conference in Beijing, July 2005, obtained from AMIC archives.

Kofi Annan as the next secretary general of the UN (which he lost to Ban Ki-moon). His talk was titled 'Weapons of Mass Distraction' and he spoke at length about the hegemony of the Western media, especially through satellite-driven television to set the global political, economic and cultural agenda.

'The media does not just reflect public opinion, it shapes it', Dr Tharoor said further adding 'with all the freedom in the world, there is no escaping the implications of the subtle influence that the media has to help us define who we are and how we behave'. He said:

> In a world where people fear a clash of civilizations, the need for tolerance and effective protection of minorities and other vulnerable groups has never been stronger. The media has an important role to play in conveying the message that it is our diversity that gives the human species its splendor and our diversity that has enabled us to make progress.

Thus, Tharoor, whom many Asians have often said as the best UN secretary general we never had, argued that the media has to go the extra mile with an urgency to teach about respect of the 'other', because the alternative may be the terrorism which so dominates our headlines. More than a decade after his speech, his prophecy unfortunately has become true.

The Difference between Hiroshima and Pearl Harbor

A good example of how the global media's news agenda is dictated by Western cultural subjectivity is the way the international media reported President Obama's visit to Hiroshima and Japanese Prime Minister Shinzo Abe's visit to Pearl Harbor, both in 2016.

In May 2016, President Barack Obama became the first sitting president of the USA to visit Hiroshima, the city where America dropped an atomic bomb on 6 August 1945 killing over 80,000 people. A week later, another atomic bomb was dropped in Nagasaki, which killed over 70,000 people. It led to Japan surrendering and the end of the Second World War.

In December 2016, Japanese Prime Minister Shinzo Abe visited Pearl Harbor, which the Japanese torpedo planes, bombers and fighter planes bombed on the morning of 7 December 1941, pounding the US fleet moored there in the hope of destroying US power in the Pacific, and pulling the USA into the Second World War.

It is interesting how the Western media outlets framed the two visits. As Hiroshima and Nagasaki are the only two cities in human history to suffer from a nuclear bomb attack, in anybody's imagination, the first visit to such a city by a sitting president of the country which was the perpetuator of such a 'war crime' (according to today's terminology) would be expected to make a formal apology to its host Japan. But that was not how the visit was framed and as far as I know, there were no calls by any MSM nor civil society groups in Japan, demanding that President Obama should make an apology if he visits the city.

When his visit was announced months before, the White House was at pains to emphasize that he will not make an apology to the Japanese people for the heinous attack in 1945. When London's *Guardian* asked if the trip might be seen as an apology, the White House Press Secretary Josh Earnest replied: 'If people do interpret it that way, they'll be interpreting it wrongly'. He declined to comment on the morality of America's decision to drop the atomic bomb, for which there have been calls for the country to apologize. He said, 'The president intends the visit to send a much more forward-looking signal for his ambition of realizing the goal of a planet without nuclear weapons'.[12]

Thus, they framed the visit as part of Obama's campaign for the elimination of nuclear weapons. As Gardiner Harris writing in the *NYT*[13] on the eve of Obama's visit noted, 'Obama's predecessors had good reasons to avoid Hiroshima. None wanted to be seen by American voters as apologizing for a decision that many historians even today believe, on balance, saved lives'. So when Americans are

---

[12] https://www.theguardian.com/us-news/2016/may/10/obama-hiroshima-japan-visit-second-world-war (accessed on 7 June 2019).

[13] http://www.nytimes.com/2016/05/26/world/asia/obama-hiroshima-visit.html?_r=0 (accessed on 7 June 2019).

involved in a 'war crime' from the American cultural perspective, 'it was done to save lives'. He added that Obama's visit to Hiroshima will 'further his efforts to curb the world's stockpile of nuclear weapons, a signature issue for him and an important reason he won the 2009 Nobel Peace Prize'. No questions asked here, why he was given the Nobel Peace Prize before he could achieve it. Harris pointed out that just 10 weeks after becoming president, he told in a speech in Prague, 'as the only nuclear power to have used a nuclear weapon, the United States has a moral responsibility to act (to abolish nuclear weapons)'. Is that enough reason to get a Nobel Peace Prize?

Benjamin Rhodes, a deputy national security adviser, was quoted in the *NYT* article as saying that the visit to Hiroshima 'is a gesture of respect for the Japanese people', and it will help to build on the growing alliance between the USA and Japan, and 'it would be meaningful for the Japanese people to pay this kind of visit'. But the report also pointed out that China and South Korea in particular have criticized the visit as endorsing Prime Minister Abe's campaign to move Japan beyond its militarist past and recast itself as a victim rather than the aggressor in Asia during the Second World War. That is another interesting culturally subjective viewpoint coming from Korea and China.

For decades, the Western media has harped upon the fact that Japan should apologize for its 'atrocious' behaviour during the war, and even *NYT* article referred to a Japanese apology in December to Korea and other nations for the 'comfort women' sex slaves taken by the Japanese army during the war.

During Obama's visit to Hiroshima on 27 May 2016, Western MSM emphasized Obama's comments at the solemn ceremony at the bombing site, where he said:

> Why do we come to this place,to Hiroshima? We come to ponder the terrible forces unleashed in the not so distant past. We come to mourn the dead ... their souls speak to us and ask us to look inward. To take stock of who we are and what we might become.[14]

---

[14] http://edition.cnn.com/2016/05/27/politics/obama-hiroshima-japan/index.html (accessed on 7 June 2019).

The reports also pointed out that Obama in his speech referred to the need to abolish nuclear weapons and urged the world to 'choose a future when Hiroshima and Nagasaki are not considered the dawn of atomic warfare but as the start of our own moral awakening'. Wow, a nice way to redefine a 'war crime' as a 'moral crusade'!

When Abe visited Pearl Harbor, the focus of reporting was different. Most Western media reports zoomed in on his condolences for the attack and the pledge to never to wage such a war again, also emphasizing that he did not apologize for the bombing. Reuters quoted him as saying: 'I offer my sincere and everlasting condolences to the souls of those who lost their lives here, as well as to the spirits of all the brave men and women whose lives were taken by a war that commenced in this very place'.[15]

The BBC also emphasized his condolences and pointed out that the Japanese prime minister has praised the USA for its efforts to mend relations with Japan since the war.[16]

In an era where the words 'war crimes' and 'crimes against humanity' are common currency in reporting about civil wars and other armed conflicts around the world, these words were completely missing from reports on the two events.

Why Nobel Peace Prize for Liu Xiaobo, Not Julian Assange?

As we look at subjectivity in news reporting, especially how it creates a hegemony of ideas and perceptions, it will be appropriate to look at how the Nobel Peace Prize is awarded and reported by the international media, as well as a largely unknown alternative: the Ramon Magsaysay Awards.

The Nobel Prizes are named after the Swedish Scientist Alfred Nobel who invented dynamite, a substance that has been used for

---

[15] https://www.yahoo.com/news/pearl-harbor-visit-abe-pledges-japan-never-wage-023911703.html (accessed on 7 June 2019).
[16] http://www.bbc.com/news/world-asia-38438714 (accessed on 7 June 2019).

generations in explosions. Before his death, on 27 November 1895, he signed his last will and testament, giving the largest share of his fortune to a series of prizes, the Nobel Prizes. As described in Nobel's will, one part was dedicated to 'the person who shall have done the most or the best work for fraternity between nations, for the abolition or reduction of standing armies and for the holding and promotion of peace congresses'.[17] This is today known as the Nobel Peace Prize announced to the world each year in October.

While there have been many worthy recipients of this award over the years, there have also been very controversial recipients such as former US Secretary of State Henry Kissinger, Palestinian Liberation Front's leader Yasser Arafat and the 2010 winner Liu Xiaobo. Indian Independence leader Mahatma Gandhi, though nominated for the prize five times, was never given it, even though he brought down the most powerful empire the world has known through a non-violent independence struggle.

In recent years, the Nobel Peace Prize has been criticized, especially in Asia and Africa for bias and espousing a Eurocentric liberal agenda. It came to a boil in 2010 when Chinese writer, former university professor and human rights activist Liu Xiaobo was given it, while he was serving an 11-year prison term for espionage in China.

China reacted furiously to the announcement seeing it as an interference on Chinese internal affairs with Foreign Ministry Spokesman Ma Zhaoxu saying that the Nobel Committee has violated its own integrity and the award would have negative repercussions in international relations. 'The Nobel Peace Prize should be awarded to those who work to promote ethnic harmony, international friendship, disarmament and who hold peace meetings. These were (Alfred) Nobel's wishes',[18] he said.

Liu Xiaobo was found guilty of violating Chinese law and sentenced to prison by Chinese judicial organs. His actions run contrary to

---

[17] https://www.nobelprize.org/nobel_prizes/facts/peace/ (accessed on 7 June 2019).
[18] http://www.theage.com.au/world/china-furious-at-nobels-violation-20101008-16c29.html (accessed on 7 June 2019).

the purpose of the Nobel Peace Prize. By awarding the prize to this person, the Nobel committee has violated and blasphemed the award.

Though he was little known inside China at the time of the award due to official censorship, he was a veteran of the Tiananmen Square protests of 1989, and a co-author of the Charter 08 manifesto[19] for which he was sentenced for 11 years in prison on 25 December 2009.

In awarding the prize, the Norwegian Nobel Committee said that Liu Xiaobo has waged a long and non-violent struggle for fundamental human rights in China. They added:

> For over two decades, Liu Xiaobo has been a strong spokesman for the application of fundamental human rights also in China. He took part in the Tiananmen protests in 1989; he was a leading author behind Charter 08, the manifesto of such rights in China, which was published on the 60th anniversary of the United Nations' Universal Declaration of Human Rights, on 10th of December 2008. The following year, Liu was sentenced to eleven years in prison and two years' deprivation of political rights for inciting subversion of state power.[20]

In an editorial in China's *Global Times*, a day after the announcement describing Liu Xiaobo as an 'incarcerated Chinese criminal', it accused the Nobel Committee of arrogance and bias. 'The Nobel committee once again displayed its arrogance and prejudice against a country that has made the most remarkable economic and social progress in the past three decades', it said, pointing out that most Chinese feel 'the prize is loaded with Western ideology'.

Continuing the theme of Western ideological bias, the daily noted that in the last century, the prize was awarded several times to pro-Western advocates in the former Soviet Union, including Mikhail Gorbachev, whose efforts directly led to the disintegration of the

---

[19] Charter 08 advocates a whole series of reforms that would result in a separation of powers, a new constitution and legislative democracy.

[20] https://www.nobelprize.org/nobel_prizes/peace/laureates/2010/press.html (accessed on 7 June 2019).

Soviet Union. Thus, it stated: 'It seems that instead of peace and unity in China, the Nobel committee would like to see the country split by an ideological rift, or better yet, collapse like the Soviet Union'.

Beijing Daily asked in a commentary[21] why the Nobel Peace Committee hadn't given the prize to Julian Assange, the Australia-born founder of WikiLeaks who 'exposed some US secrets' that posed a threat to world peace. It pointed out that he was 'imprisoned' at an embassy in London because the Western countries (i.e., Sweden) were trying to charge him for a suspected rape and sexual harassment, which is a lifestyle issue.

'Assange's experience shows that United States's advertised freedom of speech is not absolute and also have sub-degrees, and there is a bottom line', argues the *Global Times*. 'If it is flat and does not hurt, it is okay to say a few words about US government's bad actions, but Assange has crossed that bottom line' and the paper went on to argue that WikiLeaks has exposed US non-transparent actions that are threatening world peace and he is now hunted by the Western governments.

Global Times challenges the Nobel Peace Prize Committee to give the prize to Assange because, using their own criteria, he has used his freedom of speech to expose powerful Western governments to protect people around the world from what it calls 'western government violence'. Thus, the Committee needs to stand up to acknowledge a 'defender of freedom of speech against Western government persecution' and if it is unable to do that, then the prize would become a tool of the USA, North Atlantic Treaty Organization (NATO) and European governments to use the winner 'as a Western tool to repress other consciousness'.

Why Is Ramon Magsaysay Prize Ignored?

When the Nobel Prizes are announced each year, the world is kept in high suspense by the media for a few weeks. But when the Ramon

---

[21] http://news.163.com/10/1210/03/6NGSVK2K00014AED.html (accessed on 7 June 2019).

Magsaysay Prizes are announced—which are sometimes dubbed Asia's Nobel Prizes—the world's media hardly takes note of it. Why?

The Ramon Magsaysay Award, Asia's premier prize and highest honor, celebrates greatness of spirit and transformative leadership in Asia. In the past five decades, the award has been bestowed on over three hundred outstanding men, women and organizations whose selfless service has offered their societies, Asia, and the world successful solutions to some of the most intractable problems of human development. The trustees of the Ramon Magsaysay Award Foundation annually select the awardees. Awardees are presented with a certificate and a medallion with an embossed image of Ramon Magsaysay facing right in profile. The Award is presented to them in formal ceremonies in Manila, Philippines on August 31st, the birth anniversary of the much-esteemed Philippine President whose ideals inspired the Award's creation in 1957.[22]

Ramon Magsaysay (1907–1957) is a Filipino independence hero, who was the president of the Philippines from 1953 to 1957. He was a son of an artisan and was a school teacher in the provincial town of Iba on the main island of Luzon. Though most Philippine political leaders were of Spanish descent, Magsaysay was of Malay stock, like most of the common people.[23]

The Magsaysay awardees are those who have dedicated a lifetime to work towards transforming their societies for the better. They are exemplary figures, who have worked on the ground to apply unique solutions and inspired many more to follow in their footsteps and offered inclusive solutions to wide-ranging problems that are workable and sustainable. Their work and personalities may have helped Asia in particular, and the world in general, to create a more inclusive and just society, if both the global media and the Asian media would have paid more attention to the awardees and their work when the prizes are announced each August.

---

[22] http://rmaward.asia/about-the-award/ (accessed on 7 June 2019).
[23] Source: Encyclopaedia Britannica.

If one checks through the list of awardees over the years, it is noticeable that the award has gone to those who have done positive work towards breaking barriers, rather than to activists who demand their rights. Among recent awardees are:

- *2017—Yoshiaki Ishizawa (Japan):* A Japanese who devoted 50 years of his life to help ensure that Cambodia's Angkor Wat survives and remains a living monument for Cambodians. He has worked side by side with Cambodians, networking with international experts and organizations, campaigning in the Japanese media to generate awareness and support, and devising programmes for Angkor's protection and conservation.
- *2017—Abdon Nababan (Indonesia):* He is an Indonesian who formed the Indonesian Indigenous People's Alliance of the Archipelago (AMAN) after the fall of the Suharto government in 1998, which developed into a mass movement with over 115 local chapters. Under Nababan's leadership, AMAN won a landmark court ruling in 2012 that declared indigenous properties as not 'state land' and over 57 million hectares have been returned to ownership of indigenous communities.
- *2017—Tony Tay (Singapore):* In 2003, he started 'Willing Hearts', a non-profit volunteer-driven organization with 11 volunteers to cook and distribute hot food to the needy in Singapore. Today, the organization cooks over 6,000 meals a day and is distributed from 40 points across the island.
- *2016—Conchita Carpio-Morales (Philippines):* An exemplary public servant who has restored peoples' faith in the public service as the government's ombudsman who fearlessly pursued the corrupt, keeping her integrity and equanimity in the face of enormous challenges. Under her leadership, she filed cases against a former president, former vice-president, senators, congressmen and governors.
- *2016—Thodur Madabusi Krishna (India):* A celebrated Indian Carnatic musicians born into a high-caste Brahmin family in Chennai, who broke convention by identifying rural gifted youth of lower caste background who lacked opportunities and bringing them to Chennai to be trained under renowned musicians and

getting them a college education. The lower castes have been traditionally excluded from sharing in India's rich cultural legacy.

- *2015—Kommaly Chanthavong (Laos):* A soft-spoken Laotian woman whose love for traditional silk weaving revived and developed the ancient Laotian art form almost destroyed by the legacy of the Indo-China war. It created livelihoods for thousands of poor, war-displaced Laotians. Today, her Phontong Handicrafts Cooperative operates in 35 villages and connects over 450 Laotian traditional artisans.

These are just a handful of over 300 awardees since 1958, who have contributed to society, sometimes in a quiet but determined manner.

Noting that people are claiming democracy has failed mankind 'because freedom has caused the poor to remain poor, while the rich gained more', Philippine Vice-President Leni Robredo said in her keynote speech at the 2017 award ceremony that there is a greater need now for people like the Magsaysay awardees.[24]

It would be good to conclude this chapter by asking the question: why is that the global media largely ignores the Ramon Magsaysay Awards and especially the work done by its awardees to make this world a better world by incorporating cultural heritage preservation (which is different to nationalism) to their work, as well as community mobilization (not by shouting slogans and taking to the streets), using the arts to break entrenched cultural barriers or indulging in quiet social work (rather than demanding reparation for alleged 'war crimes') to overcome years of trauma from war?

Covering the work of Ramon Magsaysay awardees may be a better way to encourage more cooperative human relations towards creating a better and peaceful world, rather than giving saturation coverage to Nobel Peace Prize winners who often use that award for political campaigning that may sometimes create more conflict than peace. In Chapter 10, we will explore how to develop such 'mindful' reporting strategies.

---

[24] https://www.mmtimes.com/news/asias-nobel-prize-now-more-ever.html (accessed on 7 June 2019).

CHAPTER 5

Dawn of the Post-Truth Era?

Some commentators, particularly in the West, are arguing that we are living in the 'post-truth' age. The *Oxford Dictionary*[1] describes it as an 'era of post-truth politics, where it's easy to cherry-pick data and come to whatever conclusion you desire'. Meanwhile, the *Cambridge Dictionary*[2] describes it as 'relating to a situation in which people are more likely to accept an argument based on their emotions and beliefs, rather than one based on facts'. But aren't the subjective reporting values we discussed in the previous chapter exactly the same?

According to Wikipedia, in 2004, American author Ralph Keyes used the term 'post-truth era' in his book by that title. In it, he argued that deception is becoming more prevalent in the current media-driven world. According to Keyes, lies stopped being treated as something inexcusable and started being viewed as something acceptable in certain situations, which supposedly led to the beginning of the

---

[1] https://en.oxforddictionaries.com/definition/post-truth (accessed on 7 June 2019).
[2] https://dictionary.cambridge.org/dictionary/english/post-truth (accessed on 7 June 2019).

post-truth era. But let us look at why post-truth era has become such a talked-about topic these days.

'Facts hold a sacred place in Western liberal democracies. Whenever democracy seems to be going awry, when voters are manipulated or politicians are ducking questions, we turn to facts for salvation. But they seem to be losing their ability to support consensus', argues William Davies, who is an associate professor in political economy at the University of London in an op-ed on *NYT*.[3] Pointing out that Poynter Institute's PolitiFact has found that about 70 per cent of Donald Trump's 'factual' statements actually fall into the categories of 'mostly false', 'false' and 'pants-on-fire' untruth, he says:

> How can we still be speaking of 'facts' when they no longer provide us with a reality that we all agree on? The problem is that the experts and agencies involved in producing facts have multiplied, and many are now for hire. If you really want to find an expert willing to endorse a fact, and have sufficient money or political clout behind you, you probably can. The combination of populist movements with social media is often held responsible for post-truth politics. Individuals have growing opportunities to shape their media consumption around their own opinions and prejudices, and populist leaders are ready to encourage them.... The problem is the oversupply of facts in the 21st century: There are too many sources, too many methods, with varying levels of credibility, depending on who funded a given study and how the eye-catching number was selected.

This produces some chilling possibilities for politics, argues Davies, the author of *The Happiness Industry: How the Government and Big Business Sold Us Well-Being*. He asks, 'once numbers are viewed more as indicators of current sentiment, rather than as statements about reality, how are we to achieve any consensus on the nature of social, economic and environmental problems, never mind agree on the solutions?' arguing that this is a recipe for conspiracy theories to prosper. 'And while we will have far greater means of knowing how many

---

[3] https://www.nytimes.com/2016/08/24/opinion/campaign-stops/the-age-of-post-truth-politics.html (accessed on 7 June 2019).

people believe those theories, we will have far fewer means of persuading them to abandon them.'

The aforementioned arguments on the post-truth era gathered momentum after the November 2016 Presidential elections in the USA and the Brexit vote in the UK a few months later. However, as discussed in Chapter 4, subjective interpretation of facts has led to misrepresentation or biased reporting for a long time, perhaps going back to the 19th century when European imperial trade and communications came together with the development of news agencies. So is this really a post-truth age? Didn't the NWICO debates of the 1970s address such practices by the Western news agencies in particular?

Leaders of the Two-Thirds World hotly contested the Western media's selective choice of 'facts' that painted their countries in a negative frame and built consensus among Western audiences (as well as global audiences who had access to only Western news sources) that these countries are corrupt, all people live in poverty and in dirt, are untrustworthy or inefficient, etc. At the same time, the Soviet media was showing selective 'facts' about the West where they concentrated on crime, discrimination against minorities, poverty among Blacks in the USA, etc., giving Soviet audiences a very negative picture of the 'decadent' Western societies. This information cold war has intensified today with the advent of the Internet and social media.

As *The Times of India* columnist Amulya Gopalakrishnan[4] points out, in India, organized distrust of what is given as facts goes back longer and deeper than the Trump and Brexit era. 'As our sources of information multiply, authoritative sources, certifying agencies, are losing their power', she argues, adding that when you don't like the news, you blame the MSM. 'Official documents can be dismissed, forensic evidence is held to be suspect. Even photographs and videos can be faked and circulated. There is no floor to stand on, no basis for certainty', notes Gopalakrishnan, adding 'while the nature of disagreements isn't new, the Internet has intensified the breakdown of

---

[4] https://timesofindia.indiatimes.com/blogs/to-name-and-address/everything-but-the-truth-what-we-share-with-the-brexit-campaign-and-trump/ (accessed on 7 June 2019).

objective assessment'. So what this has led to is that when we have a gut sense, a received belief system, we then find evidence to support it. 'We may be willing to change our mind on the details, but not the fundamentals', she concludes.

Let us take a couple of recent examples of international news coverage. When the Russian and Syrian forces were liberating Aleppo from the Islamic terrorists, if you watch the Western media channels, they will show pictures from Aleppo and describe the attacks as a 'war crime' and that civilians are being killed. But Russia's RT channel will show the same footage and say they are flushing out the terrorists who have held civilians as human shields. Similar reporting happened in 2009 when the Sri Lankan armed forces crushed the terrorist group Liberation Tigers of Tamil Eelam (LTTE) in a fierce battle to end the 30-year Civil War. Western media, often source from LTTE propaganda claims that it was a 'war crime' where 40,000 people perished. The Sri Lankan government said that it was a 'humanitarian mission' that saved thousands of human shields the terrorists held within areas they controlled.

The Sri Lankan government vehemently denied such huge casualties and over the past years provided numerous reports to quash the claim, but Western media, particularly British media, continued to use the 40,000 figure asking the Sri Lankan government to account for it. Even the United Nations Human Rights Council (UNHRC) had fallen for this, though no one had even produced 400 names— leave aside 40,000—of those civilians killed. The UN says it is more likely to be around 7,000, but they are not able to produce names of such people missing or killed. But the fact is, as Gopalakrishnan says, if you are in a 'received belief system', you will find evidence to support it. Thus, if that belief system is a belief in the notion that once their 'benevolent' European colonial masters left, these countries have drifted back into chaos, the propaganda material provided by the LTTE fits very well as 'evidence'. Even Britain's Channel 4 used unverified video clips provided by activist groups as such evidence.[5]

---

[5] https://www.youtube.com/watch?v=z5O1JAfRXew&t=561s (accessed on 7 June 2019).

Fact-Checking and Media Bias

Often we hear arguments that media bias in the 'post-truth' world could be tackled by better fact-checking of stories. But the question that will naturally arise is on what basis are you fact-checking the source? The criteria adopted would itself give rise to bias, especially subjective cultural or political bias. For example, liberals hold conservative viewpoints as 'extremist' or 'bigotry', while conservatives hold liberal viewpoints as taking 'political correctness too far'. Tamar Wilner, a Dallas-based freelance journalist and researcher writing in the *Columbia Journalism Review*, asks:

> If I say an article is biased, you'd be right to ask, biased compared to what? Choosing a baseline is fraught with issues, journalistic and philosophical. How can we judge an individual outlet's choice of stories without knowing the whole universe of stories the outlet had to choose from?[6] Depending on the question you're asking of the data, a widely acceptable baseline may not always be possible.

These days, the academic discussions on fact-checking often make me wonder if content analysis media researchers have done for decades is any different in trying to make sense of media bias. Wilner discusses various technologies, tools and sites being developed for fact-checking such as by Google and *NYT* (Third Eye), but argues that these efforts 'suffer from the very problem they're trying to address: Their subjective assessments leave room for human biases, or even simple inconsistencies, to creep in'.

'Fact-checkers are no longer the fresh-faced journalistic reform movement pushed forward by the tailwinds of positive expectations. We are wrinkly arbiters of a take-no-prisoners war for the future of the Internet', said Alexios Mantzarlis,[7] director of International

---

[6] https://www.cjr.org/innovations/measure-media-bias-partisan.php (accessed on 7 June 2019).
[7] https://www.poynter.org/fact-checking/2018/fact-checkers-are-no-longer-a-fresh-faced-movement-theyre-fighting-for-the-future-of-the-internet/ (accessed on 7 June 2019).

Fact-Checking Network (IFCN) in opening remarks to their 5th Global Summit in June 2018. He warns:

> A dark cloud hangs over us. The disaffection and distrust that have plagued mainstream media outlets for many years is now spilling over to fact-checkers. In Turkey, the Philippines and especially Brazil it broke out in the form of concerted campaigns aimed to vilify fact-checking as an instrument.

If fact-checking organizations like his are to succeed as a media reform movement, then Mantzarlis posed that they need to address six questions, such as:

1. Are we effective enough at keeping public figures accountable?
2. Are we doing enough to correct ourselves?
3. Are we doing enough to dispel concerns about bias?
4. Are we equipped to reassert the primacy of facts in the face of political movements that are inherently suspicious—at the time with good reason—of the fact-generating institutions we rely on?
5. Are we truly taking advantage of this network of fact-checkers to build collaborations larger than the sum of our parts?
6. Are we putting in place mechanisms to ensure that our delegated powers over Google and Facebook don't have unintended consequences?

Poynter Institute[8] in a new-year prediction in January 2019 noted that in 2018 there have been many incidents around the world, where proper fact-checking may have avoided a disaster, such as cross-national hoaxes in Europe, mob lynching incited by WhatsApp rumours in India and attacks against fact-checkers in Brazil and the Philippines. Poynter Institute warned:

> The stakes for fact-checking have only gotten higher (and) in 2019, we predict that fact-checkers will have to contend with the rise of government actions against misinformation around the world.

---

[8] https://www.poynter.org/fact-checking/2018/heres-what-to-expect-from-fact-checking-in-2019/ (accessed on 7 June 2019).

They'll see even more attempts to undermine their debunking efforts—particularly when it comes to videos. Technology companies will be coaxed into implementing more projects addressing the spread of misinformation on their platforms.

Ironically, the Internet, which was celebrated a decade ago as a tool that would democratize communication around the globe, would become the battleground to tighten the screws on free speech. Even fact-checkers, wittingly or unwittingly, could be drawn into it.

In Chapter 8, we will be discussing the redefining of journalistic ethics and in Chapter 9 the fake news hysteria in the so-called post-truth era. But, in this book, as you may have noted already and will find out more as we proceed with the coming chapters, I will be arguing that misrepresenting or twisting of facts is not new and we need to look at it through media bias and subjective interpretations. So let us take a few more examples.

Tsunami Is 'Yes'—Why Fallujah Is 'No'?

The Asian Tsunami of 2004 that hit Indonesia, Thailand, Sri Lanka and India killed over 250,000 people. There was a tidal wave of media coverage across the world, but just a month before the Asian Tsunami happened, an equally devastating—but a human-made—calamity took place in Fallujah in Iraq, of which we hardly heard anything about, not until a few months later, that too mainly via alternative media (see Seneviratne, 2005).

Fallujah was a city of over 300,000 people, and US sources have claimed that some 6,000 insurgents were holed out in the city, and in order to flush them out, the US forces destroyed the whole city. Fallujah's compensation commissioner has reported that 36,000 of the city's 50,000 houses have been destroyed, along with 8,400 shops, 60 nurseries and schools, and 65 mosques and shrines.

Didn't the big waves which hit Aceh or the southern coast of Thailand and Sri Lanka do the same? But why should we be kept in the dark about what human-made calamities can do to communities? Why are we not shown the piled-up bodies of Iraqis? It depends who is responsible for this calamity.

We must also ask the question that if fact-checking sites existed then like today, would they have picked on it? What is not reported here is more important than what was reported. Are fact-checkers equipped to do that, especially if that happens outside the USA or Europe?

The global Western media not only ignored the event, they ignored its first anniversary in 2005 while revisiting the Asian Tsunami with documentaries and analysis to mark the occasion. One year after the attack on Fallujah, coincidentally, the US forces in Iraq made an admission that they used burning phosphorus weapons during their assault on Fallujah a year ago.[9]

Fallujah is a place name that has become a symbol of unconscionable brutality, noted Mike Marqusee, co-founder of Iraq Occupation Focus, writing in London's *Guardian*[10] on the first anniversary of the Fallujah attack.

> The assault was preceded by eight weeks of aerial bombardment. US troops cut off the city's water, power and food supplies, condemned as a violation of the Geneva convention by a UN special rapporteur, who accused occupying forces of 'using hunger and deprivation of water as a weapon of war against the civilian population'. Two-thirds of the city's 300,000 residents fled, many to squatters' camps without basic facilities.

This by itself should have been big news—not just one off news report—that would have led to calls for war crimes investigations by the International Criminal Court (ICC). This is what the fourth estate's 'watchdog' journalism is supposed to do.

When the media ignores such brutality, turns a blind eye to refugees fleeing from the carnage and the human suffering that it entails, people across the world are left in ignorance on why Iraq and Arab world's resistance against American occupation has intensified over the years. We are told that is because 'young people are brainwashed' by Islamic

---

[9] http://news.bbc.co.uk/2/hi/middle_east/4440664.stm (accessed on 7 June 2019).

[10] https://www.theguardian.com/world/2005/nov/10/usa.iraq (accessed on 7 June 2019).

fundamentalist ideas of a shortcut to heaven via suicide bombing. Getting out of the hell created by such brutality should be heaven to them anyway. As Dr Tharoor said (see Chapter 4), most of today's intercultural conflicts are due to a 'perceived cultural humiliation' of their voices been kept out of what Galtung and Vincent (1992) call the 'centre'.

In Chapter 10, we will discuss these issues and ways to develop an international reporting culture that could promote peace and not hatred.

Revisiting Agenda-Setting Theory

Subjectivity in reporting is not merely about reporting lies or 'fake news' (in today's jargon), but it is also about reporting part of the truth or interpreting news according to what the journalists perceive as important for their audience. This has been theorized over half a century ago as 'agenda setting' by Maxwell McCombs and Donald Shaw (1972). The main concept associated with agenda setting is gatekeeping, which was used to be practised by news editors and directors in framing the news in a selective information control process.

There are two ways in which framing a news creates a meaning to its audience. First, through a news content that is typically shaped and contextualized within the same frame of reference to which the audience can relate; and second, by making the audience adopt the frame of reference to see the world in a similar way the journalist has framed the news.

While McCombs and Shaw came up with their theory in 1968 after analysing the US Presidential Election that year, five years earlier, Bernard Cohen (1963) in his book *Press and Foreign Policy* argued that the press 'may not be successful much of the time in telling people what to think, but it is stunningly successful in telling its readers what to think about. The world will look different to different people', Cohen continues, 'depending on the map that is drawn for them by writers, editors, and publishers of the paper they read'.

The advent of the Internet, some argue, has weakened the agenda-setting role of the MSM's news editors and directors, while others would argue that it has created other forms of much more complex regimes of agenda setting as we discuss in this chapter and others to follow.

The Difference between Aleppo and Mosul

In July 2017, after the Iraqi forces with US support retook an Islamic rebel stronghold of Mosul in northern Iraq, British media watchdog 'Media Lens' did a comparative study[11] of the UK media reporting of the liberation of Aleppo by the Syrian forces helped by Russia and the liberation of Mosul by Iraqi forces assisted by US-led coalition forces.

In December 2015, British Conservative politician Boris Johnson, writing in *The Telegraph*[12] of London, said that after he voted for bombing missions in Syria, people in the streets used to ask him, why he voted for war? His response was that

> innocent lives are being lost now; tens of thousands of people ... because they belong to the wrong strand of Islam. I don't want to have them on my conscience, and I don't want these sickos from Daesh/Islamic State of Iraq and the Levant (ISIL) to continue to exult in their so-called caliphate, and to be allowed indefinitely to promote their terrorist campaigns.

The British will be bombing and killing Muslims in Syria to save 'good' Muslims ... so goes the logic! Even more daring was that Johnson argued that they should work with the 'Devils'—Russian President Vladimir Putin and Syrian President Bashar al-Assad—to stop the Islamic terrorists getting a foothold in Syria.

Just over a month later, when Russian and Syrian air forces were bombarding Islamic rebel-held East Aleppo, newspapers and television screens in the UK were full of anguished reporting about the plight of

---

[11] http://medialens.org/index.php/alerts/alert-archive/2017/852-mass-media-siege-comparing-coverage-of-mosul-and-aleppo.html (accessed on 7 June 2019).

[12] http://www.telegraph.co.uk/news/worldnews/middleeast/syria/12036184/Lets-deal-with-the-Devil-we-should-work-with-Vladimir-Putin-and-Bashar-al-Assad-in-Syria.html (accessed on 7 June 2019).

civilians killed, injured, trapped, traumatized or desperately fleeing. Syrian and Russian leaders were demonized, with UK's *Evening Standard*[13] describing Assad as a 'monster' but at the same time arguing that working with him is the best chance for peace in Syria.

Aleppo was once the second largest city in Syria, and it has been one of the key symbols of resistance to the Assad regime since 2012, when anti-Assad groups took control of parts of it. Many of them were supported by the West and its allies and called the 'moderate' opposition to Assad rule. On 29 July 2016, London's *Guardian* in an editorial[14] said that 200,000–300,000 people are trapped in Aleppo's eastern neighbourhoods surrounded by Syrian government forces assisted by Russian air power. They warned that the uprising is facing an 'irreversible defeat' and it would be the 'beginning of a new, humanitarian catastrophe of unprecedented proportions' in Syria.

The Guardian also added 'Aleppo has been so massively shelled and bombed these past weeks that it has become an inferno for those who struggle among the ruins'. It claimed that Syrian and Russian governments are 'resorting to a tactic of siege and starvation' and called for Aleppo's siege to be immediately lifted. What it did not say was that these people are held as human shields by the Islamic rebels.

On 15 December 2016, BBC's Moscow Correspondent Sarah Rainsford delivered a classic subjective viewpoint on the battle for Aleppo. Showing footage of Russian ground forces in Syria on state television for the first time, she said that the 'commentary is all about a heroic fight against terrorists. No mention here of any civilians caught up in the bloodshed'. At the end, in a piece to camera, she says:

> For Russia, the conflict in Syria was always about projecting its power and influence. As the West stalled (sic), Moscow moved in. The message to Russians here is that they were helping to protect

---

[13] https://www.standard.co.uk/comment/comment/assad-a-monster-and-dictator-but-he-s-the-best-option-for-peace-in-syria-a3191741.html (accessed on 7 June 2019).

[14] https://www.theguardian.com/commentisfree/2016/jul/29/the-guardian-view-on-the-battle-for-aleppo-stop-it-now (accessed on 7 June 2019).

the world from terrorism. The message to the world, that Russia under Vladimir Putin is a political and military power to be reckoned with.

Towards the end of the report, she showed footage of the damage done by Russian forces in Grozny in Chechnya many years ago and used an on-camera interviewee to say that 'Putin also called (this) a war on terror. In this latest conflict, he's faced no calls at home for restraint'.

On 16 December 2016, Russia's RT channel took a completely different slant and reported that the liberation of East Aleppo has been completed, quoting the Russian Defense Ministry's Centre for Reconciliation. All women and children have been evacuated from militant-controlled parts of East Aleppo. Sourcing TASS news agency, RT stated: 'In the liberated areas of Eastern Aleppo Syrian soldiers had uncovered several warehouses of food which had been delivered from abroad. These products were only consumed by terrorists and members of their families while the population of Aleppo suffered from malnutrition.' RT reporter on the ground showed how Aleppo streets have erupted in celebrations with happy people waving flags and shooting in the air as reports of the Syrian Army taking control of the last militant-held areas in eastern part of the city emerged. They showed a lot of destroyed buildings in the city. They also broadcast interviews with orphaned boys and girls who described how their parents were killed by the rebels.

In contrast, what 'Media Lens' found from the UK coverage were mainly reports suggesting a great massacre and a war crime in East Aleppo. The British media focused on stories such as last calls by tweeter of children caught in the 'siege' of Aleppo as the Syrian forces closed in; *The Independent* carried videos on its website of women pleading for help as they claimed that they were about to witness a 'genocide'—the information obviously fed by activists either inside or outside the conflict zone. Media Lens noted: 'There were heartbreaking accounts of families, children, elderly people, all caught up in dreadful conditions that could be pinned on the "brutal" Assad and his "regime"; endless photographs depicting grief and suffering that tore at one's psyche'.

In such a situation when the MSM decides to base their reporting on video or audio provided by activists, there are serious issues of authenticity. How do you know if it is concocted or not? They could record these anywhere in the world and feed it to you via an Internet link. The media will say that they have authenticated these from unnamed 'trusted sources', but is that term 'trusted' a subjective viewpoint as well?

There were very little of such sources appearing in the Western MSM when the Iraqi forces supported by US fire power started pulverizing areas in Iraq's second largest city Mosul occupied by Islamic rebel forces opposed to the USA. In 2014, Islamic State of Iraq and Syria (ISIS) leader Abu Bakr Al-Baghdadi declared a caliphate in this northern Iraqi city on the steps of the 12th-century al-Nuri mosque. In October 2016, the US-led coalition stepped up its bombing raids and artillery attacks on Mosul over and above what had already been an intensive military campaign following the city's capture by ISIS almost three years ago.

According to a report released by Amnesty International (AI)[15] in July 2017, they claimed that ISIS has used civilians as human shields in West Mosul moving them systematically to conflict zones resulting in 5,805 civilians killed and over 600,000 displaced from West Mosul as a result of attacks launched by the US-led coalition between February and June of 2017. AI has also accused the Iraqi government and the US-led coalition of a serious failure to protect civilians and says that the real death toll may never be known. The report says the people of Mosul were subjected to 'a terrifying barrage of fire from weapons that should never be used in densely populated civilian areas'.

Though there are now reports of the plight of civilians leaving the destruction of Mosul and the BBC have noted AI's concerns, initially the coverage in the UK, says that Media Lens, omitted the atrocities committed by the Western forces in alliance with Iraqi army. On 9 July 2017, BBC reported about the 'Iraqi army mopping up final IS

---

[15] https://www.amnesty.org/en/latest/campaigns/2017/07/at-any-cost-cvilian-catastrophe-in-west-mosul-iraq/ (accessed on 7 June 2019).

pockets',[16] but there was no mention of the human catastrophe AI talked about. The BBC even provides a 5-minute video of a '360-degree' tour of the city of Mosul with an embedded BBC journalist in a 'live combat helicopter' that shows the city below looking very peaceful until the helicopter started firing at something which the reporter said was 'responding' to ground fire from ISIS.

BBC Reporter Jonathan Beale was embedded with the Iraqi troops for months before and after the attacks on Mosul and as Media Lens noted much of his reporting had a propagandist theme such as these reports they have listed as follows:

- 'The US-led coalition appears confident that fighters of the so-called Islamic State (IS) will be defeated in Mosul'.
- 'A brutal fight for every street'.
- 'The troops both battle hardened and battle weary'.
- 'We hear coalition aircraft overhead. Then a whoosh and a thud, followed by an explosion.... There's another whoosh, thud and boom and then a plume of smoke from an air strike'.
- 'No-one can question the bravery of the Iraqi forces'.
- 'This is unforgiving, urban warfare and for the Iraqi forces there is still a mountain to climb'.

'This was a bang-bang style of "journalism" that obscured or blanked the deaths of civilians being killed in the "Battle for Mosul," as the BBC News television studio graphic called the massive bombardment for months on end', noted Media Lens. 'It was always "Battle for Mosul" never "US air strike massacres civilians" or "US seeks hegemony in the Middle East." It's Good (Us) vs Evil (Them).'

'The Iraqi city of Mosul. The Syrian city of Aleppo. Both "liberated" in recent months from radical jihadist terror groups. But while one anti-terrorist operation has been lauded in the West, the other was fiercely denounced', noted British journalist Neil Clarke in an

---

[16] http://www.bbc.com/news/world-middle-east-40547131 (accessed on 7 June 2019).

op-ed piece on the RT website published on 14 July 2017.[17] 'The very different ways in which the respective "liberations" were portrayed tell us much about the way war propaganda works in the so-called free world'.

Turning his attention to how the 'liberation' of Aleppo was reported by the Western media, Clarke noted:

> Then, the anti-terrorist operation of the Syrian army and Russia, to free the east of the city from al-Qaeda/al-Nusra front control, was roundly condemned. The Mayor of Aleppo told Sky News[18] that a *holocaust* was taking place and blamed the international community for doing nothing. Sky News ran special all-day coverage on 14th October, entitled 'Aleppo, Death of a City'.
> In the House of Commons, Foreign Secretary Boris Johnson broke with diplomatic protocol to call for protests outside the Russian Embassy. The lights of the Eiffel Tower were even turned off in a *gesture of support for the people under bombardment in Aleppo.*
> Prominent media coverage was given to unverified reports from anti-government activists, such as the so-called 'White Helmets', that Syrian and Russian forces had targeted civilians. The tweets of an anti-Assad, anti-Putin, seven-year-old girl caught up in the battle, Bana Alabed, were publicized by leading western celebrities, such as the Harry Potter author J. K. Rowling, which was tweeted by Bana's mother.

As reflected in the earlier discussion, what we have seen in the coverage of the liberation of East Aleppo and West Mosul are facts presented from a subjective viewpoint. How fact-checkers would respond to this challenge is an interesting question. Perhaps there cannot be a better example than this on how news presented by subjective perspectives could constitute propaganda.

[17] https://www.rt.com/op-edge/396295-mosul-aleppo-tale-liberated/ (accessed on 7 June 2019).
[18] http://news.sky.com/story/aleppo-mayor-blames-west-for-doing-nothing-over-holocaust-in-city-10614937 (accessed on 7 June 2019).

Influencer Marketing and 'Donor'-Funded Social Media

The year 2011 was marked by what is called the Arab Spring movement, where the Anglo-American media—such as the BBC, CNN and a host of others including Al Jazeera—have manipulated news feeds to cheerlead some 'uprisings' such as in Libya and Syria while quickly forgetting others such as in Bahrain.

In the context of 'Influence Marketing' (IM) by companies in social media, it will be interesting to examine whether another type of IM is happening in the political arena—in the marketing of human rights and democracy—through NGOs funded from overseas. Where would the 'post-truth era' theories fit into this? (See Chapters 6 and 10 for more discussion.)

Are young people who are being trained in the use of various social media tools, also at the same time, fed with a political ideology to serve the needs of the 'donors'? (see Seneviratne, 2012). Are the media-oriented civil society groups the new missionaries using an influence marketing techniques to spread a new gospel of human rights and democracy that is presenting a Western ideology as a 'civilizing' force?

A very useful tool for such IM is the video clip produced and supplied by 'citizens groups' or 'citizen journalists' that have been funded by Western donors (Box 5.1). Western media and social media sites have used these often to claim human rights violation in Two-Thirds World countries.

Box 5.1: Video Clip—The Weapon of 'Dollar Chasing Democracy Vendors'

Are civil society movements, created by Western funding, designed on a dependency model, where the local NGOs become 'dollar chasing democracy vendors' that produce social media message to attract further Western funding?

This is a question asked in many parts of the world where such movements have destabilized governments and even led to 'regime

---

(Continued)

(Continued)

change' that have created an aftermath of chaos as what has happened in Libya. If these are peoples' movements, they need to be committed to the welfare of their own people as well as their nation and not influence marketers for their funders.

A very useful tool is the video clip produced and supplied by 'citizens groups' or 'citizen journalists' that have been funded by Western donors. Western media has used these often to claim human rights violation in Two-Thirds World countries. Channels such as the BBC, CNN and Channel 4 (in Britain) use these video clips provided by activists taken on mobile phones. Often they broadcast these without proper authentication, and international human rights agencies including some UN agencies lap onto these to accuse governments for human rights violations. Syria, Myanmar, Sri Lanka, Libya, Iran, Russia, Venezuela and a host of other countries whose leaders are not subservient to Western interests have faced the wrath of this news manipulation.

With the case of Sri Lanka, after the government defeated the terrorist group LTTE, their Western-based Tamil refugee propaganda networks provided Britain's Channel 4, in particular, video clips of so-called 'war crimes' of Sri Lankan troops against Tamils. These surfaced mysteriously just before the six monthly meetings of the Geneva-based UNHRC—where Western countries were trying to mobilize support for a resolution calling for 'war crimes' investigation against Sri Lanka (as discussed in Chapter 6). Channel 4 gladly broadcast these clips claiming 'new evidence' of war crimes, even though these don't indicate a date, time or place. Then it gets picked up by other media—like *The Times* of London or even the BBC—and it becomes an international story. Sri Lankan government is then forced to scramble their foreign office and defence ministry sources to refute these allegations, which the Western media dismisses as 'government propaganda'.

Referring to these media campaigns, presidential media advisor Lucien Rajakarunanayake (2010) describes the modus operando of what he calls an 'ugly pattern of distortion' in the way Channel 4 used unidentified video clips claiming human rights violations, thus:

> You get one side of the pro-LTTE operators abroad, especially in the West, to produce the fake and highly sinister material. You then get a western media outlet that is known for lack of attention to veracity and an open agenda against Sri Lanka and pro-LTTE to air it, you get a so-called independent news organization such as the BBC to spread the story wider, and then comes HRW (Human Rights Watch) or any such others, pontificating how the unverified news item in question, underscores the need for an international commission of inquiry into possible war crimes

committed (of course by both sides, but one side not available in Sri Lanka anymore), during the armed conflict in Sri Lanka.

An irate Sri Lankan Foreign Minister Professor G. L. Peiris,[19] speaking to the media from Geneva where he was leading the Sri Lankan delegation to the UNHRC meeting in April 2010, said 'there is a limit to selectivity' in news reporting and claimed that human rights organizations using such material have done irreversible damage to the UNHRC process. He said that the Sri Lankan delegation had raised the issue of double standards on human rights practised by the very nations who are trying to mount war crimes investigations against Sri Lanka. He was referring to US and NATO actions in Afghanistan, Iraq and Pakistan.

The same strategy has been adopted by the anti-Assad groups in Syria and as Global Research's Peter Koenig[20] notes, poison gas has become weapon of choice for 'false news' to justify attacks on Syria with a view to remove President Assad. The allegations are made via video clips provided by activist groups who are often not even based in Syria.

'The recent fake gas attack on Douma outside of Damascus, has allegedly killed 80 to 120 people, mostly women and children. Of course, that sells best in the propaganda theatre—women and children. But there is not proof, none whatsoever', he points out. 'People living in Douma say they haven't heard of any nerve gas attack. Strangely, like last time, the infamous White Helmets discovered the gas victims, including a gas canister-like bomb laying on a bed, having been shot through the roof of a house.'

The White Helmets, officially known as the Syria Civil Defence, is a humanitarian organization made up of 3,400 volunteers. Their website[21] states:

> When the bombs rain down, the Syrian Civil Defence rushes in. In a place where public services no longer function these unarmed volunteers risk their lives to help anyone in need—regardless of their religion or politics. Known as the White Helmets these volunteer rescue workers operate in the most dangerous place on earth.

The Western MSM often cites them as 'reliable' sources of information on Syria. They have also mastered the art of providing first-hand video

(Continued)

---

[19] http://srilankabrief.blogspot.com/2012/02/gosl-refers-to-us-hr-record-demands.html (accessed on 7 June 2019).

[20] https://www.globalresearch.ca/poison-gas-weapon-of-choice-for-false-news/5635839 (accessed on 7 June 2019).

[21] https://www.whitehelmets.org/en (accessed on 7 June 2019).

(Continued)

> footage of what they claim are 'war crimes' of the Syrian and Russian military, especially the accusations regarding chemical attacks. Their work was the subject of an Oscar-winning Netflix documentary and two Nobel Peace Prize nominations, according to London's *Guardian*.[22] But many news sources outside the Western MSM have accused them of being a Western-funded NGO that is spreading 'fake news' and not being based in Syria.
>
> A day after the USA, UK and France lobbed missiles into Syria in April 2018, *The Jerusalem Post*[23] reported that the Pink Floyd leader Roger Waters during a concert in Barcelona described the White Helmets as a fake organization that provides propaganda for terrorists and jihadists in Syria. He told his audience that listening to 'propaganda of the White Helmets and others we would be encouraged to encourage our governments to go and start dropping bombs on people in Syria'. He told his audience that he has refused to let someone who supports White Helmets to make a statement on stage.
>
>> This would be a mistake of monumental proportions, in terms of us as human beings, what we should do is be persuading our governments not to go and drop bombs on people and certainly not until we have done all the research that is necessary so that we have a clear idea of what is going on.
>
> Waters told his young audience. He also alleged that 'we live in a world where propaganda appears to be more important than the reality of what is going on in places'.

Influencer Marketing—A Weapon in ISIS Armoury

While the Western 'donor'-funded NGOs are being trained in using such IM techniques to spread political messages and even to mount 'regime change' movements, perhaps an unwelcomed addition to this club is the Islamic terror group ISIS (Islamic State of Iraq and the Levant [ISIL]), which has alarmed the West.

---

[22] https://www.theguardian.com/world/2017/dec/18/syria-white-helmets-conspiracy-theories (accessed on 7 June 2019).

[23] http://www.jpost.com/International/Roger-Waters-slams-Syria-intervention-attacks-White-Helmets-as-fake-549894 (accessed on 7 June 2019).

'Isis is a brilliant example of a deviant brand, keeping the headlines big and their aura powerful and persuasive', notes Mark Borkowski writing in *the Drum*.[24]

> In pure creative marketing terms though, perhaps most important, is their devotion to symbology and visualization and for all those brands that are highly committed to the value of data, market research, and focus groups, take a hard look at Isis. They use their hater's thoughts as inspiration.

He argues that ISIS has a clearly understood single vision and common purpose and uses emotion to drive engagement, while it understands disruption and deals with the haters using social media to its advantage far beyond any brand.

Brendan Koerner writing in The Wire in March 2016[25] argues that ISIS is winning social media war because they have mastered how to use emotions—good or bad—to peddle their message and influence their target audience. 'The Islamic State has been singularly successful at that task, thanks to its mastery of modern digital tools, which have transformed dark arts of making and disseminating propaganda', he notes. 'Never before in history, have terrorists had such easy access to the minds and eyeballs of millions'. ISIS is, in fact, as much a media conglomerate as it is a fighting force, argues Koerner. They use photo essays, audio clips, pamphlets and even full-length documentaries dubbed to many languages in their IM activities.

'The group's closest peers are not just other terrorist organizations, but also Western brands, marketing firms, and publishing outfits—from PepsiCo to BuzzFeed—who ply the Internet with memes and messages in the hopes of connecting with customers', he notes. 'And like those ventures, the Islamic State hews to a few tried-and-true techniques for boosting user engagement.'

---

[24] http://www.thedrum.com/opinion/2014/06/25/isis-and-propaganda-war-how-social-savvy-extremists-are-dominating-headlines (accessed on 7 June 2019).
[25] https://www.wired.com/2016/03/isis-winning-social-media-war-heres-beat/ (accessed on 7 June 2019).

CHAPTER 6

Human Rights
The New Missionary Religion

When European gunboats went across the world, Christian missionaries who wanted to 'civilize' the people—to whom the Bible was an unknown entity—accompanied the colonizers. Today, when US or NATO missiles ram into countries, their foot soldiers, Western human rights organizations and their activists follow, with their media in tow. They also have a similar mindset—to 'civilize' the people with notions of freedom and democracy. However, the debacle of the Arab Spring and the double standards practised in the war on terror have exposed the hypocrisy of this gospel.

'Human Rights' and 'Democracy' have become contentious notions in international communication discourse today. These have become much abused words in journalism practices that have led to accusation of human rights and democracy becoming the new gospel backing a new wave of Western imperialism.

Yet the principles behind democracy and human rights covenants could be a very powerful tool for journalism practice to develop a people-focused paradigm of journalism—the very concept prescribed by the Libertarian Theory (which was discussed in Chapter 1). If applied and practised without the widespread hypocrisy we see today, this gospel could be a useful guiding tool for a reincarnated 'watchdog' model of journalism, where the media will be the friend of the citizen, not its manipulator.

As discussed in the earlier chapters, human rights have become such a contested concept because of subjective journalism. It has often been used for political purposes such as 'regime change' projects of Western imperialist designs as we will discuss later in this chapter and the next chapter.

As Professor Michel Chossudovsky[1] of Global Research argues, 'the world is at a dangerous crossroad' because of the 'lies of omission' practised by the very media that claims to promote human rights and democracy. 'America's wars are portrayed by the media, as humanitarian endeavours. The "Responsibility to Protect" (R2P) doctrine provides a framework, which justifies military action', he notes. 'When war is upheld as peacemaking, conceptualization is no longer possible. Once the lie becomes the truth, there is no moving backwards. Insanity prevails. The world is turned upside down', warns Professor Chossudovsky.

Fundamental Flaw of Human Rights Discourse

A fundamental flaw of the human rights discourse in the media is the focus given to the 1947 UN Human Rights Declaration (that was mainly drafted by Western countries) and often ignoring the 1976 International Covenant on Civil and Political Rights (ICCPR), which was drafted with the active involvement of many Asian countries.

As 20th-century Indian Independence campaigner Aurobindo Ghose (cited in Mishra 2012: 223) noted, when the age of democracy, nationalism and imperialism came together, the British needed a different philosophy to justify their imperial designs as the principle of 'might is right' was no longer valid.

> The idea that despotism of any kind was an offense against humanity, has crystallized into an instinctive feeling, and modern morality

---

[1] https://www.globalresearch.ca/independent-media-reveals-the-criminal-nature-of-us-foreign-policy/5620556 (accessed on 10 June 2019).

and sentiments revolted against the enslavement of nation by nation, of class by class or of man by man. Imperialism had to justify itself to this modern sentiment and could only do so by pretending to be a trustee of liberty, commissioned from on high (ground) to civilize the uncivilized and train the untrained until the time had come when the benevolent conqueror had done his work and could unselfishly retire.

Today, the rise of Asia—within basically a generation—to the level of economic progress that took Europe more than two centuries to achieve—that too after enslaving and plundering two-thirds of the world—is a marvel of the modern age. Yet, if you were to base your judgement of particularly China's impressive rise in the past two decades on Western media discourse, you may believe that China achieved this by transforming the country to a despotic nation which abused and exploited its own people to conquer the world with the supply of cheap manufactured goods, and now they are using that wealth to set up 'debt traps' for poor nations.

Singaporean Political Science Professor Kishore Mahbubani speaking at Harvard University[2] in April 2015 told his American audience that as the world prepares for an international order where the USA is no longer number one, there are some frightening developments that are related to the way Americans see the world. He added that during his 10 years at the UN as Singapore's ambassador, it was somewhat tragic to watch in the UN that the institutions that were essentially created by the USA after the Second World War (which) 'were basically American inspired institutions' are being been undermined by American policies. He said that though the USA may have the freest media in the world, the best financed newspapers, the best financed television stations in the world

> but I can tell you this (as) someone who travels to at least 30 to 40 countries a year, when I come to the United States and I go

---

[2] https://www.youtube.com/watch?v=bVkLqC3p0Og (accessed on 10 June 2019).

to my hotel room and turn on the television, I feel that I've been cut off from the rest of the world, and literally the insularity of the American discourse is actually frightening.

Professor Mahbubani pointed out that if you read *The Wall Street Journal*, the *NYT* or *The Economist*, you cannot but notice the constant belief there that the best thing that can happen to China is to have a collapse of the Chinese Communist Party and have a democratic system. In a concluding comment, he left the American audience to ponder a different point of view.

> Be careful what you wish for, because of the Chinese political system (if it) becomes more democratic, it could very well become far more nationalist [and] the great paradox here is that the Chinese Communist Party is actually delivering a global public good by restraining Chinese nationalism, and if you didn't have a strong Chinese Communist Party in charge, you might actually get a more nationalist a more assertive China.

He also pointed out to his American audience that when he first went to China in the 1980s, there wasn't a single Chinese tourist leaving China. In 2014, 100 million Chinese went overseas freely, and a 100 million Chinese returned to China freely. 'Now, if there's no freedom in China, if China was this despotic, oppressive state, would a hundred million Chinese come back to China?' asked Professor Mahbubani.

Ibrahim Saleh[3] of Egypt's Nile University argues, FOE needs to come from the grassroots. We need to add local perspective (on human rights), if we are going to talk about corruption, role of political economy—the depoliticization of journalism need to be on the agenda. Noting that, if the media does not provide a sense of belonging to face problems and deal with that, peoples' enthusiasm for FOE would be faded out and they would become desperate. This type of polarization would result in dire economic situation of confusion and long years of political corruption. Though he did not go so far, this is perhaps what we see in the Middle East today.

---

[3] Interview with the author in Kuala Lumpur, November 2016.

Pradip N. Thomas (AMIC 2000: 7) argues that the question of how to safeguard human rights in a mediated world is difficult to answer, and while media ranks among the central definers of reality, they are not the only definers of reality. The education system and religion, along with the family, also play a role in providing us with frames of reference, he argues. All these institutions are influenced by society and, in turn, influence society. However, it could be argued that in the context of our times, the media does play a pre-eminent role in defining public agendas.

It is this dilemma which we will address in this chapter. Whether there is just one way of looking at democracy and human rights—the way Western media defines it to us? I hope the discussions that follow will motivate young budding journalists, in particular, to look at human rights and reality not through slogans and rhetoric, but the reality of life at the grass roots. What does freedom mean at the street level? Let me give you an example to stimulate your thinking.

Mugabe, Zimbabwe and International Media

The betrayal of the collective agenda we set at Rio[4] is a compelling manifestation of bad global governance, lack of real political will by the North and a total absence of a just rule of law in international affairs. The unilateralism of the unipolar world has reduced the rest of mankind to collective underdogs, chattels of a rich, the willful few in the North who beat, batter and bully us under the dirty cover of democracy, rule of law and good governance. Otherwise how would they undermine at global level the same values of good governance and rule of law they arrogantly demand from the South?

Institutionally, we have relied for much too long on structures originally set to recover and rebuild Europe after a devastating war against Nazism. Over the years, these outdated institutions have been unilaterally transformed to dominate the world for the realization of the strategic national goals of the rich North. That is why, for example, the International Monetary Fund has never been a fund for poor peasants seeking sustainable development. Even the

---

[4] Here, he was referring to the Rio de Janeiro Earth Summit of 1992.

United Nations, a body that is supposed to give us equal voices, remains unreformed and undemocratic, largely because of resistance from the powerful and often selfish North.
—President Robert Mugabe of Zimbabwe, addressing the World Summit on Sustainable Development in Johannesburg on 2 September 2002.[5]

At the end of the speech, he told delegates, that included Britain's Prime Minister Tony Blair, in reference to his criticism of Zimbabwe's land reform programme that was taking land away from rich White farmers and giving it to the landless Blacks to farm: 'Blair, keep your England, and let me keep my Zimbabwe!' He received thunderous applause from the audience dominated by Africans, who saw him as a champion of the African Renaissance. Mugabe's anti-colonial message has always been popular with a good number of nations in the Two-Thirds World.

When I watched on television Mugabe's dramatic comments at the UN Summit, my mind went back to a visit to South Africa just over a year before the event. I was driving a rented car from Kruger National Park in South Africa to Johannesburg a good six hours or so by road. For most of the journey, we travelled through White-owned farmland, which reminded me of driving in the countryside in Australia (where I have lived for 20 years). Most of the farms were mechanized and the only Blacks we saw were a handful of labourers and maids playing with White children and every car we passed were driven by Whites. The farmlands seemed prosperous and the Whites very rich. But when we came to the outskirts of Johannesburg, we came across the teeming Black townships on the hills with its tin sheds, lack of infrastructure and poverty.

I told my wife, 'I wonder for how long these people will be patient with the ANC government.' Very soon, they are going to turn around and ask from the ANC, 'where are the dividends of the liberation

---

[5] http://www.un.org/events/wssd/statements/zimbabweE.htm (accessed on 10 June 2019).

struggle for us?' Six years later, I wrote a feature on Zimbabwe for Sri Lanka's *Daily News* after being sick of hearing on the BBC Radio or reading in newspapers, even in Asia where I was living now, reports on Zimbabwe. What I saw in South Africa always came to my mind. What we hear about Zimbabwe are reports about a brutal dictator (Mugabe), not about how Black aspirations could be satisfied in a Zimbabwe liberated from White colonial rule over 25 years ago. As a journalist, I always wonder, some 50 years after liberating ourselves from White colonial rule, are we yet to liberate our minds from White colonialism? Why are we still swallowing their propaganda coming to us as (subjective) news? My article was a critical assessment of the Western media reporting of Zimbabwe at the time.[6] Let me summarize this article.

Beginning in 1889, diamond miner Cecil Rhodes and his band of British imperialists systematically grabbed land occupied by the Shona people for over 1,000 years. Each volunteer in these imperialist wars was given 6,000 acres of captured land. When the villagers returned to their land, they were treated as tenants. Gradually, the Whites developed commercial farming in these lands and the Blacks became their workers—if not slaves.

In 1966, Robert Mugabe, along with fellow Black Nationalist Joshua Nkomo, began a guerrilla war of liberation where the 'land question' was the major issue. The 1979 Lancaster House Agreement hammered out in London paved the way for independence in the 1980s and Mugabe's subsequent landslide election win. Under the Lancaster House Constitution, the Zimbabwe government could only buy White Land from willing sellers. When this condition expired after 10 years, the government passed a law empowering it to make compulsory purchases.

Twenty years after the 1980s liberation from White rule, some 4,500 White farmers owned 70 per cent of the best farmlands in the country. Thus, since March 2000, a group of war veterans of Mugabe's Zimbabwe African National Union–Patriotic Front (ZANU–PF) ruling party has occupied many White-owned farms claiming this as

[6] https://kalingasen.wordpress.com/2016/01/25/why-swallow-western-propaganda-on-zimbabwe/ (accessed on 10 June 2019).

their dividends for fighting the war of liberation. Addressing the FAO Food Summit in Rome in June 2008, President Mugabe explained that over the past decade, Zimbabwe has democratized the land ownership patterns in the country, with over 300,000 previously landless families now proud landowners.

Mugabe complained that in retaliation for the measures he took to empower the Black majority, the UK has mobilized its friends and allies in Europe, North America, Australia and New Zealand to impose 'illegal economic sanctions' against Zimbabwe. He went on to list the economic sanctions it has imposed, which includes cutting off all development assistance, disable lines of credit, prevent the Bretton Woods institutions from providing financial assistance and order private companies in the USA not to do business with Zimbabwe. 'All this has been done to cripple Zimbabwe's economy and thereby effect illegal regime change in our country', he claimed, adding that funds are being channelled through NGOs to opposition political parties, which are a creation of the West to topple him at election time.

While the Anglo-American media has dismissed Mugabe's complaints as the ranting of a dictator hell bent on clinging to power, it is important that we analyse these comments and subsequent developments in the economic and political spheres with an objective mindset. While researching for that article, I read many commentaries written in African websites by Africans many of whom are sceptical about British and Western concern for democracy in Zimbabwe. It is interesting to analyse whether the economic sanction imposed by the West was designed to undermine those land reforms and ensure the policy failed, rather than promoting democracy in the land.

In a commentary I came across in a Rastafari (African nationalist) website[7] after Mugabe won another election in 2013 (described by the Western media and human rights organization as 'rigged'), it noted:

> The recent Zimbabwe elections saw an escalation of attempts by external forces to intervene in the supposedly sovereign and

---

[7] http://www.africaspeaks.com/reasoning/index.php?topic=5306.0;wap2 (accessed on 10 June 2019).

independent nation of Zimbabwe. Given the complex circumstances surrounding Zimbabwe, for the millions of people in the Caribbean and around the world, it has been difficult to get balanced views of what is going on in Zimbabwe, ever since the government under President Robert Mugabe, started to make moves to reclaim land that was stolen during British Colonial rule. Since the start of the land reclamation exercise to now, the events in Zimbabwe have exposed how irresponsible and lazy the local mainstream media are. Mainstream media seem quite content to jump on the anti-Mugabe bandwagon as they parrot news from the international media sources such as BBC, CNN, Reuters and Associated Press.

This was also a point I argued in the 2008 article titled 'Why Swallow Western Propaganda on Zimbabwe?' which was picked up and published in a number of African websites, including in Zimbabwe.

The Rastafari website argues:

Make no mistake about the situation. Things are desperate in Zimbabwe, but contrary to media reports, it is not because of the evil or excesses of Mugabe, but because of the deliberate actions of the US and the UK working through, and/or sponsoring a complex web of actors including opposition forces, NGO's, Western Media. It is understandable that some Zimbabweans will support the opposition, especially given that it is being said by Western leaders that sanctions will be lifted and life made better if Mugabe is removed. Persons inside of Zimbabwe may have some very valid reasons for being against Mugabe, as will many people in any country will have reasons for being against the present leader. That is okay, if such is the case, then elections will allow them to elect and change as they want. What I'm saying is that the people of Zimbabwe should determine their leader without foreign imperialistic intervention. People should be wary about puppet governments being installed to simply look after Western interests and perpetuate Western domination.

Aged 92, he was still planning to fight another election battle in July 2018, but was deposed by an army 'coup' in November 2017, which was supported by his own ruling ZANU–PF party.

An article written by African journalist Ata Ikiddeh[8] and widely circulated within Africa gave a fascinating account of how Mugabe's wife Grace—some 30 years younger—was manipulating her ailing 92-year-old husband to make her the head of ZANU–PF. She pressured President Mugabe to sack his Vice-President Mnangagwa to pave the way for Grace's rise, which led the army commander Chiwenga to move in demanding Mugabe to step down. The army never called it a 'coup' and when Mugabe finally agreed to step down after days of tense negotiations, Mnangagwa who had fled to South Africa came back and took the presidency. Mugabe was given immunity from persecution, though Grace's situation was not clear. Thus, ZANU–PF remains in power and so is Zimbabwe's power structure. Mugabe continues to live with his wife Grace in Harare, often visiting Singapore for medical treatment.

Now Mugabe is gone, international media focus is not on Zimbabwe anymore. But his party is still in power and so are most of his trusted supporters. They will continue supporting the Black farmers—supporters of ZANU–PF—who are now owners of land previously occupied by White farmers. For Zimbabwe to feed itself—as they did in the first few years of Mugabe rule—the farmers have to be supported and international community may be able to help. Right to both land and food is also human right as argued later in this chapter.

United Nations and Human Rights Covenants

In order to understand and apply human rights principles in a fair and balanced manner, we need to be familiar with not only the Universal Declaration of Human Rights (UDHR) of 1948 but also the ICCPR that was adopted by the UN General Assembly in 1966. Let us look at the major components of the two UN human rights covenants.

Universal Declaration of Human Rights

The UDHR adopted by the UN General Assembly on 10 December 1948 came at a time when most UN member states were Western or

---

[8] https://www.lusakatimes.com/2017/11/16/kiss-married-woman-eventually-scattered-mugabes- kingdom-lesson-men/ (accessed on 10 June 2019).

tightly controlled by the West. It also came at a time just after the Second World War when the world, especially Europe and Japan, were traumatized by the destruction and inhumanity of war. Thus, the world was prepared for a new beginning where rights of people could be protected so that another global tragedy of these dimensions will not be repeated.

The UDHR said in its preamble that the recognition of the inherent dignity and of the equal and inalienable rights of 'all members of the human family is the foundation of freedom, justice and peace in the world' and it reflected upon the fact that disregard and contempt for human rights have resulted in barbarous acts which have outraged the conscience of mankind and that it is essential, if man is not to be compelled to have recourse, as a last resort, to rebel against tyranny and oppression, and that human rights should be protected by the rule of law.

The Declaration includes 30 Articles[9] and in Article 1 it declares: All human beings are born free and equal in dignity and rights. Article 2 defines this further: Everyone is entitled to all the rights and freedoms set forth in this Declaration, without distinction of any kind, such as race, colour, sex, language, religion, political or other opinion, national or social origin, property, birth or other status. It is Article 19 that is directly related to the work of the media and which has been often quoted in defending FOE. It states:

> Everyone has the right to freedom of opinion and expression; this right includes freedom to hold opinions without interference and to seek, receive and impart information and ideas through any media and regardless of frontiers.

The UDHR is generally regarded as the foundation of international human rights law.

---

[9] http://www.un.org/en/universal-declaration-human-rights/ (accessed on 10 June 2019).

International Covenant on Civil and Political Rights

The ICCPR was adopted by the UN General Assembly on 16 December 1966 and came into force on 23 March 1976.

The ICCPR[10] took the individual focus of the UDHR a step further by bringing in collective rights. As the preamble reflects in accordance with the UDHR, the ideal of free human beings enjoying civil and political freedom and freedom from fear and want can only be achieved if conditions are created whereby everyone may enjoy his/her civil and political rights, as well as his/her economic, social and cultural rights and it further elaborates that realizing that the individual, having duties to other individuals and to the community to which he/she belongs, is under a responsibility to strive for the promotion and observance of the rights recognized in the present covenant.

The focus on collective rights is regarded as being influenced by the Asian nations, who have by now increased their representation and influence at the UN. While the focus on individual rights could be regarded as influenced by Judeo-Christian concepts of the freedom of the individual, a result of the Christian protestant reformation movements in Europe of the 16th century, the idea of collective rights is very much a reflection of the Indic-Buddhist civilizational influence in Asian cultures.

The ICCPR is also sometimes referred to as a document that sets out development rights. It is referred to in Article 1 itself, where the right to self-determination and to economic, social and cultural development are spelled out. Peoples' right to their natural wealth and resources are also acknowledged and it says in no case may a person be deprived of his/her own means of subsistence.

While individual rights are protected in this covenant, it is also related to a country's or a society right to development. Though scholars and development experts, especially in the Two-Thirds World, have often referred to this Covenant as a yardstick to measure human

---

[10] http://www.ohchr.org/EN/ProfessionalInterest/Pages/CCPR.aspx (accessed on 10 June 2019).

rights with respect to social and economic development of a nation, the Western media has usually played this down, seeing it as an excuse for authoritarian governments to justify its repression in the name of development.

Poverty Reduction before Human Rights— A View from the South

At a side event during the 38th Session of the UNHRC in Geneva, in July 2018, the South Centre[11] organized a seminar on development rights and poverty reduction. In a statement delivered by Yuefen Li (South Centre 2018), senior advisor on South–South Cooperation and Financing for Development of the South Centre, she mentioned the important role of the State in formulating the right development strategies and the required policy space to implement them and called upon the international community to provide an enabling and supportive global economic environment for it.

'Human rights cover different levels and dimensions including civil, political, economic, cultural and other rights. However, without economic development, all these rights would be difficult to be attained', she argued, posing the question. 'How much human rights and human dignity people living in absolute poverty in remote areas can enjoy?'

Li added that poverty is a pressing human rights concern with 800 million people across the world still living in extreme poverty. Thus, they enjoy 'very, very little' of the human rights we talk about. 'When people have no access to education, roads, medicine, clean drinking water and other things we deem as basic needs, it is impossible for the population to achieve and enjoy human rights', she argues. 'Many kinds of human rights would be sacrificed and, most sadly, people

---

[11] The South Centre is the intergovernmental organization of developing countries that helps developing countries to combine their efforts and expertise to promote their common interests in the international arena. The South Centre was established by an international agreement which came into force on 31 July 1995. Its headquarters are in Geneva, Switzerland.

would not even be aware of it. Therefore, the right to development is closely linked with poverty alleviation and promoting and protecting human rights.'

While also arguing that poorer countries need to be allowed to provide government support and subsidies to build up their industrial base and diversify economies, Li pointed out that debt traps by investors and trade wars are a major threat to development rights. This should also involve technology transfers, while trade agreements should benefit both the importers and exporters.

'Unfortunately, after decades of debate and struggle by many countries and academia, the world still does not have a sovereign debt restructuring mechanism and no international rules can stop vulture funds from reaping billions out of a debt crisis', warned Li, noting as an important milestone the 2015 Belgian legislation curtailing the activities of vulture funds and unethical financial speculation. The law will effectively place a limit on how much investment funds can claw back from government debt, which they buy incredibly cheaper from countries that are in serious financial difficulty.[12]

The first draft of a legally binding treaty in International Human Rights Law was submitted to the UNHRC on 16 July 2018. The question is: would they have the courage to stand up for the people against powerful TNCs? If a 'free media' is the fourth estate that stands up for the rights of the people, they need to keep an eye on the progress of this draft treaty at the UN body (see commentary in Appendix A.2).

Cuba and the Castro Legacy—A Model of Development Rights

The passing of Fidel Castro at 90 years of age provided opponents of the Cuban Revolution with an opportunity to pick up their ideological mantra in favour of some abstract notion of democracy, while ignoring the Revolution's social achievements and human development. But Cuba's foreign policy has also been of a

[12] https://www.valuewalk.com/2015/07/belgium-passes-law-against-vulture-funds/ (accessed on 10 June 2019).

remarkable consistency, and its impact has been lauded by many people, including its enemies. (Gleijeses 2016)[13]

The aforementioned comments were made by Professor Piero Gleijeses, a renowned scholar of Cuban affairs at the School of Advanced International Studies at Johns Hopkins University in the USA.

While watching and reading all those corporate media obituaries on the death of Fidel Castro on 25 November 2016 that depicted him as a ruthless dictator that has imprisoned the Cuban people for over half a century, my mind went back to the time of the inauguration of South Africa's first Black President Nelson Mandela on 10 May 1994, which was attended by the Cuban leader. When he took to the podium to speak, he had to wait for a few minutes before the chants of 'Fidel, Fidel' from thousands of Mandela's ANC cadres died down. Living in Australia at the time, I can remember watching a broadcast on Australian television where the reporter expressed bemusement at this and asked why they did not greet Britain's Prince Charles—who was representing the British government—the same way? The Australian broadcaster said that Britain has paved the way for Mandela's rise to power. But I knew the reason why Castro got such a reception, though he didn't.

The ANC cadres firmly believed that it were the Cuban troops fighting alongside Angolan troops in the famous (not in the West though) 'Battle of Cuito Cuanavale' in 1987–1988 that broke the back of the White South African army and its aura of 'invisibility'. Cuban air power in what is now known as the biggest battle on African soil since the Second World War humiliated a South African incursion force into Angola. They had to withdraw and most importantly it showed to the Black African forces that the White army of South Africa could be defeated. This battle is credited with having convinced the White regime in South Africa that time was up for giving into Black demands for liberation and negotiate. Cuba sent troops to fight

---

[13] http://www.investigaction.net/en/in-fighting-against-apartheid-cuba-defended-the-most-beautiful-cause-of-mankind/ (accessed on 10 June 2019).

alongside the African forces with no favours asked other than revolutionary solidarity.

What ANC cadre demonstrated on this day was its gratitude to Comrade Fidel. It is unfortunate that much of the Western media was not able to pick up this story as demonstrated by the Australian broadcast. I was aware of it because I was doing a weekly radio broadcast on a university radio station in Sydney at the time called 'Voices from the South' and I have been following up on alternative news sources from the Two-Thirds World such as the Malaysia-based Third World Network (TWN) which covered issues such as the victory of Cuban forces in the battle at Cuito Cuanavale.

'Cuba and Fidel Castro, for instance, played a decisive role in changing the course of history in Southern Africa, in the struggle against apartheid', argues Professor Gleijeses.

> They saved Angola from the attack of apartheid South Africa, they helped the Namibian guerrillas, they helped the (Black) South Africans, asking for nothing in return. And when I say for nothing I really mean absolutely nothing. Not only this, but Cuba paid a high price to help the Africans, because that meant increasing the enmity of the United States.

The *NYT* (DePalma 2016) in a lengthy article published a day after Fidel's death—which was more than 2,500 words long—mainly painted him as a dictator who brought the Cold War to America's doorstep. Though admitting that he became a towering international figure far exceeding what one would expect from a leader of a small Caribbean island with 11 million people, the article had lengthy discussions on his life and how he controlled his people. 'He wielded power like a tyrant, controlling every aspect of the island's existence', DePalma argued. 'He personally sent countless men to prison. But it was more than repression and fear that kept him and his totalitarian government in power for so long. He had both admirers and detractors in Cuba and around the world'. The theme of the article was mainly about how he 'prolonged a dictatorship' and denied 'the long suffering Cuban people' a chance to control their lives.

While acknowledging that his legacy in Cuba and elsewhere 'has been a mixed record of social progress and abject poverty, of racial equality and political persecution, of medical advances', which has given a degree of advancement compared to the conditions that existed in Cuba when he entered Havana, yet there was no discussion of this progress. The only reference to Cuba's involvement in Africa was the following paragraph:

> In 1989, when frustrated veterans from Cuba's African ventures began rallying around Gen. Arnaldo Ochoa, who led Cuban forces on the continent, Mr Castro effectively got rid of a potential rival by bringing the general and some of his supporters to trial on drug charges. General Ochoa and several other high ranking officers were executed on the orders of Raúl Castro, who was then the minister of defence.

The BBC[14] in its obituary was not much better. It did acknowledge that when Fidel took power, 'Cuba had become a haven for the playboy rich, and was run largely by organised crime syndicates. Prostitution, gambling and drug trafficking were endemic.' But it did not go on to discuss how the Cuban revolution eradicated these and raised the human development index of the country. The BBC also fell into the same trap of looking at Cuba's progress through multiparty democracy prism. 'Castro kept the red flag flying right on the doorstep of his greatest enemy, the United States', it noted. 'A divisive figure, his supporters praised him as a champion of socialism, the soldier-politician who had given Cuba back to the people. But he faced accusations of brutally suppressing opposition and pursuing policies that crippled the Cuban economy'.

There was no discussion whatsoever of the success of his social policies, especially in education, healthcare and agriculture. There is no mention about Cuba's role in South Africa's anti-apartheid battle, except one sentence: 'He also took sides, especially in Africa, sending his troops to support Marxist guerrillas in Angola and Mozambique'. Referring

---

[14] http://www.bbc.com/news/world-latin-america-10744408 (accessed on 11 June 2019).

to the fall of the Soviet Union and the loss of Soviet economic support, the BBC said, 'the country Fidel Castro called the most advanced in the world, had, in fact, returned to the age of ox-drawn carts' and it went on to describe how, by the mid-1990s, many Cubans had had enough and thousands were now taking to the sea in a waterborne exodus to Florida. But it acknowledged that 'Yet Cuba registered some impressive domestic achievements. Good medical care was freely available for all, and Cuba's infant mortality rates compared favourably with the most sophisticated societies on earth' but did not go to elaborate on this. It ended the report by noting: 'While many Cubans undoubtedly detested Castro, others genuinely loved him. They saw him as a David who could stand up to the Goliath of America, who successfully spat in the "Yanqui" eye. For them Castro was Cuba, Cuba was Castro.'

> Following the death of 90-year-old Cuban revolutionary Fidel Castro on November 25, 2016 corporate Western media has been fixated on depicting Fidel as the mastermind of a two-dimensional 'dictatorial regime'. For those with a three-dimensional perspective, however, Fidel Castro's death provides an opportunity to celebrate victories from the 56 years of the Cuban Revolution for which many people around the world are profoundly grateful and even owe their lives. (Bartlett 2017)

The above observation made by Stephen Bartlett, an American agro-ecological farmer, was carried by the TWN to mark Castro's death which talked about a different legacy Castro had left behind, quite in contrast to what was the focus for the *NYT* and BBC. He discussed about the Cuban 'medical internationalism' which, by 2014, was sending 50,000 Cuban doctors and nurses to 60 developing countries. As he points out, 'this unparalleled solidarity has barely registered in the western media'.

In 1999, Cuba founded the Latin American Medical School (ELAM) and offered 10,000 scholarships to students in countries where Cuban medical teams were assisting the local health systems. The idea behind the ELAM is for graduates to eventually replace the Cuban doctors in their countries, according to MEDICC, a non-profit organization, which promotes Cuban public health programmes. The

ELAM currently has 19,550 students from 110 countries, making it one of the largest medical schools in the world. All students receive a full scholarship and those graduating are well known to focus on the field work and preventive healthcare that could be somewhat different to the drug-focused treatment in most developing countries supported by the big pharmaceutical companies.

Since 1998, some 6,000 Cuban doctors have treated over three million patients in Haiti. In 2005, Fidel Castro offered to send a large Cuban medical team to help in the disaster relief operation in New Orleans after Hurricane Katrina, but the Bush administration rejected the offer.[15] In 2008, newly independent Timor-Leste in Southeast Asia had nearly 300 Cuban health workers, while around 850 Timorese students were studying medicine in Cuba and in a newly created Faculty of Medicine in Timor-Leste. 'Cuban approach to aid is different', argues University of Sydney Political Economics Lecturer Tim Andersen, in a paper analysing Cuban aid to Timor-Leste. 'First, they regard cooperation as a matter of solidarity between peoples, not of financial flows or financial leverage.'[16]

Another area where Cuba has made some innovative progress in recent years is in sustainable agriculture, which the BBC described as 'returned to the age of ox-drawn carts'. This was necessitated when Cuba lost markets and support for its agriculture sector when the Soviet Bloc collapsed in the early 1990s. As Miguel Altieri,[17] Professor of Agroecology at the University of California, explained in a recent article, 'it encourages local production by small-scale farmers, using sustainable strategies and combining Western knowledge with traditional expertise'.

'Cuban farming has become a leading example of ecological agriculture', added Professor Altieri. 'Thousands of oxen replaced tractors that could not function due to lack of petroleum and spare parts.

---

[15] http://edition.cnn.com/2005/WORLD/americas/09/05/katrina.cuba/ (accessed on 11 June 2019).

[16] http://citeseerx.ist.psu.edu/viewdoc/download?doi=10.1.1.525.9559&rep=rep1&type=pdf (accessed on 11 June 2019).

[17] https://theconversation.com/cubas-sustainable-agriculture-at-risk-in-u-s-thaw-56773 (accessed on 11 June 2019).

Farmers substituted green manures for chemical fertilisers and artisanally produced bio pesticides for insecticides'. He also pointed out that from 1996 through 2005, per capita food production in Cuba increased by 4.2 per cent yearly during a period when production was stagnant across Latin America and the Caribbean.

During President Obama's visit to Havana in March 2016, US Agriculture Secretary Tom Vilsack signed an agreement with his Cuban counterpart, Agriculture Minister Gustavo Rodriguez Rollero, to promote sharing of ideas and research. Professor Altieri warns Cuba that they need to manage this new relationship carefully with US Agribusiness, otherwise 'Cuba will revert to an industrial approach.'

Malaysian sociologist and Islamic scholar Dr Chandra Muzaffar (2008) believes that Castro's Cuba has provided a good example of sustainable development for the entire world, especially to small countries. He points out that their health care system is perhaps the best in the world with neighbourhood clinics, polyclinics and hospitals covering the entire 104,944 sq. km of the island with one doctor for every 160 people. He argues its network of kindergartens, primary and secondary schools constitutes the foundation of the nation's education system that has provided the human resources for its great accomplishments in health care and agriculture. Its economy dominated by state and municipal corporations, cooperatives and collectives in agriculture, commerce and industry provides an alternative model of development to that of the capitalist model.

> Whatever the future holds for Cuba, it is undoubtedly one of the most outstanding success stories in social transformation in history. There are few other places on earth where justice, equality and solidarity have been given such concrete expression. What makes Cuba's achievements even more unique is that it has—in spite of the US blockade—given so much help to the poor and needy millions in other countries. Indeed, it is this—Cuba's unparalleled humanity—which has enhanced its dignity in the eyes of the world. (Muzaffar 2008: 61)

The Western media's subjective viewpoints and interpretations of development issues in Two-Thirds World countries focusing excessively on a narrow view of human rights, democracy and human development has deprived the world from learning about a unique development path—that of Fidel Castro's Cuba. If objective coverage was given to Cuba's achievements, it could also provide inspiration to other developing countries to adopt development models that are not excessively dependent on global corporations and Western-controlled funding sources such as the IMF and the World Bank (WB).

Freedom of Expression—Is That All?

FOE is a complex right which is rooted in the Article 19 of the UN Human Rights Declaration of 1948 which says, among others, that everyone has the right to freedom of opinion and expression. It is also supported by the first Amendment to the US constitution that says that the Congress must make no laws that infringe on the freedom of speech, the press and religion. But this right is not absolute because it comes with responsibilities and duties towards society and the nation. Sometimes these may be seen as hindering freedom of speech and create tensions between government and the citizens or between segments of the population.

In an FOE toolkit prepared by the UNESCO in 2013, especially targeted at students, it lists five commonly used tactics to silence people as follows:

1. When a licence to publish or broadcast is denied.
2. When there are physical or emotional intimidations such as reporters investigating sensitive issues receive death threats or dissidents held for long hours in interrogation that are designed to break them.
3. When access to information is being unduly denied or limited. This is subject to the fact that some sensitive information can be justifiable restricted from the public for a certain amount of time, for example, information concerning someone's medical records or the whereabouts of military personnel or weapons storage facilities.
4. When defamation, libel or slander suits are being abused where defending oneself against these suits could bankrupt a person.

5. When there are restrictive laws or regulation such as widely applied sedition laws or national security laws.

In recent years, there have been many instances where FOE could be taken to the extremes that offends others and lead to the phenomenon called 'hate speech' that triggers violence. The 2006 French Charlie Hebdo cartoons led to offending Muslim sensitivities and to violence right around the world, which ultimately led to a terrorist attack on its offices in 2015 that killed 12 journalists. This is an example of such restrictions in the modern world. Though not condoning the terrorist attack, this culminated in a series of events that included Charlie Hebdo publishing numerous cartoons and satirical pieces that lampooned the Prophet Muhammad and upset Muslims. One may argue that in a free society, one should learn not to get emotionally upset with cartoons and satire, but different cultures could see it differently.

For long, governments have been held responsible for violations of the FOE principles, but increasingly it is non-state actors that are becoming a threat to FOE. As a special investigation by *The Economist* in June 2016 pointed out: From the mosques of Cairo to the classrooms at Yale, all sorts of people and groups are claiming a right not to be offended. This is quite different from believing that people should, in general, be polite. A right not to be offended implies a power to police other people's speech. As Flemming Rose, editor of *Jyllands-Posten*, a Danish newspaper, told *The Economist*, 'taking offence has never been easier, or indeed more popular' (*The Economist* 2016). Certain people could create an offence and a conflict when it could be easily ignored and forgotten (we will look at the July 2012 Sam Bacile YouTube video later in this chapter).

While Xi Jinping's Chinese government may employ thousands of censors to block 'subversive' online messages that are distributed via the Internet sometimes by Western-funded Chinese NGO activists overseas, in the USA, student groups are demanding that speakers whose ideas they don't agree with be banned from speaking on campus; or in Bangladesh, an Islamist activist shoots-dead a fellow Muslim writer who questions certain tenets of Islam and speaks in favour of 'gay rights' (they claim he was promoting 'Western imperialism'); or in the Philippines, a 'hired killer' would shoot-dead a radio journalist while he is riding to work or is marketing with his family for exposing corrupt businessmen or crime syndicates operating in the province. Thus, threats to FOE not necessarily come from the usual culprits—governments or the military; however, some governments like in Bangladesh have not pursued the killers but made statement that implicitly tend to condone the killings. 'Our society does not allow any movement that promotes unnatural sex', said the Bangladeshi Home Minister Asaduzzaman Khan Kamal after a gay rights magazine editor Xulhaz Mannan's murder. Sheikh Hasina, the prime minister, has likened the slain bloggers' writing to 'porn' (*The Economist* 2016b).

As *The Economist* observes, in the Muslim world, by contrast, speech is under attack from state and non-state actors in roughly equal measure. The assassin's veto is exercised keenly in such places as Bangladesh, Iraq, Nigeria, Somalia and Syria. In several Arab countries, after a brief flowering of free debate during the Arab Spring, regimes even more repressive than the old ones have taken charge. Media outlets supportive of the Muslim Brotherhood, which Abdel Fattah el-Sisi, Egypt's present ruler, has branded a terrorist organization, have been closed down. In Spain, in February 2016, two puppeteers were arrested in Madrid. Their show, 'The Witch and Don Cristóbal', was provocative: a nun was stabbed by a crucifix; a judge was hanged with a noose. What upset the police, however, was a scene where a puppet policeman accused a witch of supporting terrorism and shoved a sign reading 'Up Alk-ETA' (a reference to Al-Qaeda and ETA, a Basque separatist group) into her hands. They were charged for 'glorifying terrorism' which carries a three-year jail term.

While those who support homosexuality have come under attack in Muslim-majority Bangladesh, in US and UK campuses it's been vice versa. *The Economist* reported that a recent survey has found that two-thirds of British students endorsed the National Union of Students' No Platform Policy, which has, for example, banned Peter Tatchell, a gay rights activist, who was a hero on campuses in the 1990s but has upset some of today's students by favouring free speech even for homophobes (*The Economist* 2016c). In Europe laws against Holocaust denial, brands its opponents as apologists for the 1940s genocide and silences them.

Yet, in other cases, a determined regime can usually think of ways to muzzle a voice that annoys it. Khadija Ismayilova, a journalist in Azerbaijan who revealed scandalous details about the ruling family's wealth, received photos in the post in 2012 showing her having sex with her boyfriend. A secret camera had been installed in her flat. A letter threatened to post the video online if she did not stop investigating corruption (*The Economist* 2016a).

Since the late 1980s, globalization and multiculturalism push, especially by liberals in the West, and advent of 'political correct speech' where offending minorities in general was discouraged and even censored in the media and public space, has created a counter movement. The current drift the other way seems to be a natural payback by majorities who are now feeling aggrieved. In Myanmar and Sri Lanka, for example, some Buddhist monks feel it is their right to talk about a 'Muslim threat' to their Buddhist heritage, citing examples from history about the spread of Islam in Asia. The same is felt by Hindu nationalists in India that make threatening comments about Muslims in order to protect India's Hindu identity. In Malaysia, Malay Muslim majority feel that their *bumiputra* (sons of the soil) rights are threatened by the richer Chinese minority, who are gaining political ground.

We may be in an age of receiving messages, images and moving pictures within seconds from the other corners of the world via our mobile phones, yet we may be entering an age where sending and receiving these may be not as free as we would like to think. As *The Economist* pointed out (*The Economist* 2016d), there are three different ways this communications could be interrupted: first, of course, by governments and its censorship devices increasingly through technology, but the more worrying one is by non-state actors through assassinations. The third is the spreading of the idea that people and groups have a right not be offended. But this is a subjective matter and who is going to police it? There could also be a looming threat from technology companies using their algorithms.

Blasphemy Laws and Threat to FOE

Following the Danish and French cartoon episodes, there have been moves by certain Muslim countries, particularly Saudi Arabia and Indonesia, to introduce an international treaty via the UN against blasphemy. But such a treaty will seriously hinder the FOE of Buddhists in particular, and also the growing numbers of atheists around the world, particularly in Europe. Both do not believe in the existence of God. The case of the jailing of Jakarta's Christian Governor Basuki Tjahaja Purnama in May 2017 under Indonesia's blasphemy laws should be a timely wake-up call for the international community, who may be thinking of an anti-blasphemy treaty to counter 'hate speech'. There should be other ways to promote and accommodate expression of different viewpoints without hurting other's feelings.

In 2004, international lingerie maker Victoria's Secret withdrew a Buddha-print bikini from the international market[18] and apologized to Buddhists after Sri Lanka's foreign ministry lodged a complaint and a US-based Vietnamese Buddhist organization collected thousands of signatures from Buddhists around the world calling for it to be withdrawn. In Buddhist-majority Thailand, for the past many years, an organization called Knowing Buddha has mounted a local and international campaign to respect the Buddha statue and not to use the image as decorations and tattoos. They have erected billboards and pasted posters at immigrations counters at Thai airports and also got police to raid bars and hotels where Buddha statues are placed inappropriately. Buddhists have never attacked Victoria's Secret outlets nor burned their bikinis, or Thai Buddhists haven't assaulted any tourists showing off a Buddha tattoo, though Sri Lanka did charge a British tourist, who happened to be a Buddhist herself, for entering the country with a Buddha tattoo on her arm.

Everyone has a right to feel offended and express it, but it needs to be tackled through public education and expressing displeasure in a non-violent way as the Buddhists have done with the 'Victoria's Secret' issue. In Europe, there have been many instances where Christians

---

[18] https://able2know.org/topic/29987-1 (accessed on 11 June 2019).

have been offended by lampooning the Christ image in the media or artistic activities. These too have been usually resolved via public education. We need to review FOE via this type of communication methodologies, where the news media could play a role. We need to talk not about religious tolerance, but respect, and respect cannot be practised if you do not know what the other believes in. The tragedy today is that some religious groups do not want to know of other peoples' faiths, ideas and philosophies. They are quick to call it 'blasphemy' without listening (or even debating) another philosophical viewpoint. Many governments play into their hands by discouraging the media from reporting about any religious issue, even the socio-economic as well as cultural issues related to religion and community.

Thus, the availability of FOE laws by itself is not enough, it has to be accompanied by public information and openness of people to listen to other peoples' point of view. Otherwise 'political correctness' in speech could also become a form of censorship.

The Assassin Model of Censorship

A serious threat to FOE has come up in recent years that no guidelines or regulations could stop. One may call it the 'assassin model of censorship', which I have already referred to in the Chapter 5.

In July 2012, a man calling himself Sam Bacile posted a short video on YouTube. It showed the Prophet Muhammad bedding various women, taking part in gory battles and declaring: 'Every non-Muslim is an infidel. Their lands, their women, their children are our spoils.' The film was, as Salman Rushdie, a British author, later put it, 'crap'. The innocence of Muslims could have remained forever obscure, had someone not dubbed it into Arabic and reposted it in September that year. An Egyptian chat show host denounced it and before long, this short, crap film was sparking riots across the Muslim world and beyond. A group linked to Al-Qaeda murdered America's ambassador in Libya citing this as the excuse. Protests erupted in Afghanistan, Australia, Britain, France and India. Pakistan's railway minister offered a US$100,000 bounty to whoever killed the film-maker and was not sacked. By the end of the month, at least 50 people had died (*The Economist* 2016a).

While the rights of people not be offended and be heard is an important issue of international communication discourse, a more recent phenomenon is a group's right to assassinate those who offend them. *The Economist* (2016a) in an article titled 'The Muzzle Grows Tighter' raised this issue arguing that freedom of speech is in retreat as a result.

While we have been debating about the 'right to communicate' for some time, in terms of communication theory, is there a need to consider if people and groups have a right not to be offended and if so, under what circumstances?

This may sound ridiculous for most of us communicators as we have been arguing for long that freedom of speech is about being able to communicate your ideas and debate it. As I have discussed in this book, the problem is when people are restricted or blocked by communicating your ideas. So should we even debate the idea that there is a 'right not to be offended'?

We know politeness and respect is a virtue and, especially in Eastern cultures, sometimes we may not say something if we feel that the other party could get upset and/or social harmony is disturbed. But if I say I have a right not to be offended, that means someone must police what you say about me, and judge it against the things I hold dear, such as my ethnic group, religion or even political beliefs. Since offence is subjective, the power to police it is both vast and arbitrary. In Australia, for example, defamation lawyers have used arguments of 'grapevine' and 'chilling' effects to claim compensation for comments made on Facebook or other social media platforms.

Rather than going into such legal minefields, we have seen a movement that is currently spearheaded by some Islamist groups, but spreading to others as well, such as so-called Hindu lynch mobs in India, and White supremacist groups in the USA, that they have a right to assassinate someone if he/she offends them, especially using tools of communication such as video and journalistic methods.

Balancing Civil Rights and National Security

At a conference organized in Brussels by the International Federation of Journalists (IFJ) and the European Federation of Journalists (EFJ) to mark the 10th anniversary of the 9/11 attacks, speakers lamented that laws introduced in the USA in the aftermath of the attacks have had a chilling effect on the practice of journalism worldwide, allowing governments to avoid public scrutiny.

To mark the 10th anniversary of the 9/11 attacks, I was involved with financial assistance from the EU Centre in Singapore to publish a research study on the impact of anti-terror laws on journalists in Europe and in Asia. The impact of the rush to adopt anti-terror laws on both civil liberties and media freedoms has been a concern in both Europe and Asia, and it continues to do so.

The European study found that in the UK there has been an increase in racist assumptions and stereotyping of Muslims in the media and exclusion of UK-born Muslims from Britishness. In Germany, the study found that Muslims are portrayed as a threat and are generally viewed as a homogenous group. While mosque raids are widely reported, the end result where nothing was found is not usually given prominence in the reporting. In France also, media reporting sees Islam as a potential threat, and treatment of Islam is always partial, covered exclusively as a crisis and a problem. And in the Netherlands, the study found that as a result of a number of high-profile terrorist attacks, particularly the murder of Dutch filmmaker Theo van Gogh, in spite of the sensational coverage, and after an initial period of confusion, there has been a marked appreciation of several structural problems faced by the migrants in the Netherlands. The researcher Ramesh Jaura in Berlin noted that member states across the EU find themselves faced with a dilemma, whether to preserve cherished democratic values of which Europe is proud of or to combat 'terrorism', which is perceived as a threat to these values (Seneviratne and Hwee 2011).

In Asia, the study noted that new anti-terror laws or amendments to criminal codes have seriously restricted journalists' ability to investigate and report freely. There have been new restrictions on what journalists can write or broadcast on acts of terrorism; access to information on investigations and persecution of terrorists has been restricted; laws have also sought to amend and restrict traditional protection given to journalists' sources while making it an offence for journalists to withhold information on terrorism from policy or security sources. The study found that in Pakistan, journalists have been killed, arrested, tortured or gone into exile as a result of reporting on terrorism. Thus, the safety of journalists was getting worse. In India, the attack on Parliament in December 2001 and the Mumbai terror attacks of November 2008 and the subsequent amendments to anti-terror laws have been a setback for investigative journalism. There have been increasing incidents of violence against journalists, particularly in states where there is tension between Hindus and Muslims. In Sri Lanka, as the war against Tamil Tiger terrorism intensified, Defence Secretary Gotabhaya Rajapaksa gave the media a stark choice—support the war effort or be labelled a traitor. Interestingly, the Sri Lankan media also had to fight a propaganda war with the Western media on the behalf of the government, as many Western media organizations were seen to be propaganda outlets for the Tamil Tiger (LTTE) terrorists. The Philippines has had the most number of journalists killed in the past two decades, not necessarily connected to terrorism, but the study found that in an environment of problematic governance, political cronyism and simmering insurgency in the southern-most island of Mindanao, there is always the chance of misuse of anti-terror laws to restrict reporting in other areas such an endemic corruption.

There is no doubt that in the era of 'war against terrorism', media's ability to report without fear or favour has been seriously restricted. The debate on 'fake news' could add another armoury to those who want to restrict media freedoms (more discussion of this in Chapter 9). Nine days after the 9/11 attacks, President George W. Bush addressing a joint session of the American Congress[19] asked, 'Why do they (terrorists) hate us?' Answering his own question, he said, 'They hate our freedoms—our freedom of religion, our freedom of speech, our freedom to vote and assemble and disagree with each

---

[19] https://www.youtube.com/watch?v=0wPuY5hI96U (accessed on 11 June 2019).

other'. He may be correct, but over 15 years later looking at the state of media freedoms around the world because of the concerns of terrorism, one is entitled to ask whether the terrorists have won the war of ideology and ideas.

The reaction to terror attacks has resulted in a campaign in the West against Islam rather than realizing the need to understand why there is outrage among Muslims about injustices meted out to them. It could be argued that these stem from Western action in the region where they have divided countries and installed puppet kings and sheikhs to rule. Many such rulers did not provide education and health for their citizens, Muslim piety took on the task of providing what the state was not providing. So large networks of religious schools and hospital were created and, when elections were finally permitted, these became the basis for legitimacy and the vote for Muslim parties. This is why, just taking the example of two important countries, Islamist parties won in Egypt and Algeria, and how with the acquiescence of the West, military coups were the only resort to stopping them, noted Roberta Savio.[20] This brutally abridged historical process is useful for understanding how anger and frustration is now all over the Middle East, and it has been made worse particularly by the overthrow of the Gaddafi regime in Libya and its aftermath as discussed later in this chapter.

In the context of not falling into a trap of fighting just one kind of terrorism, it is also interesting to give a thought to how you define a terrorist. This came to my mind when I saw reports of the US' biggest mass murder in Las Vegas in September 2017. According to the *Oxford Dictionary*, terrorism is defined as *the unlawful use of violence and intimidation, especially against civilians, in the pursuit of political aims*. So wouldn't it be offensive to a Muslim that when someone with a Muslim name or background is involved in such a terrorist attack the whole religion is guilty as we call him/her 'Islamic terrorist'? And when a Black shoots someone that will be called 'Black Gangster Terrorism'. But when a White shooter is involved in a mass murder like the Las

---

[20] http://www.ipsnews.net/2015/01/opinion-the-paris-killings-a-fatal-trap-for-europe/ (accessed on 11 June 2019).

Vegas murderer Stephen Paddock, he is described as a 'mentally troubled lone wolf'. Even the *NYT*[21] was confused about what to call someone, who is clearly terrorizing but not a terrorist, was how they posed the question. In that case, we could well use the same terminology to ask the question about those so-called 'home-grown Islamic terrorists' in the West. Are they also 'mentally troubled lone wolfs'?

Is 'War Crimes' Hypocrisy Killing Human Rights?

Before closing this chapter, I would like to draw attention to a couple of issues that though espousing to promote human rights and democracy may do exactly the opposite because of the hypocrisy involved in the media narrative and its influence on implementing these policies. This is about the narrative on 'war crimes' and 'crimes against humanity'.

When a terrorist attack happens in Europe these days, and I read and hear about how Europeans react to it by going after not only Muslim youth in their own countries labelling them as 'persons of interest' or 'home-grown terrorists' but also firing missiles via drones to Muslim communities overseas that kills innocent civilians. The Western media reports these as a 'surgical strike against Islamic terrorist'.

True that majority of Europeans believe in the principles of human rights enshrined in the UDHR and they cherish that. But they also need to practise it, especially when they are fond of preaching that to others. I can remember, in the early 1980s, when the Dalai Lama visited Australia and gave a talk at the Sydney Town Hall to a packed audience, he was asked by an Australian, how can you practise compassion you preach towards China, when they have invaded and enslaved your people for so long? His response was that when you have an enemy, that is the time to practise what you preach. 'Chinese government provides me a subject to practice my compassion towards' was his response. Well, the Chinese government

[21] https://www.nytimes.com/2017/10/02/us/politics/terrorism-las-vegas-attack.html (accessed on 11 June 2019).

may disagree on whether the Dalai Lama does practise compassion towards them as they often describe him as an 'insurgent' out to divide China.

Anyways, let me take two issues here with regard to this subject of hypocrisy of the Western media towards human rights issues in the West and elsewhere, especially in Africa and Asia. The first case is about the ICC in The Hague and the other is the Geneva-based UNHRC.

ICC and 'War Crimes' Allegations against Africa

In January 2017, at the end of a closed-door meeting of the African Union (AU) in Addis Ababa, it was announced that they had adopted a strategy for Africa to collectively withdraw from The Hague-based ICC. African nations have for some time been unhappy about the narrow nature of investigations by the court on genocide, war crimes and crimes against humanity and they feel that Africa has been unfairly targeted as a continent. Some have even gone to the extent of labelling the ICC as a 'racist' organization dominated by Whites and, in 2016, South Africa, Burundi and Gambia expressed its intention to quit.

The ICC caused an uproar among some African nations in 2007 when it indicted Kenyan President Uhuru Kenyatta on charges of crimes against humanity for post-election violence in which more than 1,000 died. The case collapsed amid allegations from ICC prosecutor that the Kenyan government did not cooperate. Some African countries have been critical of the ICC for pursuing existing heads of state such as Sudanese President Omar al-Bashir for allegedly orchestrating atrocities in Darfur.

In March 2017, South Africa withdrew its notice of leaving the ICC after the Supreme Court ruled that the Cabinet could not make the decision by itself without it being passed by the parliament. South African Cabinet took the decision to leave in October 2016 after the ICC riled it for not arresting Sudanese president and handing him over to the ICC, when he came to attend an AU summit in South Africa in 2015.

Africa's former UN Secretary General Kofi Annan who was instrumental in setting up the ICC has warned countries against leaving the ICC as it will allow crimes against humanity to go unpunished.

Writing in London's *Guardian*,[22] he said:

> We also made the most use of the institution from the outset: of the nine investigations on the African continent, eight were requested by African states, six African states referred their own situation to the ICC, and African states voted in support of the UN security council referrals on Darfur and Libya. Kenya was the only case in Africa opened independently by the court, but it enjoyed the enthusiastic support of a majority of Kenyans. They wanted justice for the 1,300 people killed and hundreds of thousands displaced in election-related violence.
>
> The ICC got involved in these African cases because national authorities did not conduct investigations into the massive crimes that had occurred. The ICC does not supplant national jurisdictions, it only intervenes in cases where the country concerned is either unable or unwilling to try its own citizens. Africans deserve justice as much as anyone else, even if their governments cannot always provide it.

But many in Africa and Asia do not agree with it. They have seen this mentality as smacking in double standards because the West has virtually got away with murder. Many see US and NATO bombing campaigns in the Middle East, Afghanistan, Pakistan and even going back to the Vietnam War era as 'war crimes' and 'crime against humanity' which go unpunished, especially because the USA in particular has refused to join the ICC and hence their citizens cannot be charged by the ICC.

In 2012, at the UNHRC, there were strong criticisms against the use of drone strikes with many member countries arguing that this violates international human rights law. The use of drones or pilotless aircraft operated by remote control, by the government in one country

---

[22] https://www.theguardian.com/commentisfree/2016/nov/18/state-impunity-international-criminal-court-african (accessed on 11 June 2019).

to strike at persons and other targets in other countries, has been increasing in the USA, Pakistan, Afghanistan, Yemen and Somalia at the same time. Instead of following clear legal standards, the practice of drone attacks has become a vaguely defined and unaccountable 'licence to kill', according to a 2010 report of a UN human rights special rapporteur. The American Civil Liberties Union (ACLU) has estimated that as many as 4,000 people have been killed in US drone strikes between 2002 and 2012 (Khor 2012).

At an event organized by the ACLU, Christof Heyns, the UN special rapporteur on extrajudicial, summary or arbitrary executions, said the US drone attacks would encourage other states to flout human rights standards and suggested that some drone strikes may even be war crimes, according to a report in the London-based *Guardian* (Khor 2012).

News portal Truthout[23] reported in 2014 that complaints have been made to the ICC about drone strikes as a 'war crime'. Lawyers with the British human rights organization Reprieve filed a legal complaint at the ICC documenting the experiences of Pakistani anti-drone activist Kareem Khan and other drone strike victims and accusing NATO-allied states of war crimes by helping to facilitate the US' covert drone programme in Pakistan. Khan has fought an ongoing legal battle with the Pakistani government and the USA. In a 2010 lawsuit he filed in the Islamabad High Court, he identified the then CIA station chief in Pakistan, Jonathan Banks, for his alleged role in the drone attack.

The ICC and the Anglo-American global media have been largely silent on this issue, often reporting such strikes as 'targeted strikes on militants' and if any civilian casualties are reported referring to them as 'collateral damage'. Thus, such terminology misleads and manipulates international public opinion creating apathy towards this issue.[24]

London's *Guardian* noted that the year he left office, in 2016, according to US own Department of Defense's figures, Obama

---

[23] https://truthout.org/ (accessed on 11 June 2019).
[24] http://www.truth-out.org/news/item/22025-nato-members-complicit-in-drone-strikes-world-court-complaint-alleges (accessed on 11 June 2019).

administration was involved in dropping 26,171 bombs around the world: 'One bombing technique that President Obama championed is drone strikes', noted *The Guardian*.

> As drone-warrior-in-chief, he spread the use of drones outside the declared battlefields of Afghanistan and Iraq, mainly to Pakistan and Yemen. Obama authorized over 10 times more drone strikes than George W Bush, and automatically painted all males of military age in these regions as 'combatants', making them fair game for remote controlled killing.[25]

This should have triggered calls in the international media for Obama's Nobel Peace Prize to be revoked, but no such calls were made.

UNHRC's Bias against Sri Lanka

In June 2018, the USA announced that they would leave the UNHRC after the UN body voted to probe the killing of Palestinian civilians by Israel in Gaza. It accused the UN body of 'chronic bias' against Israel. 'We take this step because our commitment does not allow us to remain a part of a hypocritical and self-serving organization that makes a mockery of human rights', US Ambassador to the UN Nikki Haley said standing alongside former CIA Head and US Secretary of State Mike Pompeo in Washington. Such comments could be music to the ears of many African and Asian governments that have accused the organization of such bias.

As a Sri Lankan, I must admit that I smiled when I heard Haley's statement. Many Sri Lankans see the UNHRC as carrying out a witch-hunt against Sri Lanka since the LTTE was eliminated in 2009. It is the cynical use of a UN human rights mechanism to interfere in the domestic affairs of a country to serve Western geopolitical interests. While many Sri Lankans would agree with the US statement, it is also puzzling why they are leaving an organization that has served US geopolitical agenda very well. The same campaign they have carried

---

[25] https://www.theguardian.com/commentisfree/2017/jan/09/america-dropped-26171-bombs-2016-obama-legacy (accessed on 11 June 2019).

out against Sri Lanka is being repeated against Myanmar of late, both strategically located countries in Asia.

Sri Lanka's former ambassador in Geneva described the role of the UNHRC in these words in 2009, when the witch-hunt was started:

> Mr President Sri Lanka noted with some degree of amusement that the EU, the United Kingdom, Ireland and France were all cheering on the notion of an international inquiry into allegations of human rights violations conducted by all sides as they put it to the Sri Lankan conflict so here's the deal—Sri Lanka will be prepared I think to regard this a little more charitably if we start from the human rights situations that precede the Sri Lankan conflict, let France institute an impartial independent inquiry into the millions of deaths in so-called French Indochina, and then in Algeria including those who are submitted to electroshock during the Battle of Algiers. Let it also have an independent inquiry into the disappearance of Mary Jane Barker from the streets of Paris and possible complicity with of all sorts of personalities in that disappearance. Let Great Britain and Ireland have an international inquiry into the events of Bloody Sunday 1972 in Londonderry but there was no fog of war like in the closing stages of Sri Lankan conflict, but dead civilians were strewn on the streets of Londonderry and after two Commissions of inquiry the only result has been the promotion of every single soldier (who) was there on that day and the commanding officer being given some sort of honors by Her Majesty the Queen. Now if these countries set an example to Sri Lanka and submit their own conduct to so-called impartial or independent international inquiries of the sort that they have commanded us, Sri Lanka would be ready (to talk).
> —Dr Dayan Jayatilleka, Sri Lanka's Permanent Representative to the UNHRC, speaking in Geneva, June 2009.[26]

The aforementioned speech was given at the UNHRC in Geneva just after the end of the Civil War in Sri Lanka. The ambassador was obviously trying to make a point about Western hypocrisy that historically, when European interests were threatened, they never cared about

---

[26] https://www.youtube.com/watch?v=IC13OaHU7m0 (accessed on 11 June 2019).

human rights. So why they care about Sri Lanka when the country's very existence was seriously threatened by LTTE terrorism. They claim—without evidence to back it—that 40,000 were killed in the final days of the end to a 30-year Civil War in the country. This figure has been bandied by international media ever since, but not even 400 names of such people killed have been given by any media organization nor the UN. No one seems to question where this figure comes from, even though the Sri Lankan government has often questioned its reliability.

In an article titled 'Implications of UK's Refusal to Release Evidence', Sri Lanka's *Island*'s editor Shamindra Ferdinando pointed out that there are conflicting claims by different parties on the casualty figures, and while the UK has been the main party pressuring the UNHRC to mount 'war crimes' allegations against Sri Lanka, the government refuses to provide any evidence even when one of their Privy Councillor's demand the government do so.[27]

Sri Lanka's battle with the UNHRC has been a long drawn out one[28] and it's still continuing. It has now bitten right into the domestic political process in Sri Lanka where domestically unpopular constitutional changes are been forced upon by the UNHRC, which most Sri Lankans feel are been forced on the government on the whims of Western powers who want to control the local judiciary under the disguise of setting up a local 'war crimes court' that may have foreign judges sitting on the bench.

Ever since the success of the Western 'regime change' project in Sri Lanka in January 2015, the new government has come under immense pressure to surrender to the dictates of the UNHRC, so much so that in late 2015 Sri Lanka co-sponsored a resolution requiring the island nations to 'account' for the so-called 'war crimes' and set up courts to try former armed forces personnel—whom most Sri Lankans see as 'war heroes' (Ranaviru)—for having got rid of terrorism

---

[27] http://www.island.lk/index.php?page_cat=article-details&page=article-details&code_title=173842 (accessed on 11 June 2019).
[28] http://www.nationmultimedia.com/opinion/United-Nations-mediation-a-warning-from-recent-his-30228533.html (accessed on 11 June 2019).

from the country. Part of the deal with the UNHRC is a new constitution that will create these mechanisms. Pushed by the UNHRC, a Sri Lankan parliamentary group has drafted a new constitution that is vastly unpopular with a large majority of the people, and it is unlikely to be passed by parliament, especially after the February 2018 nationwide local government elections that saw vast gains made by the opposition led by former President Mahinda Rajapaksa.

In a commentary published in Sri Lanka's *Island* in April 2018, former Sri Lankan ambassador to the UNHRC in Geneva, Tamara Kunanayakam[29] (an ethnic Tamil), argued that the UNHRC is trying to turn an independent republic to a vassal state. She noted:

> The demands articulated in the US-led resolution are being fast incorporated into the law of the land through a series of radical reforms and the drafting of a new Constitution. Ever since Yahapalana (good governance) government was installed in power in January 2015, we have seen a flurry of activity in making, breaking, reforming and amending institutions of State and laws of the land. Some reforms are known, others are being drafted and negotiated behind closed doors. Many are being hurriedly rushed through without consultation with the people or debate in Parliament, particularly when these violate the country's Republican Constitution.

Kunanayakam said that it is not only the UN that is being used but also the WB and the IMF. She argues that the hidden agenda behind the UNHRC resolution 30/1 which Sri Lanka co-sponsored is to turn a fiercely independent people into a slave state for US geopolitical interests. Interestingly, it is done in Sri Lanka via interference in the electoral process through funding NGOs and through so-called development assistance to a client government. Pointing out that underlining this resolution is the controversial R2P, she warns:

> We must remember that it (resolution 30/1) was not formulated by the Sri Lankan people, but by a foreign power, the USA, whose sole interest is to turn our country into an aircraft carrier to contain

---

[29] http://island.lk/index.php?page_cat=article-details&page=article-details&code_title=182626 (accessed on 11 June 2019).

and roll back China as part of its imperial ambition of maintaining global hegemony. R2P is the modern version of the 'White Man's Burden' of the late 19th century used by the US and Great Britain as justification for their savage colonial wars. It is a project of re-colonization, associated with bringing countries under their tutelage.

It is an irony of our times that a UN instrument—UNHRC—that was set up to protect human rights of the people has become a tool in the hands of big powers to subjugate people.[30] The bigger tragedy is that the international media—nor the Asian media—is reporting about it. As I have discussed earlier about subjective reporting, it will be too much for us to expect the Western international media to report this issue from the perspective presented here. But the Asian media needs to be alert to it and, in this age of the Internet, they could easily pick up commentaries like Kunanayakam in the Sri Lankan media. If the Asian media does not pick up this story, there will be other Asian countries on the chopping block, especially countries such as Myanmar, Cambodia, the Philippines, Malaysia and Thailand. In fact, the UNHRC is trying to get involved in Myanmar using the Rohingya minority, and their strategy is exactly the same as that used against Sri Lanka.

The War on Libya and R2P

When youth uprisings in Tunisia and Egypt got rid of long-serving pro-Western dictators, it seemed as if the youth of the Arab world were finally rising against dictators who had served Western capitalism well but not their own people. But when the revolution spread to Libya and the haste at which the controversial R2P formula—for long espoused by the International Crisis Group led by former Australian Foreign Minister Gareth Evans—was adopted by the EU and the USA to create a no-fly zone in Libya under the pretext of protecting civilians in Benghazi from a possible assault by pro-Gaddafi forces,

---

[30] http://www.nationmultimedia.com/opinion/United-Nations-mediation-a-warning-from-recent-his-30228533.html (accessed on 11 June 2019).

the Western powers' manipulation of the Arab Spring uprisings soon became blatantly clear. Once China and Russia were pressured into abstaining from vetoing the 'no-fly zone' resolution at the UN Security Council, the path was paved for regime change.

The NATO bombing campaign in Libya against civilian population centres under Gaddafi rule made a mockery of the R2P formula. As many critics inside and outside the West have pointed out, these NATO bombing campaigns and the way Gaddafi and his son were killed amounted to war crimes.

On 1 November 2011, Luis Moreno Ocampo,[31] ICC's chief prosecutor, told the UN that NATO troops would be investigated alongside rebel soldiers and regime forces for alleged breaches of the laws of war during the battle to overthrow Colonel Muammar Gaddafi. But, compared to the hounding of the Sri Lankan government after it crushed the LTTE to end the 30-year-old Civil War there, the Western media and the human rights organizations, which consistently accuse developing country governments of war crimes, have been silent on this one.

Rape and torture have become standard issue in the propaganda arsenal of Western media. Reports from organizations such as Human Rights Watch (HRW) or AI that claim to document the systematic use of rape and torture by the 'enemies' of the West have become usual fare in the soft war against whomever the Western powers choose to attack. We have seen these claims used to legitimize aggression against Libya, Iraq and Syria as well as attempts at interference in internal affairs of Sri Lanka and Myanmar, and a number of African countries.

In the run-up to the attacks against Libya in 2011, the lie that Gaddafi forces were using rape as a weapon was planted in the public mind, providing NATO the human rights cover they so desperately needed for their intervention. Of course, as is so often the case, the fact that these claims were later proven untrue went conveniently

---

[31] http://www.telegraph.co.uk/news/worldnews/africaandindianocean/libya/8866007/Libya-Nato-to-be-investigated-by-ICC-for-war-crimes.html (accessed on 11 June 2019).

missing from the standard narrative. But, by the time the myth was debunked, the PR damage was done: Gaddafi was a monster, the Benghazi 'rebels' and National Transitional Council (NTC) were heroic freedom fighters, and Libya was in dire need of the benevolent bombs of NATO to get rid of a tyrant.

Who makes these claims is also important in the propaganda war. The UNHRC, HRW, AI and countless other organizations, which are dependent on funding from sources mainly within the USA and EU, lent credence to such charges. The fact that they are often quoted by the Western media and in turn relayed without criticism or questioning by the MSM around the world gives legitimacy to Western interventions and 'regime change' campaigns.

How Gaddafi was overthrown and a new government was set up is a very important lesson for countries of the Two-Thirds World who are either rich in resources or strategically important for Western powers in their geopolitical battles. While demonizing Gaddafi with trivial stories, the Western media ignored facts, which would have shown that Gaddafi did look after his people well, even though they were not allowed to criticize him like the dictators in most pro-Western Arab regimes, such as Saudi Arabia does.

For example, in Gaddafi's Libya, education was free to everyone from elementary school right up to university and post-graduate study, at home or abroad. Libyans enjoyed free health care, with a ratio of 1 doctor per 673 citizens. Libyans were given interest-free housing loans and free land for farmers. In 2010, Libya had no external debt and its reserves amounted to US$150 billion.[32]

The West does not just overthrow a regime and let the people elect their representatives. They bring back a stooge who has obtained refuge in the West, particularly in the USA and plant him/her as the new ruler or ruling alliance. Abdurrahim Abdulhafiz El-Keib, who served as Libya's interim prime minister after the overthrow of Gaddafi, from 24 November 2011 to 11 November 2012, has spent

---

[32] https://www.sailanmuslim.com/the-cost-of-killing-gaddafi-by-shenali-waduge/ (accessed on 11 June 2019).

decades in the USA teaching at the University of Alabama. He is also a former employee of the Petroleum Institute, based in Abu Dhabi, and sponsored by British Petroleum (BP), Royal Dutch Shell and France's Total S.A. His successor, Prime Minister Ali Zeidan, was a Geneva-based human rights lawyer, who is believed to have played a crucial role in persuading the French President Nicolas Sarkozy to support the anti-Gaddafi forces.

Malaysian journalist Bunn Nagara (2015) reflecting on US fetish for invasions in the post-Cold War era beginning with Afghanistan, then Iraq and now Libya, asked whether it is an unreal fantasy process where the real-life consequences are forgotten? Among these consequences are the human suffering on the ground and the flood of refugees emerging from the broken societies that bombings produce and leave behind, that are flooding into Europe, he points out.

'Europe's present generation has not seen anything like the current tide of human beings washing over their territory. So they cannot respond rationally or react intelligently. Several local communities revert to vile subhuman behaviour. Even child refugees have been assaulted', noted Nagara. He blames the European media for not educating the populations to cope with the refugee influx that is a result of Western incursions into the Muslim world, and the destruction of their communities and economies.

He argues:

Saddam and Gaddafi were no doubt tyrants, as is Bashar al-Assad, but it had been tyranny that kept terrorism and other destabilising factors down and out. Remove the tyrants and the tyranny, and terrorism and chaos would rush in before the glory of human rights and a golden age of democracy.

Naturally, that obvious connection may not be widely acknowledged in Western establishment circles. Ideology and its consequences are seldom acknowledged by ideologists, as Nagara points out.

Nagara thinks that with all the petty and hideous xenophobia against refugees on display in Europe, the benefits, which migrants bring to their new countries are often forgotten. The media need to educate the people regarding this process. But the question is: can an adversarial media do it?

Adversarial Reporting a Threat to Human Rights

This brings us back to the question whether journalism's focus on events reporting that leads to adversarial journalism—not education—is the real problem that is contributing to growing conflict and tension around the world.

If European audiences are educated about the horrors of their governments' (i.e., NATO) military adventures in the Arab world, it may create peoples' movements that would oppose war rather than refugees arriving on their shores. They may perhaps see NATO as an unnecessary burden on European taxpayers. Like what happened during the Vietnam War days, such media reporting may lead to a peace movement that could help to bring these conflicts and the resulting mysteries to an end. Which will, of course, stop the refugee flow.

It is ironic that five years after the fall of Gaddafi, young Libyans—who used to be funded by the Gaddafi government to go to Europe for studies—are now been transported by human traffickers via treacherous waters of the Mediterranean Sea to the shores of Europe where they are not welcomed. When they brought in the money to British and European universities, they were welcomed with open arms. And most of them returned to Libya after graduation to serve their country under Gaddafi.

That is not the way CNN saw Libya five years after its 'liberation'. In a report to mark the occasion, CNN said that since coming to power in 1969, Gaddafi systematically stripped the country of its ability to self-govern, installing a cult of personality where his mercurial political predilections prevailed. In short, he was creating a state ready to fail as soon as he died. The report did admit that the country is in a mess with no clear ruler, but did not say that it is due to Western intervention. It talked about ISIS filling a vacuum and an illegitimate governing clan shipping Libya's oil which is only half the output of one million barrels a day during Gaddafi's time. The report did not analyse any ghastly Western miscalculations that have wrecked a country, which was well-governed sans democracy. Nor did they try to investigate who exactly is making the money out of Libya's oil exports and also what has happened to the billions of dollars of Libyan reserves that were banked in the West.

The reality in Libya makes a mockery of West's claim to have toppled dictators to bring democracy to the people. If the CNN is to get an honest opinion from many of the Libyan refugees who are living in mystery in refugee camps in Europe, I have no doubt they would talk glowingly about the good old days under Gaddafi. But would CNN broadcast such interviews?

Irish journalist and a Middle East correspondent for the *Financial Times*, Patrick Cockburn (2013) writing in the *British Journalism Review* noted of the wars fought by the West since the 9/11 attacks thus:

> The four wars fought in Afghanistan, Iraq, Libya and Syria over the past 12 years have all involved overt or covert foreign intervention in deeply divided countries. In each case the involvement of the West exacerbated existing differences and pushed hostile parties towards civil war. In each country, all or part of the opposition have been hardcore jihadi fighters. Whatever the real issues at stake, the interventions have been presented as primarily humanitarian, in support of popular forces against dictators and police states. Despite apparent military successes, in none of these cases have the local opposition and their backers succeeded in consolidating power and establishing stable states.
> More than most armed struggles, the conflicts have been propaganda wars in which newspaper, television and radio journalists played a central role. In all wars there is a difference between reported news and what really happened, but during these four campaigns the outside world has been left with misconceptions even about the identity of the victors and the defeated.

Cockburn argues that Libya's descend into anarchy has hardly been covered by the Western media as they have now moved to Syria. Even the fact that 1,000 Iraqis are killed each month is not covered. He argues that the very concept of a war reporter is misleading and gives the reporter a sense of reporting conflict, when what happens after an invasion and regime change is a political process that goes largely unreported. These political developments need to be interpreted by journalists on the ground who usually look for battlefields.

As we have been discussing in this chapter the double standards, especially in the Western media narrative on human rights, it will be appropriate to end this chapter with this quote from Singaporean academic Kishore Mahbubani,[33] who responds to criticism from the Western media of Singapore lacking FOE:

> I can tell you the Western media gets it completely wrong because you read the Western media you got the impression that Singapore is just a nicer version of North Korea and everybody's suppressed or repressed and so on. Guess what—you know virtually every Singaporean travels overseas every year and comes back to Singapore so obviously this is not an oppressive State. The reason why Singapore has restrictions on press freedom is precisely because of the 1964 ethnic riots that Singapore experienced. We've seen in many other countries, press freedom like in Rwanda is to (allow) hate speech against minorities. We want to ensure that, that doesn't happen in Singapore and therefore there are these restrictions on press freedom in Singapore.
>
> But I know on the question of civil liberties there's a very important point that Americans should bear in mind when they speak about civil liberties you know one of the big shocks that the world experienced after 9/11 was when they watch America, the world's most advanced open democratic society walked back from some civil liberties as soon as they began to feel insecure and because they were frightened of terrorists. They said I'm happy to give up my privacy come have surveillance cameras everywhere I'm not worried, I want my safety in security.
>
> Now if America the world's most powerful country is prepared to give up some of its civil liberties in exchange for security right, then you begin to understand why smaller and much more

---

[33] https://www.youtube.com/watch?v=u8sykIHdvoI (accessed on 11 June 2019).

vulnerable states like Singapore have also develop a compact, with the government [that] is it okay we'll give up some of our civil liberties, we'll give up some of our press freedom but continue to keep this place peaceful and prosperous and strong.

On this point of how to balance security with human rights, we will go to our next chapter looking at why people are dissolution with neoliberal economics with its ability to control people and the media.

CHAPTER 7

Neoliberalism Breeding Inequality
Who Is Telling the Truth?

> Like other sciences, economics strives for objectivity. In the process, however, subjective values, such as ethics, are excluded. With no consideration of subjective, moral values, an economist may say, for instance, that a bottle of whisky and a Chinese dinner have the same economic values, or that drinking in a night club contributes more to the economy than listening to a religious talk or volunteering for humanitarian work. These are truths according to economics.
>
> But the objectivity of economics is short sighted. Economists look at just one short phase of the natural casual process and single out the part that interests them, ignoring the wider ramifications. Thus, modern economists take no account of the ethical consequences of economic activity. Neither the vices associated with the frequenting of nightclubs nor the wisdom arising from listening to a religious teaching is its concern. (Payutto 1992: 16)

What the well-known Thai Buddhist monk venerable Prayudh Payutto says about economists may also be applied to describe economic or business reporters, who report on the figures at the 'bottom lines' without giving much emphasis to the social and cultural aspects of economic activity. In this chapter, we will explore how influences of neoliberal economics have tainted economic and business reporting, where the main element—the people—is often missing from the reporting.

London-based Oxfam International in its second Commitment to Reducing Inequality (CRI) Index released in October 2018[1] pointed out that over the past 30 years, the gap between the rich and everyone else has worsened in many countries across the world. Since 2001, the poorest half of the population has received just 1 per cent of the total increase in global wealth, while the richest 1 per cent has received 50 per cent. Extreme inequality reduces economic growth, threatens women's rights and worsens health and other outcomes, argues the report, noting that each year, 100 million people are driven below the poverty line by having to pay for health care. Almost 70 million young people are working but still living in extreme poverty, surviving on less than US$2 a day. Women make up the majority of the world's low-paid workers, getting by on wages that leave them trapped in a cycle of poverty. The report stated that 2017 has seen the biggest increase in billionaires in history—one more every two days. Billionaires saw their wealth increase by US$762 billion in just 12 months (March 2016–March 2017). This huge increase could have ended global extreme poverty seven times over. Eighty-two per cent of the new wealth created has gone to top 1 per cent, while 0 per cent has gone to the world's poorest 50 per cent.

> Large corporations and rich individuals play a key role in widening this gap. They use their power and influence to ensure government policy works in their interests. And big business is ruthlessly focused on maximizing returns to their shareholders by any means—whether that's driving down wages or dodging taxes.
> —Oxfam CRI Report 2017

Neoliberal Economics and Globalization

The predicament that the world's richest 1 per cent own most of the world's wealth has been facilitated by the advent of neoliberal

---

[1] https://www.oxfam.org/en/campaigns/even-it/reducing-inequality-what-your-country-doing-tackle-gap-between-rich-and-poor (accessed on 13 June 2019).

economics in the 1980s and globalization process beginning in the 1990s after the fall of the Berlin Wall and the dismantling of the Soviet Union. The whole world has become their market without much regulation to protect national interests and the people at the grassroots of the society.

These two processes have played a major role in a remarkable variety of crises, argues George Monbiot (2016), author of *How Did We Get into This Mess?* He lists some of these crises as the financial meltdown of 2007–2008; the offshoring of wealth and power, of which the Panama Papers[2] offer us merely a glimpse; the slow collapse of public health and education; resurgent child poverty, the epidemic of loneliness; the collapse of ecosystems and the rise of Donald Trump and his brand of populist politics. Monbiot provides a very simple explanation.

> Neoliberalism sees competition as the defining characteristic of human relations. It redefines citizens as consumers, whose democratic choices are best exercised by buying and selling, a process that rewards merit and punishes inefficiency. It maintains that 'the market' delivers benefits that could never be achieved by planning.
> Attempts to limit competition are treated as inimical to liberty. Tax and regulation should be minimised, public services should be privatized. The organisation of labour and collective bargaining by trade unions are portrayed as market distortions that impede the formation of a natural hierarchy of winners and losers. Inequality is recast as virtuous: a reward for utility and a generator of wealth, which trickles down to enrich everyone. Efforts to create a more equal society are both counterproductive and morally corrosive. The market ensures that everyone gets what they deserve.

Oxfam points out that the most commonly cited source of wealth for billionaires on the *Forbes* richest list comes from sectors that are not productive industries—in the sense that it produces goods and services

---

[2] https://www.theguardian.com/news/2016/apr/08/mossack-fonseca-law-firm-hide-money-panama-papers (accessed on 13 June 2019).

that are essential to human survival/well-being—they are mainly speculative industries, where the players make a lot of money, of course, as long as the governments and the media leave them alone or cheerlead them.

Among the 10 richest people in the world, they have mainly made their fortunes due to the opening up of markets and the globalization process assisted by the Internet. As of March 2018, *Forbes*[3] has pinned down a record of 2,208 billionaires from 72 countries. Americans lead the way with a record of 585 billionaires, followed by mainland China with 373. Topping the list is Amazon Chief Jeff Bezos who has become the first person to top the US$100 billion mark. Next is Bill Gates followed by Warren Buffett. While Gates has made his fortune through a virtual global monopoly with his software, Buffett would not have become so rich if not for the opening of global markets for rich investors from overseas. The global media narrative usually focuses on their philanthropic activities rather than about the ethics of their business activities. Next is Bernard Arnault who owns some 70 brands including Louis Vuitton—again globalization and global media exposure has helped in building his global brands. And the fifth is Facebook Founder Mark Zuckerberg who is worth an estimated US$61 billion in 2014 and growing.

While we hear a lot about his company these days in respect to the 'fake news' frenzy and other technological aspects of his operation, we rarely hear much discussion on how Facebook is taking away advertising revenue from the local media in most countries they have access to, which has contributed to a crisis in the economic viability of local media. If there is a 'free media', we should be having a global debate about the need to devise a tax regime where businesses such as Facebook, Google and Amazon should be taxed in each country they generate revenue from. This may go into a fund to help local media development.

Oxfam also pointed out that the biggest and most successful companies come from both the finance and insurance sectors and the

---

[3] https://www.forbes.com/billionaires/#2437a291251c (accessed on 13 June 2019).

pharmaceutical and health care sectors. All these have been facilitated by globalization. They have achieved extremely high profits and therefore command substantial resources which they use to compensate their owners and investors, helping to accumulate their personal wealth. But these resources could also potentially be used for economic and political influences. One way that companies explicitly use their resources for influence is through the direct lobbying of governments, particularly on issues and policies, which affects their business interests. Some of them also fund NGOs to influence the national political agenda in countries where their business interests could be threatened by nationalist sentiments or other political developments.

As we have discussed in Chapter 1, in the libertarian free media model, the media is expected to be the watchdog of the governments' abuse of power and protect the people from such abuse. When such a small wealthy elite is having enormous power, who is going to be the watchdog of them? Today, especially with the advent of globalization, this group of people is much more powerful than any government or government leaders, and many of them also control the leavers of the media as we have discussed in Chapter 2.

9/11 Scuttling the 'Global Justice' Movement

At the time World Trade Centre towers came tumbling down in New York on 11 September 2001, there was a huge 'global justice' movement that was building up across the world with activists from both the First and Two-Thirds World joining hands to protest against the injustices of globalization. The movement gathered steam in the 1990s through the use of the Internet for global mobilization—it opposed what they see as large multinational corporations having unregulated political power, exercised through trade agreements and deregulated financial markets, facilitated by governments. Their main targets were World Trade Organization (WTO), International Monetary Fund (IMF), OECD, WB and other international trade agreements.

It brought 'civil society' people from the North and South together under common goals. There was also the 'Jubilee 2000', an international movement led by Christian/Catholic churches calling for the cancellation of Two-Thirds World debts—it aimed to wipe out US$90 billion of debt owed by the world's poorest nations, reducing the total to about US$37 billion. The activities were initially directed through church channels, and youth groups in particular became heavily involved. It also involved music and entertainment industry.

As Alan Shipman (2002: 14) noted in his book *The Globalization Myth*, 'Globalization shaped around Western economies and their multinational companies has been challenged, from within that privileged minority, for its apparent indifference towards the majority of mankind'. Pointing out that these movements were led from the West on behalf of the Two-Thirds World people, 'though large in numbers, these victims lack a voice', he argues. 'Their own governments, forced to look abroad for financial and logistical support, are frequently indifferent to their complaints. So their words of dissent are increasingly spoken for them by "anti-globalization" campaigners based in the rich world'. But all these attempts were annulled by the 9/11 attacks and the global justice movement (which the Western media called the 'anti-globalization' movement) lost its momentum as a war against terrorism materialized. Today, mounting such protest action has become illegal in most countries due to new anti-terror laws.

Backlash Against Neoliberalism

However, the backlash against globalization continues with some momentum given to it by the economic crash in the West in 2007–2008 beginning with the unsustainable debt burden of American homebuyers and derivatives scandals of the banking sector. The Western governments came to the aid of their bankers bailing them out to the tune of billions of dollars. Ten years earlier, when Asia faced a similar crisis and the Malaysian government bailed out its banks with cash infusions, the Western media called it 'crony capitalism' but in 2008 when the West did the same, it was because the banks were 'too big to fail' as such failure would pull down the whole economy, so went the argument.

In late 1997, when Malaysia's 'booming' economy was about to crash, Prime Minister Mahathir Mohamad blamed George Soros for it and publicly called him a 'moron' and a 'criminal'. Addressing an Asia-Pacific Economic Cooperation (APEC) conference in Chile, he called these financial speculators who were making billions of dollars as 'rich people from rich countries' who have no compulsion about impoverishing the poor 'in order to enrich themselves'. He went on to describe them as 'shadowy figures whose trading is far from open' with no published records of the transactions, the volume, the funds and the individuals involved. Thus, he suggested that currencies should be linked to the economic indices of the countries concerned (Seneviratne 1998).

During his long stint (1981–2003) as prime minister, Mahathir was a strong critic of the Western media's double standards in reporting about Asia's economic rise. You don't need to go any further than the *Time* magazine's cover story published at the height of Mahathir's criticism of Soros and the hedge funds with the heading 'George Soros: He's Spending Millions to Save the World—And Getting Blamed for Wrecking Asia's Currencies' (*Time* 1997) to get Mahathir's point. Though the article did explain the somewhat shadowy way the hedge funds operate which have brought in annual returns of 33 per cent for Soros's Quantum Fund, the 8-page article was mainly praising Soros for his 'philanthropic' activities around the world to create what he calls 'open societies'. There was no discussion about how open is the industry from which he earns the money and how globalization has opened the doors for the rich to get richer and, as Mahathir argues, make the poor further impoverished.

As Jeffrey Sachs (2012) argues in the preface to his book *The Price of Civilization*:

> The US has been very quick to give stern lectures to other countries, for example in the wake of the East Asian financial crisis in 1997. 'Crony capitalism' cried the American government officials who swooped in for the kill in Jakarta, Seoul and Bangkok. Yet a decade later, it was Asia that was booming while America was collapsing in the throes of crony capitalism. Wall Street's meltdown in 2007–08 had all the makings of a morality tale, with greedy bankers claiming to be doing 'God's work', corrupt politicians fawning on

Wall Street in search of campaign contributions, and a hapless public left to foot the bill for trillions of dollars of newly added public debt.

Sachs says the purpose of his book is to encourage readers in all parts of the world to examine the workings of their own national economies in the wake of the lessons that could be learned from the American experience of 2007–2008. He warns the 'buyers beware' of America's economic advice as America's economic and social strengths have been 'squandered by a political system in the grip of corporate lobbies and the spin masters of the media'. He argues that the society that led the world in financial liberalization, round-the-clock media saturation, television-based election campaigning and mass consumerism 'is now revealing the downside of a society that has let the market institutions run wild over politics and public values'.

IMF and the Neoliberal Agenda

The American-controlled IMF has been a prime mover of the neo-liberalism agenda for over two decades and in June 2016 they produced something of a shocker to the global financial community when three of their senior economists published an article titled 'Neo-liberalism Oversold?' (Ostry, Loungami and Furceri 2016).

They argue:

> The neoliberal agenda—a label used more by critics than by the architects of the policies—rests on two main planks. The first is increased competition—achieved through deregulation and the opening up of domestic markets, including financial markets, to foreign competition. The second is a smaller role for the state, achieved through privatization and limits on the ability of governments to run fiscal deficits and accumulate debt. There is much to cheer in the neoliberal agenda. The expansion of global trade has rescued millions from abject poverty. Foreign direct investment has often been a way to transfer technology and know-how to developing economies. Privatization of state-owned enterprises has in many instances led to more efficient provision of services and lowered the fiscal burden on governments.

This is, however, what you normally expect to hear from IMF economists, but the shocker came in the next paragraph, when they said, 'there are aspects of the neo-liberal agenda that have not delivered as expected'. They criticized two hallmarks of IMF policy—the removal of restrictions on the movement of capital across a country's borders and the imposition of austerity measures that cuts government spending in order to reduce debt levels. They argued that these measures have stymied growth, increased inequality and hurt sustainable growth (development).

Some economists in Asia have indicated that the IMF has finally come to realize that the biggest economic success story in the world in the past two decades—China—has not followed the neoliberal economic path to its success. Also, China and India, which have limited capital account liberalization, have come out virtually unscratched from the 2007–2008 Global Economic Crisis.

Major criticism of IMF's 'Structural Adjustment Programme' (SAP) has been its pro-business focus that affects ordinary citizen and keeps them worse off. 'The IMF report on the destructive nature of neoliberalism may have come too late for many African countries', noted William Gumede,[4] chairman of the Democracy Works Foundation, South Africa.

> The neoliberal structural adjustment programmes have led to economic hardships, political instability and conflict in most African countries where they have been implemented. These policies may have in some cases lifted economic growth, but brought little equity, jobs or social security; and the irony has been that the structural adjustment often enriches the already well-off African political and economic elites, autocratic regimes and leaders—and impoverishes ordinary citizens.

When governments sign SAPs and cut government spending and subsidies for the people, it has often led to riots and even suicides. The international media reports about the riots and suicides but rarely goes

---

[4] https://www.twn.my/title2/resurgence/2016/310-311/cover04.htm (accessed on 13 June 2019).

beyond that to go to the people affected by these policies to listen to them and write stories from their perspectives. It is also important to look at Africa as a resource-rich continent and how the international economic system is keeping it poor. Rather than talking about African nations needing to introduce cost-cutting austerity measures to overcome debt burdens, international media should ask whether Africa is getting a fair price for its resources extracted and exported by foreign companies. The whole mining taxation issue needs to be investigated and debated (Box 7.1).

Box 7.1: Mining Taxes and Development

An article by Efam Dovi in *Africa Renewal* argued that mining contracts must benefit communities and promote economic linkages. He took the case of Obuasi, about 200 km northwest of Accra, Ghana's capital, which is home to one of the world's richest gold mines.

For more than a hundred years, the precious metal mined there has been taken to jewellers in the West and beyond, earning millions of dollars for mining companies and their shareholders. But for inhabitants of villages around this rich mine—the 10th largest in the world at the end of the 20th century—years of extracting what lies beneath the rocks have brought only hardship. Cyanide-polluted streams and farmland contaminated by toxic water are just two of the harmful outcomes. As in many mining communities in Africa, infrastructure is very limited.

Yao Graham of the TWN, a civil society group, told *African Renewal*, 'Obuasi is the ultimate example of how mining is developed in Africa. The resources are taken out and very little is left for the community or the country where the mineral is produced'.

The paradox is that African nations possess an enviable share of the world's reserves of minerals. These include the six most traded commodities on the London Metal Exchange—aluminium, copper, lead, nickel, tin and zinc. Other valuable minerals coming out of Africa include chromium, cobalt, diamonds, gold, iron, manganese, phosphate, platinum, rutile, uranium and vanadium. The unprecedented industrial expansion of China, Brazil and India depends in part on Africa's vast natural resources. Experts contend, however, that African economies are net losers in this global trade. Through taxes, they earn only a fraction of the profits from the decades-long mineral boom.

The workers employed by mining corporations receive low wages, while they and their communities pay a hefty price in environmental pollution and social disruption, breeding feelings of resentment.

(Continued)

(Continued)

> In 2010, net profits for the top 40 mining companies grew by 156 per cent over the previous years. However, Africa's 'own share of windfall earnings has been minuscule', laments Stephen Karingi, a director at the UN Economic Commission for Africa.[5]

Economics Professor Jomo Kwame Sundaram, a former UN assistant secretary general for economic development, argues that there has been a silver lining in the economic crash in the West in 2007–2008. 'There has been a growing realization in the West that economic conditions for working people, which had been rising for decades, have been slowly but steadily deteriorating', he notes 'This has been associated in the popular imagination with globalization and some of its major manifestations, including increased inflows of cheaper goods and migrants.' But he argues that it is dangerous for the establishment to ignore the popular political, social and cultural reactions as populisms. He warns that it is the wrong path to take by tendency of dismissing these concerns as 'xenophobic and racist' and often reinforced by connecting it to terrorists.

Panama Papers and Globalized Corruption

Offshoot of the globalization process is how criminal activity and tax avoidance have been globalized as well. An expose of leaked documents in early 2016 by the Washington-based International Consortium of Investigative Journalists (ICIJ) unearthed a massive web of corruption that involved details of the hidden offshore financial dealings of 12 current leaders and 128 more politicians and public officials around the world.[6] The documents, some dating back to the 1970s, were leaked from a Panamanian law firm and corporate services provider Mossack Fonseca in 2015 by an anonymous source to a German journalist.

---

[5] http://www.un.org/en/africarenewal/vol26no2/beyond-mining-taxes.html (accessed on 13 June 2019).

[6] https://panamapapers.icij.org/20160403-panama-papers-global-overview.html (accessed on 13 June 2019).

The cache of 11.5 million records shows how a global industry of law firms and big banks sells financial secrecy to politicians, fraudsters and drug traffickers as well as billionaires, celebrities and sports stars. The files expose offshore companies controlled by the prime minister of Iceland, the king of Saudi Arabia and the children of the president of Azerbaijan, the prime minister of Pakistan and reveals how associates of Russian President Vladimir Putin secretly shuffled as much as US$2 billion through banks and shadow companies. Even world leaders who have embraced anti-corruption platforms such as Chinese President Xi Jinping and British Prime Minister David Cameron were implicated indirectly in some of the dealings.

One would argue that this is a good example of 'watchdog' journalism that goes beyond making only governments accountable for abuse of power and privilege. The expose showed yet again how economic liberalization and globalization have helped the rich to enrich themselves, where seemingly illegal activity are practically legal now. Even before these dealings were exposed, Nayan Chanda (2014), editor-in-chief of the YaleGlobal Online noted: 'Globalisation does not cause corruption. But the opening up of a country to trade and investments by foreigners has created opportunities for bribery and malfeasance on a scale greater than at any other time in the past'. He added, 'fortunately the Internet and global diffusion of media have also enabled citizens and organizations to shine light on bribery and the darker side of the nexus between politics and business'. He cited a number of cases of how these new networks have been able to expose corruption in high places in India, Turkey, Thailand and China. In the latter case, he pointed out that ICIJ has published on their website a 'devastating' series of reports on how China's leaders have slashed away trillions of dollars in offshore heavens.

At the height of the economic crisis of 2007–2008, G7, the group of Western-dominated rich countries, raised the issue of how the very rich as well as companies have taken refuge in so-called tax havens around the world. As Roberto Bissio,[7] executive director of the Third World Institute in Uruguay noted:

[7] http://archives.dailynews.lk/2009/03/16/fea22.asp (accessed on 13 June 2019).

These heavens or havens, with their banking secrecy, anonymous numbered accounts, facilities to establish 'shelf' companies and tax exemption for these companies, are a real hell to the tax collectors in the rest of the world. Every year it is estimated that between USD one and 1.6 trillion escape from their nets and, according to the World Bank, half of this amount comes from developing countries. If this income were to pay a modest tax of say 25%, the governments would obtain an additional income between three and four times greater than the total foreign aid poor countries receive. It is twice the amount considered necessary to end extreme poverty in the world.

Bisso also pointed out that the UK has traditionally been opposed to any international regulation of tax havens, many of which are or were British colonies (the Cayman Isles, the Bahamas, Hong Kong and Jersey and the Isle of Man, among others). Meanwhile, Barack Obama, who in 2008, while still a senator, proposed passing a bill to limit banking secrecy in the USA, has been silent on this issue after becoming president.

The question is whether the global media is doing enough to put up the issue of banking transparency as a major item in the global financial system reform agenda? Or even that of the UN? Or are they simply not interested because the global and local media owners themselves are part of it? We need to ask these questions—if not in the MSM—at least in the academia and civil society forums.

Laundering Corrupt Money in the West

Though it is well and good to expose corrupt politicians outside the West, what the Anglo-American global media fails to acknowledge and investigate is how these corrupt leaders, politicians and the rich slash their ill-gotten money in very legitimate investments in the West, especially in countries such as the USA, UK, Canada, Australia and Germany. They buy expensive real estate, send their children to study in schools and universities there, even invest in stock exchanges and other investment funds, go for medical treatment in expensive hospitals, etc. The media in these countries could easily ask questions from these people how they could afford it on their meagre salaries as politicians or government officials?

An investigation by London's *Guardian* (Doward 2017) has found that since the 2008 economic crash, world's super rich have flooded into London. While the glut of funds flowing into the UK can be viewed as a sign of confidence in its economy and confirmation that it is one of the most attractive countries in the world to live, yet, *The Guardian* points out that there are grounds to suspect; some of the foreign money inflating property bubbles and private school fees has been acquired through the proceeds of corrupt practices.

The IMF assesses that the value of illicit wealth laundered globally per year is between 2 per cent and 5 per cent of GDP, which suggests the total laundered through the UK could be anything up to £90 billion. Much of the money being laundered has come from assets plundered from the former Soviet Bloc countries and African states. A wave of privatizations in the 1990s saw the illegal transfer of billions made from the corrupt sale of mining rights, telecoms contracts, gas and oil concessions.

More recently, following the Arab Spring chaos, deposed dictators and their cronies have siphoned off hundreds of millions of pounds of their countries' assets, much of which is believed to have been recycled through the UK's property market. One notable example is a £10 million house in Hampstead, which Colonel Muammar Gaddafi's son, Saadi, bought from funds diverted from Libyan state assets. Among other notable property buyers in London are Gulnara Karimova, the daughter of the late former Uzbek leader Islam Karimov, who is believed to have owned several flats in Belgravia worth millions of pounds. James Ibori, a former governor of one of Nigeria's oil-producing states, who has been jailed there for admitting to stealing millions of state funds, owns six houses in London, and Maxim Bakiyev, the playboy first son of a former president of Kyrgyzstan, who has been convicted in absentia of stealing from the Kyrgyz people, lives in a £3.5 million Surrey mansion claiming that the charges were politically motivated.

The Guardian points out that in some of the expensive leafy suburbs of London, a picture emerges of children coming out of expensive private schools more likely to be Chinese or Nigerian, waiting rooms of the UK's leading fertility clinics, orthodontists and cosmetic enhancement consultancies play host to wealthy families from the Middle East and the former Soviet Bloc. From private schools to private health care, from Mercedes dealerships to Michelin-starred restaurants, the capital has benefited from a massive influx of foreign money. Doward (2017) says:

> [I]t appears more than a coincidence that much of the money has washed up following a concerted effort aimed at enticing the super wealthy to live in the UK. Eight years ago, in return for investing £2m, foreign investors were offered a 'golden visa' allowing them to live in the UK. After five years they qualified for permanent residency.

Analysis by Transparency International shows that, out of the 3,048 visas granted since the scheme began in 2008, 60 per cent were awarded to Chinese and Russian nationals. *The Guardian* says that experts have indicated the fact that the corrupt seek to launder money through the UK property market and, in particular, London should be no surprise because the capital boasts a vast army of seasoned PR professionals who are skilled in 'reputation laundering'—helping dubious individuals enhance their social standing by ensuring that they are invited to the important parties and fundraisers.

Also, the USA, Australia, Canada, New Zealand, Portugal and Singapore have immigration laws that give permanent residency and ultimately citizenship to the rich, especially from Asian countries like China, if they bring in a given threshold, to invest legally in the country such as buying large orchards in Australia. In the USA, it was as little as US$1 million if you invest in a high unemployment rural area. In Australia, you need to invest at least AUD5 million in items such as government bonds, managed funds, Australian companies for four years and property such as in the depressed rural sector.

Singapore's *Straits Times* Beijing correspondent Grace Ng (2014) noted, 'getting a foreign passport is an exit strategy in case the corruption probes that (the government of President Xi Jinping) have been expanding over the past year targets them'. On 24 October 2014, *The*

Sydney Morning Herald reported that the Australian and Chinese governments have agreed to cooperate to flush out illicit funds invested in Australia by Chinese migrants. Earlier, the USA, Canada and Australia have been reluctant to cooperate with the Chinese government's anti-corruption drive citing privacy issues and concerns about a fair trial in China if they are extradited.

In Portugal, under a scheme called 'Golden Visa' if you invest €500,000 in property, you are granted a permanent residence visa and could obtain citizenship after six years. This has created an interesting irony, as reported by *NYT*,[8] where Portugal which earlier colonized and plundered the southern African state of Angola is now facing the prospect of many of its prestigious properties, companies and sites being owned by Angola's super-rich. Isabel dos Santos, a billionaire from Angola, has become one of Portugal's most powerful figures by buying large chunks of the country's banking, media and energy industries. Africa's richest woman has her business headquarters in the centre of Lisbon's grandest boulevard. The African nation is a major oil producer that has been led for the last 38 years by Ms dos Santos's father, President José Eduardo dos Santos. *NYT* noted:

> Angola's ruling class has profited so much during his tenure—and channeled so much of that money into Portugal—that when Angola threatened to cut off ties in recent years in response to reports that Angolan officials were being investigated for corruption in Portugal, Portugal's foreign minister promptly apologized, setting off an intercontinental debate about the changing power dynamics between the two nations.

While the Western corporate media often reports about corruption at high places in China, Russia and other non-Western countries, something they prefer to play down is the supporting role Western countries and their big banks and corporations play in all this. In August 2013,

---

[8] https://www.nytimes.com/2017/08/22/world/europe/angola-portugal-money-laundering.html (accessed on 13 June 2019).

Bloomberg[9] reported that a US investigation into hiring practices of JPMorgan Chase has expanded beyond the borders of China to see if the bank has hired the children of powerful Chinese officials to help get lucrative business deals in China. The inquiries are believed to be focused on their operations in South Korea, Singapore and India. In December 2013, *NYT* reported[10] that federal authorities have obtained confidential documents that shed new light on JPMorgan Chase's decision to hire the children of China's ruling elite. The spreadsheets included about 30 employees with ties to state-owned companies or Communist Party officials, including the daughter of the deputy minister of information and a relative of a Chinese financial regulator. The scrutiny of JPMorgan has also led to US authorities investigating Citigroup, Credit Suisse, Deutsche Bank, Goldman Sachs and Morgan Stanley.

In July 2014, WikiLeaks published a court order in Australia that has issued a gag order in publishing any material from a sensitive bribery case there which involves serving or former leaders from Indonesia, Malaysia and Vietnam.[11] They have been named in a criminal case involving alleged bribes given to these leaders by Australian business executives to obtain lucrative currency printing contracts. Singapore's *Straits Times*[12] reported in November 2013 that giant Australian construction company Leighton Holdings is being investigated over claims that they paid millions of dollars in kickbacks to secure multi-million dollar contracts in Indonesia, Malaysia, India and Iraq.

What was discussed earlier is just the tip of an iceberg of huge corruption scandals that have gripped the world and continue to do

---

[9] https://www.bloomberg.com/news/articles/2013-08-29/jpmorgan-bribe-probe-said-to-expand-in-asia-as-spreadsheet-found (accessed on 13 June 2019).

[10] https://dealbook.nytimes.com/2013/12/07/bank-tabulated-business-linked-to-china-hiring/?mtrref=www.google.com&gwh=63359821C689105D28ADA5D72FB77409&gwt=pay (accessed on 13 June 2019).

[11] https://www.theguardian.com/world/2014/jul/30/wikileaks-australia-super-injunction-bribery-allegations (accessed on 13 June 2019).

[12] http://www.straitstimes.com/business/australian-building-giant-leighton-in-graft-scandal (accessed on 13 June 2019).

so as economies are deregulated, business and movement of capital are globalized and even the movement of people. As seen from the earlier examples, it takes two to clap and the corrupt should be both the giver and the taker. That means both the Two-Thirds World and the First World are equally to blame. Unfortunately, we far too often see fingers directed only at the corrupt in the Two-Thirds World, a typical example being the reporting of the May 2016 Anti-Corruption Summit British Prime Minister David Cameron hosted, which focused on the corrupt in Africa and Asia, but not about how Britain facilitates their money laundering.

Though Cameron is gone, there is no shortage of Western leaders more interested in handwringing about 'corrupt African governments' than in examining the system that enabled and promoted this corruption, such as tax havens and investment/immigration policies that are facilitating the flow, where corrupt local officials and leaders, and Western banks are comrades in arms in the plunder of Two-Thirds World wealth that should be invested to help their own people. It is very rarely, if ever, you see Two-Thirds World people consulted in reports that are done about global corruption.

Just reporting about the riots back home against these corrupt leaders is not the type of reporting we need, but a more mindful people-centric approach where the flow of capital outside is seeing as creating suffering for people back home.

'Aid': The Biggest Misnomer

Princeton University Professor of Economics Angus Deaton,[13] the 2015 Nobel Prize winner for Economics, believes that foreign aid is a misnomer. He argues that by trying to help poor people in developing countries, the rich world may actually be corrupting those nations' governments and slowing their growth.

---

[13] https://www.weforum.org/agenda/2015/10/does-foreign-aid-always-help-the-poor/ (accessed on 13 June 2019).

According to Deaton, and the economists who agree with him, much of the US$135 billion that the world's most developed countries spent on official aid in 2014 may not have ended up helping the poor. Deaton opposes foreign aid to developing countries in large part because he believes that aid can distort political institutions and foster corruption. He would rather see forms of help that do not directly meddle with a country's markets. Rich countries that wanted to help could devote more resources to malaria research, for instance, or open their doors to more immigrants. Deaton suggests that the WB could help developing countries secure more favourable trade deals.

In the mid-20th century, economists widely believed that the key to triggering growth—whether in an already well-off country or one hoping to get richer—was pumping money into a country's factories, roads and other infrastructure. So in the hopes of spreading the Western model of democracy and market-based economies, the USA and Western European powers encouraged foreign aid to smaller and poorer countries that could fall under the influence of the Soviet Union and China. As was discussed earlier, foreign 'aid' (the word is a misnomer) was used by Western powers to manipulate local economies and increase dependencies on the West, such as through the IMF's SAP.

Professor Deaton is not the first person to argue as such. The 2006 Nobel Peace Prize winner and Bangladeshi Economist Muhammad Yunus argued this over two decades ago when he set up the Grameen Bank to give small loans to women to start a self-employment project. Today, known as 'micro-credit', it has become an alternative form of aid where the poor are helped to help themselves. Professor Yunus started a global movement where he questioned why the poor are poor, not why they should be given charity. This has also encouraged the media to look at structures of economic exploitation rather than focus on the do-gooders who hand out the 'aid'. Unfortunately, giving 'aid' has become a business and a lot of unscrupulous organizations have got into the business such as so-called 'faith-based' organizations that are more interested in converting the poor to their religious beliefs rather than genuinely helping them out of poverty.

London's *Economist* pointed out in a May 2017 report that 'doing good is doing well'[14] for private firms in the aid business. *The Economist* noted how a cable from the American ambassador to Haiti described the descent of foreign firms upon Port-au-Prince in early 2010 as 'The gold rush is on!' During the following two years, US$6 billion in aid flooded into a country of 10 million people for everything from rebuilding homes to supporting pro-American political parties. Of US$500 million or so in aid contracts from the US Agency for International Development (USAID), roughly 70 per cent passed through the hands of private companies.

Though not all countries break down aid spending according to the type of contractor used, data from those who do suggest that a growing share of aid is funnelled, not through charities or non-profit foundations but through consultancies and other private sector contractors that profit from the work, noted *The Economist*. Nearly a quarter of USAID spending in 2016 went to for-profit firms. According to Britain's Department for International Development (DFID) in 2015–2016, 22 per cent of bilateral spending went to contractors, most of them for-profit companies.

AID/WATCH, an Australian independent watchdog on aid and trade in a report card released in June 2016[15] on Australia's foreign 'aid' programme argued that there is now almost no public information on projects financed by Australian aid and their outcomes. Just one in five freedom of information requests are granted in full and a quarter are outrightly refused. 'The reality of the "economic diplomacy" approach is that aid money is being used to benefit Australian companies by opening up markets. This has nothing to do with poverty reduction and everything to do with discredited neoliberal fantasies of the Liberal/National coalition (government).' AID/WATCH

---

[14] https://www.economist.com/news/international/21721635-they-need-diversify-growing-share-aid-spent-private-firms-not-charities (accessed on 13 June 2019).

[15] https://www.aidwatch.org.au/stories/media-release-australian-aid-monitor-releases-report-card-on-the-aid-program-under-the-liberalnational-government/ (accessed on 13 June 2019).

argues: 'We need a new aid agenda founded on global justice and climate justice to address the pressing problems of growing inequality and climate change. Aid is for partnership, not for market ideology.' As pointed out in Chapter 4, Australia's 'aid' project to build a bridge across the Mekong between Laos and Thailand is a typical example of how 'aid' benefits Australia's own companies to expand overseas.

Zoe Williams[16] of *The Guardian* argues that the UK peddles a cynical colonialism and calls it 'aid'. Pointing out that there is a debate in the country about whether Britain should spend money on foreigners when there are unmet needs within the country, she argues, 'we (should) stop talking about aid and start talking about investment, so that this debate may have more focus'.

Williams gives an example of an 'aid' project where Britain invested £600 million in a private African agribusiness project which was supposed to 'raise 500 million people out of poverty by 2020' but it was 'in fact nothing of the sort' and it has worsened land insecurity among small holders and accelerated seed privatization. The report also points out that you could now become an 'aid consultant' and earn half a million dollars a year. It pointed out that one such London-based firm Adam Smith International, specializing in giving advice to governments on economic reform, has won £450 million worth of contracts from the British government's foreign aid budget.

It is a well-known fact—at least in Asia and Africa—that during colonialism Western powers have enriched themselves by extracting resources and slave labour from their colonies. But the Western media will say that's all in the past, today they give over US$125 billion in aid each year and there will be numerous UN agencies and others, providing the data to support it—solid evidence of their benevolent goodwill—the media will tell us. But that is one subjective way of looking at it. Recently, London's *Guardian* gave a different perspective to this whole story (Hickel 2017).

---

[16] https://www.theguardian.com/commentisfree/2017/jul/23/uk-colonialism-aid-spending (accessed on 13 June 2019).

It pointed out that the US-based Global Financial Integrity (GFI) and the Centre for Applied Research at the Norwegian School of Economics have published some fascinating data. They tallied up all of the financial resources that got transferred between rich countries and poor countries each year: not just aid, foreign investment and trade flows (as previous studies have done) but also non-financial transfers such as debt cancellation, unrequited transfers such as workers' remittances and unrecorded capital flight. In 2012, the last year of recorded data, developing countries received a total of US$1.3 trillion, including all aid, investment and income from abroad. But that same year, some US$3.3 trillion flowed out of them. In other words, developing countries sent US$2 trillion more to the rest of the world than they received. If we look at all years since 1980, these net outflows add up to an eye-popping total of US$16.3 trillion.

What this means is that aid is really flowing in the backward direction. Other than the occasional story from publications like London's *Guardian* or US *Huffington Post*, we rarely read such analysis. This means, Asian media, for example, whose news radar is mainly programmed in the West, misses out on putting on the public agenda this unfair international economic system. Regional forums like the Association of Southeast Asian Nations (ASEAN) or SAARC Summits don't discuss it. The NAM used to but not anymore. For example, should ASEAN put on their agenda discussing the economic impact on the Philippines of millions of their medical professionals (especially nurses) trained in the Philippines going overseas (many to richer Asian countries and the Middle East) to work and its impact on local health services? Should SAARC be discussing about how their IT professionals are lost to other countries, especially to the USA and Europe? What would be the economic benefit to their own countries and the region if these people could be persuaded to remain in the country and how can opportunities be given for them to remain at home and earn a good living wage? Perhaps more focus could be given to the business model of Indian multinational IT companies that are creating jobs at home serving global markets rather than accusing them of 'taking jobs away from developed countries'.

Media would also need to talk to the migrants to find out what their hopes and aspirations are as well. Instead we often hear about the remittances flowing back home or how well they have done overseas—which encourages others to follow suite. When Satya Nadella, an Indian-born migrant, became the CEO of Microsoft, according to international media reports, there were celebrations in India. But these reports did not question what are they celebrating about? What benefits that would bring to India and Indians who live in India other than encouraging more Indians to migrate? Even the Indian media did not ask these questions.

In terms of the aid narrative, perhaps the Chinese are more honest, since they talk about their foreign assistance programmes not in terms of 'aid' but investments in infrastructure and building trade routes, especially their new Silk Route projects. But the Western media has dubbed these 'debt traps' conveniently forgetting what we have discussed in this chapter, especially IMF's SAPs. Also, the new Silk Route project—what the Chinese call the Belt and Road Initiative (BRI)—is really about creating opportunities at home and in your own region. If it succeeds, the world's economic centre of gravity would shift permanently to Asia, and the West would not have the power to impose unjustified economic sanctions on countries anymore nor the East would be dependent on markets in the West for their prosperity. Unfortunately, Asian journalists have not grasped this point to look for win-win stories on this topic, rather than locking on to the Western news radar.

Pharma Lobby and Secrecy of Trade Negotiations

> Whether it's the rising price of the EpiPen, or new outbreaks of diseases, like Ebola, Zika and yellow fever, the rising costs of health technologies and the lack of new tools to tackle health problems, like antimicrobial resistance, is a problem in rich and poor countries alike.
>
> —UN Secretary-General's High-Level Panel on Access to Medicines (September 2016)

If you have been closely following international trade negotiations, including the free trade agreements (FTAs), especially since the Seattle WTO meeting in 1999 was closed down by a huge groundswell of a global peoples' movement, you would find that the word 'free' in these trade agreements is free only by name but not deeds. Even the meeting and the negotiations are held in secret and the media only finds out what is going on by leaks from parties that are worried about what is going on inside. Yet, many of these leaks are often reported not by the mainstream corporate media, but by alternative media networks such as the Malaysia-based TWN that provides information from over 100 civil society and academic groups in both First and Two-Thirds World countries.

While there was much hype created about the Trans-Pacific Partnership (TPP) trade agreement during the US Presidential campaign in 2016 and the subsequent withdrawal of the USA from it as one of the first policy decision of the Trump administration, yet this coverage missed out on an important aspect of the agreement—the power it would have given to the Western pharmaceutical industry. Yes, Bernie Sanders talked about it, but he was often given that space only in the US social media.

As of late 2018, there are two trade agreements that are on the table—one is what to do with the TPP now that the USA is not going to be part of it which means that may need to be renegotiated; the other is another trade deal that is being negotiated between the 10 members of ASEAN and their regional partners. This agreement is called the Regional Comprehensive Economic Partnership (RCEP). A tangible issue at the centre of both these agreements is intellectual property (IP) and affordable drugs for the people.

TPP is a so-called agreement that was initiated by the USA and included 12 countries from Asia and the Pacific region—Australia, Brunei, Canada, Chile, Japan, Malaysia, Mexico, New Zealand, Peru, Singapore, USA (withdrawn in January 2017) and Vietnam. Negotiations started in 2008 and a final agreement was reached in October 2015 and signed in New Zealand by all the 12 countries in February 2016. It will not enter into force until ratification by at least two states, which together have more than 85 per cent of the GDP of all signatories. Thus, when the USA announced its withdrawal in January 2017, the agreement was basically scuttled.

Sixteen countries are negotiating the RCEP—the 10 countries of the ASEAN—Brunei, Cambodia, Indonesia, Laos, Malaysia, Myanmar, the Philippines, Singapore, Thailand and Vietnam—and the six countries that have FTAs with ASEAN—Australia, China, India, Japan, New Zealand and South Korea. Of these 16 RCEP countries, 7 are also in the TPP and 3 are least developed countries (LDCs)—Cambodia, Laos and Myanmar.

Reuters reported[17] in October 2015 just after the TPP deal was struck that after the signing of the TPP, the negotiating teams at RCEP have started to publicly frame the process as a 'stepping stone' towards the convergence with TPP and all compassing 'free trade area of the Asia-Pacific'. It said that having being left out of the TPP, China and India are eager to frame their own regional FTA through a 'huge Asia-wide equivalent' through RCEP. The report did not refer to the contentious issue of IP rights and affordability of medicines. Instead they focused on the 'free' trade interests of China, Japan and the USA and their eagerness for such agreements.

In a joint paper prepared by Medecins Sans Frontières (MSF) and two Australian researchers,[18] the authors warn that while the RCEP's areas of negotiation are not as extensive as the 30 chapters in the TPP agreement, yet looking at the draft negotiating texts for an IP chapter in the RCEP, which were leaked and made available online, some countries, such as Japan and South Korea, that are also a part of the TPP, are pushing to include similar detrimental IP provisions in the RCEP that, if adopted, could affect millions of people across the region by delaying access to affordable and essential generic medicines. India, which is known as the 'home of the generic medicine industry', is coming under increasing pressure to agree to harmful IP provisions in the RCEP that 'would endanger millions of people globally who rely on life-saving generic medicines sourced from Indian generic manufacturers', the report warns.

[17] http://www.reuters.com/article/us-trade-tpp-rcep/china-backed-trade-pact-playing-catch-up-after-u-s-led-tpp-deal-idUSKCN0S500220151011 (accessed on 13 June 2019).

[18] https://www.twn.my/title2/resurgence/2016/314-315/cover04.htm (accessed on 13 June 2019).

In 1995, the WTO Agreement on Trade-Related Aspects of Intellectual Property Rights (TRIPS) had delivered a blow to growing generic competition by ensuring the introduction of the product patent system in key middle-income countries. This gave pharmaceutical companies 20-year patents and the opportunity to seek multiple 'evergreening' patents on essential medicines that would further delay low-cost generic versions from becoming available. However, global campaigns by public health organizations and developing country governments achieved some 'flexibilities' for developing countries in the TRIPS Agreement in subsequent years. Though, in order to become compliant with its obligations under WTO rules, India still had to amend its patent law in 2005, yet pro-public health legislators in India secured health safeguards in the Patent (Amendment) Act by referring to and interpreting relevant flexibilities in the TRIPS Agreement, all of which provide significant benefits to people in India and across the developing world.

The MSF report says that the

> impact was clearly felt with the early entry of generic antiretroviral drugs used for HIV treatment. This has succeeded in reducing the cost of first-line treatment drugs by 99% (MSF Access Campaign 2014). Countries like Indonesia, Malaysia and Thailand have also been able to import low-cost medicines, 'in spite of patent barriers'. (https://msfaccess.org/sites/default/files/AIDS_Report_UTW16_ENG_2013.pdf)

One of the most contentious issues of the TPP deal, for civil society groups as well as many developing country governments including India, was the almost complete surrender of governments to multinational corporations, especially pharmaceutical companies, where IP rights were granted to them over the rights of the people for affordable drugs.

By allowing pharmaceutical companies to delay the release of a new drug in a low-priced market, it will stop a generic medicine being produced. They could also delay the approval process in such a market, thus denying life-saving drugs; and the agreement also opens the prospects of the drug companies holding monopoly status in developing countries after their legal patent period has expired.

Of the 30 chapters in the TPP agreement, it is the chapter dealing with investment that has been the most dangerous for peoples' rights. This is because even though the TPP is a government-to-government treaty, it empowers a foreign private investor to sue a host government. Of particular concern is Chapter 9 on investment and investor-state dispute settlement (ISDS). This chapter gives extraordinary rights to foreign investors and protection of their investments and profits. In a WTO agreement, where governments are the parties, only governments can sue each other. However, what is astonishing about the TPP is that although it is a government-to-government agreement, it allows an individual foreign investor to sue the host government through the ISDS system. 'The size of ISDS claims can have a chilling effect on the policies and regulations of the governments that face them', argues Karina Wong (2015), legal consultant for the TWN.

'The intellectual property provision in the TPP's investment chapter will curtail governments' ability to use a compulsory license as a tool to negotiate the price of a medicine with the rights holder', notes D. G. Shah, secretary general of Indian Pharmaceutical Alliance. 'The TPP's investor-state dispute settlement (ISDS) mechanism, also empower the private rights holder investors (and not end consumers) to bring cases against governments.'

This is a dangerous provision in the TPP—the right granted to foreign companies to sue governments of sovereign countries if laws are passed that will interfere with the profitability of their investments in the country—that many civil society groups and academia have pointed out as serious infringement of human rights.

As Shah points out, a case in Canada where multinational drug company Eli Lilly and Company sued the Canadian government for CAD500 million under the NAFTA after the Canadian Federal Court's invalidation of the Zyprexa (Olanzapine) patent held by the company. '[This] is a portent of the shape of things to come,' he warns. 'Not only the government but also the judiciary of a country will be subject to arbitration proceedings by a private investor.'

The 19th round of the RCEP held in Hyderabad in July 2017 has seen some heated debate between India and Japan in particular about the IP issues with regard to drug companies. Since the talks are held in secrecy, an American NGO Knowledge Ecology International (KEI) has leaked a document that stated, 'like most FTAs that involve India, the pharmaceutical-hosting countries, like Japan and South Korea, want India to rein in its thriving generic industry, which has given India its moniker as the pharmacy of the developing world' (Mitra-Jha 2017). Also, the leaked draft text asks for the setting up of an ISDS mechanism, which would allow private parties to drag governments to private courts, including for IP matters.

India manufactures two-thirds of all generic medicines, including 80 per cent of all HIV medicines, while China is a big producer of active pharmaceutical ingredients (API) for the drug industry. 'If the most aggressive provisions in the RCEP are in the final agreement, it will create a host of new barriers to making, selling and obtaining generic drugs and vaccines. Prices will be even higher and monopolies will last longer for new drugs', warns Jamie Love, director of KEI. Health activists such as MSF have warned that if Japan, South Korea and Australia's push for IP rights get into the RCEP agreement, such IP enforcement would ensure that there 'is such a chilling effect that no generic manufacturer or third-party challenges their patents in court. They are skewing the judicial system in their favour', argues Leena Menghaney, regional head of South Asia, MSF Access Campaign (Mitra-Jha 2017).

Against this backdrop of heightened RCEP negotiations, the report of the UN Secretary-General's High-Level Panel on Access to Medicines was released in September 2017. The Panel had been mandated to recommend solutions to, among others, remedy the growing 'incoherence' between the right to health and trade agreements. Its report clearly recognizes that today all countries—developed and developing—face challenges in ensuring the availability and affordability of pharmaceutical products that people need to live healthy lives. The report recommends that countries undertake rigorous public health impact assessments of proposed trade agreements as an imperative to inform the negotiations. It also encourages countries to better use the legal flexibilities available under the TRIPS Agreement to ensure affordable medical products.[19]

What I have discussed earlier is a serious issue that needs wide coverage in the international and national media of countries around the world. It is no point spending tens of thousands of dollars to send out reporters to countries when a medical crisis such as the Ebola outbreak or a cholera epidemic occurs and report about the helpless victims and Western do-gooders (relief agencies at work on the field). Vittachi (1980) called such journalists 'news vultures'. We need to be mindful of the international trade agreements, IP regimes, corruption of governments and their trade negotiators that succumb to the financial clout of the 'Pharma Lobby'. The latter's chanting of 'investor-rights' must be compared with the sell-off of the peoples' right to affordable medicines.

Where is the freedom of speech in the media if the media is unable or unwilling to report in a sustainable fashion all these attempts—influencing trade negotiators, possible bribing or pressuring of them by the 'Pharma Lobby', justification for investor protection, the need for affordable drugs, etc.—that are depriving the people of a most basic human right, that is, to be able to live a healthy life and have access to affordable medicines, when needed.

In April 2015, a UN expert called for human rights impact assessments to be urgently undertaken on the numerous bilateral and multilateral free trade and investment agreements treaties currently under consideration and the potential risk they represent for the enjoyment of human rights.

The media needs to mindfully report on the failure of the UN system to hold governments accountable for the human rights implications of trade treaties they are negotiating in secret. This is what the 'fourth estate' model of journalism was originally meant to do.

---

[19] http://www.unsgaccessmeds.org/final-report/ (accessed on 13 June 2019).

How the Elites Overrule the People

The World Economic Forum (WEF) meeting and the 'World Social Forum (WSF) are two different events that take place almost simultaneously in two different locations, but their motives are different and the media coverage (or lack of it) in the global media for the two events gives a good indications of the lack of people-centric news values in the globalized MSM.

The WEF website[20] says in its mission statement: 'The World Economic Forum, committed to improving the state of the world, is the International Organization for Public–Private Cooperation.' However, the word 'public' here does not mean the people, it refers to governments. Then it goes on to say: 'The Forum engages the foremost political, business and other leaders of society to shape global, regional and industry agendas', again 'other members of society' rarely means civil society, unions or farmers. Established in 1971 as a not-for-profit foundation headquartered in Geneva, Switzerland, it is mainly a forum for the world's richest individuals and world leaders to meet for champagne and verbal intercourse—basically a feel-good gathering. But the mission statement says further: 'Our activities are shaped by a unique institutional culture founded on the stakeholder theory, which asserts that an organization is accountable to all parts of society.' However, the global media has hardly made an attempt to dissect this statement and investigate where the people and their views come into this Forum? Who are the 'stakeholders' they talk about?

In a report filed by CNBC[21] at the end of the 2017 WEF from the Swiss ski resort of Davos where this annual gathering is held, it did address the issue of whether this is all about the world elite drinking champagne and discussing the world's problems, and they referred to a panel discussion where CEOs of Royal Philips, Bank of America (BOA) and Save the Children International took part. They argued that business leaders were not turning away from their obligations to

---

[20] https://www.weforum.org (accessed on 13 June 2019).
[21] https://www.cnbc.com/2017/01/20/co-chairs-of-the-world-economic-forum-annual-meeting-at-davos-discuss-responsible-leadership.html (accessed on 13 June 2019).

be responsive and responsible, and BOA's CEO was quoted as saying that they spent a lot of time discussing the Sustainable Development Goals (SDGs). The report did not question about how they could discuss that when the people who are supposed to be the beneficiaries of the SDGs were not represented at the Davos meeting.

The WSF was launched in 2001 and the first three meetings were held at the same time as the WEF in the southern Brazilian city of Porto Alegre. WSF is a result of the mobilization of social movements in Latin America in the 1990s, and in recent years the gathering has moved to Dakar in Senegal, Mumbai in India, Tunis in Tunisia and Montreal in Canada. The goal of the WSF is to gather tens of thousands of people from civil society organizations and social movements who want to build a sustainable and inclusive world, where every person and every people has its place and can make its voice heard. It is an open meeting place for reflective thinking, democratic debate of ideas, formulation of proposals, free exchange of experiences and interlinking for effective action by groups and movements of civil society that are opposed to neoliberalism and domination of the world by capital and any form of imperialism. Though thousands of people from around the world attend this Forum every year—much more than that attending Davos—global corporate media has virtually ignored this gathering, which is not surprising at all.

Oeffner (2005: 53) in a master's thesis looking at the IPS coverage of the WSF notes:

> Mainstream media coverage of the World Social Forum—an event that is according to traditional news values not at all newsworthy—[has] generally been perceived as insufficient and often even distorted. A closer look at the individual reporting by the international news agencies AP and AFP shows a very different picture compared to the coverage by IPS. The former concentrates on elite sources and 'spot news' reporting, with a clear cultural and political bias evident in AP copy, which presents the WSF as merely anti-US gathering of leftist rebels, ignoring the reality and real motives of the Forum. IPS on the other hand provides a more diverse coverage, attempting to put the news into context and give a voice to civil society. Despite a very selective reporting with a focus on 'elite' civil

society sources, IPS can be regarded as useful alternative to the mainstream agencies. This claim becomes even more justified when considering that IPS reporting is much more in line with the WSF principles, writing about the structure of the Forum and the issues discussed there, and acknowledging its diversity.

I was part of the IPS team that covered the WSF in Porto Alegre in January 2003. Though I have been part of the IPS team at the UN International Conference on Population and Development in Cairo (1994), Social Development Summit in Copenhagen (1995) and Habitat II in Istanbul (1996), this was by far the most enriching reporting experience, where tens of thousands of people were in attendance from all over the world and represented a more diverse cross-section of the world's population, though no CEOs of global corporations seemed to be in attendance nor were government leaders. Latter were actually not allowed to address any of the forums, which is in the charter of WSF. There were over 4,000 journalists covering the meeting but most were from 'alternative media', thus one of my reports focused on the need for diverse media coverage of the event (Seneviratne 2003a).

The well-represented alternative media (now known as social media) represented community radio, cable television channels that were non-commercial in nature, webcasters, Internet-based news networks and documentary film-makers carrying their small digital video cameras. Referring to the label given by the corporate global media to the event as a 'gathering of leftists', Martin Khor, head of the Malaysia-based TWN, told me:

> If you define the left as the traditional communist party and the communist ideology, I don't see much present here. What we do see here is a lot of people who are disillusioned with the way the free market system operates, and they are asking, not for the old socialist kind of system where the state commands the whole economy, but for the government to play their proper political role of regulating the market, so that the market could be used for the social good. That this regulation be done both at the national and international level.

He further pointed out that to call this WSF an 'anti-globalization movement' is wrong because what the participants are calling is for international cooperation to 'make a better world possible' as the Forum theme says. At a panel discussion on the role of the media held at the local indoor stadium attended by a capacity crowd of about 5,000 people, they cheered loudly when Malaysian feminist Susanna George asserted that the media is utilized today to subjugate the minds and hearts of the people when guns are too crude or blatant to use. She said this just a few weeks before the US-led invasion of Iraq. When fellow panellist, French communications professor, Ignacio Ramonet, said the media is now 'exploiting and oppressing' the people—not protecting them—for commercial gains, people need to develop an ecology of information and 'we have to demand that the global media has a basic responsibility to tell the truth', he was also cheered loudly by the capacity crowd of mostly young people.

Media—A Key Dimension of Social Inequality

In Chapter 4, when the campaign for a NWICO was discussed, it was emphasized that the core arguments were about access and equality rather than 'free flow'. These are the same issues that are reflected in the discussions in this chapter on economic reporting. Be it cross-border or within borders, it is not the 'free flow' that matters but whose voices and whose perspectives are reflected in media reporting. Global or national media systems cannot effectively contribute to social progress until opportunities not just for access but also for active participation are more widely shared. Then only could we call a media 'mainstream' and 'free'. These issues will be expanded upon further in later chapters.

Especially in Asia, education is required outside the currently available textbooks on economic reporting, on what the late Thai King Bhumibol called 'sufficiency economics' in the late 1990s and British economist E. F. Schumacher called 'small is beautiful' in the 1970s. Today, the new UN jargon in development economics is the SDGs as it is often referred to in the media. A good understanding of the aforementioned concepts would help young journalists to better grasp the complex realities of economics, especially the relationship between economic data and peoples' well-being (see Chapter 10 for more discussion).

Professor Jeffrey Sachs argues that the achievement of the SDGs is at risk because of American 'militarism' and powerful business interests that drive President Trump's agenda. In a live Facebook interview[22] posted on 28 September 2017, he said that while economists work on technical things, 'the real obstacles that we are fighting every day are the political obstacles, the headwinds of powerful interests, bad ways of doing things'.

Professor Sachs told Thomson Reuters Foundation[23] news that because governments—like the USA—are not willing to take action on climatic change, he will be launching a campaign to encourage the people—who are affected—to take legal class action against companies that contribute to it, the same way tobacco companies were held liable for health damage due to smoking. He believes class action could target major oil companies such as ExxonMobil and Chevron for seeking damages from people suffering from extreme weather and sea level rising that scientists have linked to climate-warming fossil fuels.

In the area of FTAs, there may also be room for class actions though not necessarily via the courts. In 2015, Australia's FTA negotiations with China hit a snag when the opposition Labour Party and unions demanded safeguards in the agreement to protect local jobs,[24] which is not dissimilar to concerns in the USA on the TPP that ultimately led to its demise there. China is already Australia's biggest trading partner and the deal is expected to boost investment and exports of agricultural products, wine and resources.

According to Australian media reports, the deal would bring in an extra AUD18 billion to the economy over the next decade and help to create over 8,000 jobs in Australia. Thus, the deal is strongly supported by state governments, business community and farming groups, but federal opposition Labour Party leader Bill Shorten—who has a strong trade union background—hit the media with interviews arguing

---

[22] https://www.facebook.com/zilient/videos/1938996129693465/ (accessed on 13 June 2019).
[23] http://news.trust.org/item/20170929132426-75g00/ (accessed on 13 June 2019).
[24] http://www.straitstimes.com/asia/australianz/australias-fta-with-china-hits-a-snag (accessed on 13 June 2019).

that it will not help Australian workers. In a subsequent national election, against all prediction, he came extremely close to grabbing the prime ministerial post. This again showed the gap between the peoples' expectations of FTAs and that of the MSM and politicians.

An FTA signed between Sri Lanka and Singapore in 2018 is facing some nine court challenges as of December 2018 by unions and civil society groups that claim the trade deal will infringe on the fundamental rights of people such as workers' rights and land rights. The groups opposing the FTA accuse Prime Minster Ranil Wickremesinghe of selling Sri Lankan workers and land to foreign corporations. With nationalist politicians taking up the issue, the FTA with Singapore, as well as others, believed to be in negotiation with China, India and South Korea, is expected to become key campaign issue in general elections in 2020. This issue is expected to be a major vote winner for the nationalist alliance led by former President Mahinda Rajapaksa.

With the 'yellow vest' movement threatening to unsettle French President Emmanuel Macron (as of December 2018) and likelihood of the movement spreading across Europe, be it in the East or West, peoples' uprising mobilized via social media platforms is challenging not only governments, globalization and FTAs but also the mainstream corporate media narrative.

CHAPTER 8

Redefining Journalistic Ethics

Nepali journalist and former Asia-Pacific bureau chief of IPS news agency Kunda Dixit wrote in the introduction to his book *Dateline Earth: Journalism as If the Planet Mattered*:

> Infotainment is a commodity, and today's news coverage reflects market forces and the desire of media moguls to rule the airwaves. The public service role of the media is being usurped by businesses for whom the definition of news is very simple: news has to sell, otherwise it is not news. It is not a coincidence that news businesses are being taken over by conglomerates that also own entertainment empires. (Dixit 1997: 7)

The essence of the 'free media' (watchdog) theory was that the media is a public service and private media owners are those who have come forward to provide this service to the people, where the media's main function is to inform the public honestly and for the public good of the people. But when the public service role of the media is usurped by business interests, does the media really subscribe to the 'watchdog' principles enshrined in the Libertarian Media Function Theory?

In their book *Global Media: The New Missionaries of Global Capitalism*, Herman and McChesney (1997) noted that neoliberalism has been applied aggressively to global media and telecommunications where its hallmarks—deregulation and privatization—have resulted in global media companies that are drivers of globalization, and who are at the same time reporting to us about the impact of globalization. Thus, it is no wonder that what we get is a rosy picture of the benefits of globalization and not its drawbacks.

When people in the Two-Thirds World rise up against globalization, the corporate media would like us to believe that these are anarchists who are against progress; and when people in the West mount anti-globalization protests, it is because of Russian interference in domestic politics driven by fake news.

UNESCO Director-General Irina Bokova noted in a message to a special issue of UNESCO Courier under the theme 'media decontamination':[1]

> Never before have we communicated so much, and never on such a large scale. The new technologies have opened up new pathways, enabling citizens across the world to gain access to more diverse and more numerous sources of information, and to play a new role in the production of this information—to become the producers of content themselves. These new media are also creating new barriers and raising new challenges in terms of regulation and ethics. Where does information come from? How is it created? Who guarantees its quality? How do we distinguish between true and false in this web, woven by billions of pieces of information coming from all sides? In the incredible tangle of the media, the traditional roles of producer, broadcaster and consumer have changed.

In journalism training programmes, for over half a century, the practice of ethics has been emphasized. In most countries, journalists' associations or unions have a code of ethics for journalists to which they are supposed to adhere. But in the commodification of news and in the age of the 'citizen journalist', these ethics are often glossed over by the practitioners or new communicators.

Let us look at some worrying trends.

---

[1] https://en.unesco.org/courier/july-september-2017/editorial?language=es (accessed on 14 June 2019).

News Provider Not Investing in Production

It is a phenomenon of our times how a non-news producer has become the world's most globalized news provider. In the process, ethical considerations could be undermined. With over 2 billion users worldwide and leading more traffic to news sites than Google, Facebook has now emerged as a major player in news distribution, even though it still evades formal responsibility by positioning itself as a 'technical platform', notes Norwegian news editor, Espen Egil Hansen[2] of *Aftenposten*, who argues that Facebook has arguably become the largest global news site, which has turned Mark Zuckerberg into 'the most powerful editor-in-chief in the world'. Interestingly how this is achieved in not in the traditional sense of a journalist/editor sitting at a desk and stifling through news copy provided to him/her by its journalists. The difference between Zuckerberg and a news editor at Fox News is what is called newsfeed algorithm that traditional media editors do not use. This is a technical platform one could argue that the Facebook's boss has control over.

As Facebook explains, algorithms allow for the arranging of periodicals in a way that is most convenient for the reader. The challenge, however, lies with thousands of newsfeeds available to Facebook every minute, they use this technical platform to filter it. Algorithms continue to shape the reading habits of 1.28 billion daily active Facebook users (as of March 2017) or one-fifth of the world's population. Facebook scans and analyses all the information posted by any given user in the previous week, taking into account every page that he/she has liked, all the groups he/she belongs to and everybody he/she follows. Then, according to a formula—which only Facebook knows—the algorithms rank the posts in the precise order they believe the user will find worthwhile. This has created questions of whether you are fed with news with which you could agree. There is also a possibility that Facebook could use an 'editorial formula' which would feed you news from certain sources only to fit into your areas of interest.

---

[2] https://en.unesco.org/courier/2017-july-september/aftenposten-versus-facebook-triggering-crucial-debate (accessed on 14 June 2019).

'Algorithms may create the so-called filter bubbles, which reinforce a negative trend of our time—one that leads to more polarized communities', argues Hansen. 'More and more people live in bubbles, where they only get the information they want, and communicate only with like-minded people'.

Paid News Phenomenon

Paid news is a phenomenon that has been around for a long time across the globe, as long as advertiser-driven media existed. But, in recent years, it has taken an added dimension as media has taken the 'Murdochization' path (see Thussu, 2007a) and newspapers, in particular, have to compete with bloggers and all sorts of digital mobile media platforms and networks. Journalists are increasingly forced to compromise their objectivity and integrity to commercial imperatives of their employers, which, in turn, impacts their own employability and job security.

Sadly, news has become a commodity today and one may argue why not trade it as such. Paid news comes in many *avatars* (spirits) such as envelopmental journalism, chequebook journalism (CBJ), advertorial supplements, influencer marketing (IM) and so on in an increasing web of commercial imperatives, lifestyles influencing and fast-spaced live communications. In such a world, often, ethical standards in journalism are kept aside for mere economic survival or sheer greed.

Paid news or paid contents are those news items in newspapers, magazines and the electronic media, which indicate favourable conditions for the institution or the individual or even the political party that has paid for it—not as a product placement but for influence peddling. The news is much like an advertisement, but without the ad tag. This kind of news has been considered a serious malpractice in the journalism profession because it deceives the citizens, not letting them know that the news is, in fact, an advertisement. Remember, it was discussed in Chapter 1 that in a libertarian media function model, the media has to act as the 'watchdog' of abuse of power by governments as well as corporate entities. This is a serious erosion of that role.

In India, paid news became a huge scandal in 2010 leading to a government-appointed committee inquiring into it that ended up creating more controversy than solving it. In 2004, the PCIJ did an investigative report titled 'News for Sale' examining how the media sold airtime and space for a price to candidates in the 2004 national elections in the Philippines. There have been similar complaints in Indonesia, Thailand, Bangladesh, Nepal and many other countries during election time, bringing into question the very notion of multiparty elections being the thermometer of peoples' will. In Australia, the practice of CBJ and its ethics have been questioned by media academics and the public for a long time, and in Korea with the entrenched power of corporate conglomerates the use of advertising supplements—especially in the aftermath of the 1998 financial meltdown—to ensure financial viability of newspapers has raised many ethical questions in the journalism profession. Facebook is coming on the 'paid news' bandwagon as well, but they would argue that it is to help publishers with a paywall.[3]

When 'paid news' phenomena—where media houses or reporters are paid or sponsored by politicians, businessmen or celebrities to give positive news coverage in the MSM—came to a boil in India in 2010 with a number of high-profile media outlets embroiled in the scandal, a Press Council of India (PCI) report that was to be released in April 2010 had to be delayed by three months because the original version mentioned a number of leading publishing houses as culprits and some council members had argued that it would destroy the publishers' credibility and hurt their long-term viability. Thus, when the report was finally released in July 2010, it was watered down and did not include any specific names of newspapers or television channels (Thakurta and Reddy 2010).

---

[3] http://www.businessinsider.com/facebook-confirms-paid-news-subscription-tool-2017-7 (accessed on 14 June 2019).

Award-winning rural reporter P. Sainath[4] writing in *The Hindu* after the release of the report said:

> The PCI has simply buckled at the knees before the challenge of 'Paid News'. Its decision of July 30 to sideline its own sub-committee's report—which named and shamed the perpetrators of 'paid news'—will go down as one of the sorriest chapters in its history. A chapter that will not be forgotten and the impact of which caused immeasurable damage to the fight against major corruption within the Indian media. Tragically, the Chairperson of the Press Council who firmly supported the exposure of the paid news offenders was outgunned by a very powerful publishers' lobby.

Paranjoy Guha Thakurta, one of the authors of the report, told *NYT*'s Akash Kapur[5] that one of its most disturbing findings was that the practice of paid content had become 'institutionalized'. He added, 'what started out as an individual aberration has become an illness, an epidemic of sorts'.

However, Election Commission (EC) of India detected hundreds of cases where politicians have paid news outlets and TV channels money to carry favourable news reports about themselves. They have identified over 1,400 cases between 2009 and 2013, a period where 17 elections were held across India for state assemblies. In a historic decision, in October 2011, the EC disqualified Uttar Pradesh Legislative assembly member Umlesh Yadav from contesting again for three years for not including in her official accounts of expenditure the amount she spent on advertisements in two Hindi dailies that were masquerading as news items (Balaji 2011).

The Public Service Trust of India (PSTI) in a documentary titled 'Brokering News—Media, Money and Middlemen' revealed that in October 2009 during Maharashtra state polls with stakes extremely high, media house sold news space for US$40,000 for 15 days coverage

---

[4] http://www.thehindu.com/opinion/columns/sainath/The-Empire-strikes-back-mdash-and-how/article16120867.ece (accessed on 14 June 2019).

[5] http://www.nytimes.com/2010/05/08/world/asia/08iht-letter.html?mcubz=0 (accessed on 14 June 2019).

and US$50,000 for seven days exclusive coverage and exclusive interviews could be had for a fixed price. Two days before polls, two newspapers in the state have published identical articles paying glowing tributes to a local politician and the same article has appeared with different bylines in other newspapers.

Rakesh Sharma, who was a reporter in provincial newspaper between 2002 and 2010 speaking on the PSTI programme, said:

> We not only take money to publish we even take money to block news ... we were given fixed targets during elections to generate revenue ... it could be in terms of advertisements or paid news. We had to bring in revenues that were at least 10 times our salaries or it was difficult to survive many waiting to replace you.

Milind Kokje,[6] who worked as a newspaper journalist in Mumbai for many years, says some newspapers started doing it openly and some clandestinely, especially during election period. 'Packages were sold to the candidates—golden package—every day one news of you will be on front page and every day a photo of you will be on inside page. There will be some charges for that', he explained, adding that the logic behind it was

> some newspaper owners said journalists were already making money on our space when they used to give news item, they took money from the people. So why should they be given to take the money we will take it directly. That is how what is now called paid news started.

In June 2013, a Standing Committee on Information Technology submitted a report to the Indian government in which it argued that guidelines given to the industry by the PCI to clearly demarcate news from advertisements is not followed properly and there is a need for tighter regulations that would allow fines, revocation of licenses or even criminal charges.

---

[6] Interview with the author in Mumbai, 8 December 2016.

Envelopment Journalism

What is known as 'envelope journalism' that involves bribing corrupt journalists for favourable coverage has been ripe in many Southeast Asian countries where salaries for journalists are very low. The term arose from the envelopes used to hold cash, given ostensibly as tokens of appreciation to journalists for attending a press conference.

In July 2006, Indonesia's Vice-President Jusuf Kalla said at the launch of a campaign by the Alliance of Independent Journalists (AJI) and anti-grafts activists to stop the practice of 'envelope journalism' that he will order all government departments to stop the practice of giving money to journalists (Hermawan 2006). 'The envelope tradition, which is widespread among the news media, could reduce their credibility and that of their profession', Heru Hendratmoko, chair of AJI, said at the launch. The campaign was launched at a time the Indonesian media was making signifi-cant contributions to boost the national anti-corruption drive with its investigative journalism and its rigid and thorough coverage on graft cases.

A survey by the AJI before the launch of the campaign has shown that 85 per cent of 400 journalists surveyed in 17 cities believed that accepting money from news sources was a form of bribery, but only 65 per cent agreed that receiving valuable goods, such as cell phones and cameras was bribery. Thirty-three per cent of the respondents believed that having their travel expenses covered by a news source was a form of bribery, while 65 per cent said it was not.

News for Sale—The Philippines Experience

In recent years, 'envelopmental journalism' has been superseded by a much more sophisticated systems of bribing the media. It is often disguised as legitimate funding models for the media such as politicians buying into low-powered community radio licenses in provinces in the Philippines, which they use for political campaigning during elections. Both in the Philippines and Indonesia, radio and television personalities and media tycoons have also gone into politics.

The PCIJ report in 2004 titled 'News for Sale' revealed how a very sophisticated network of celebrity endorsements, sale of airtime and coverage packages circumvent Philippine's election laws. In addition to buying straightforward advertising slots in the media, in the 2004 elections, PCIJ pointed out that many candidates for national office purchased celebrity endorsements paying off showbiz press to get good coverage in the entertainment pages of newspapers and entertainment programmes on radio and television. With the restrictions in advertising expenditure for elections lifted in 2004, candidates were able to buy service packages offered by radio (which is the most popular media in the provinces) that included legitimate political ads, but with some clever add-ons such as airing of press releases, interview and reports on campaign sorties. These packages were more reliable than giving journalists envelops for good coverage.

However, in the 2016 election in the Philippines, with restrictions on campaign spending and social media playing a bigger role in election campaigning, candidates while spending billions of pesos on campaign advertising on radio and television, some have also gone viral on the Internet via Facebook and Twitter.

Advertorial 'Journalism'

An advertorial is an advertisement in the form of editorial content designed to ostensibly look like a legitimate and independent news story. These sections are usually printed with a smaller font to distinguish it from real news but this division is now increasingly becoming blurred as print media fights for survival.

The Center for Media and Democracy's 'PR Watch' website in the USA provided some interesting examples in a 2006 posting[7]:

> If McDonald's makes the case that fast food is nutritious or ExxonMobil argues against higher taxes, it looks like simple self-interest. But when an independent voice makes the case, the ideas

---

[7] https://www.prwatch.org/spin/2006/09/5163/corporate-spin-can-come-disguise (accessed on 14 June 2019).

gain credibility. So big corporations have devised a form of idea laundering, paying hundreds of thousands of dollars to seemingly independent groups that act as spokesmen under disguise. Their views wind up on the opinion pages of the nation's newspapers—often with no disclosure that the writer has financial ties to the companies involved.

Thus, they gave the example such as a prominent columnist writing a critical commentary about the movie *Super Size Me* (the movie was critical of McDonald's) on his syndicated column. What the byline did not say was that his website is sponsored by McDonald's. An analyst with the Competitive Enterprise Institute has written a column for *Washington Times* siding with the oil industry and critical of the windfall taxes (discussed by Congress at a time of high oil prices). Readers did not know that groups closely related with the writer has received at least US$180,000 from ExxonMobil.

In a survey conducted by the Korea Press Foundation in 1999, they found that journalists consider advertisers as the biggest obstacle to FOE (Kim, in George 2008). This economic clout became particularly pronounced after the 1998 economic crisis when the media faced severe funding shortfalls. They resorted to advertising supplements to increase revenue. They started to publish advertise-friendly article in special supplements that covered real estate, credit cards, cosmetics, motoring, education, travel, golf, food and drinks. Advertising supplements would also be published in commemoration of special days such as Water Day, Parents' Day, Trading Day, etc.

Korean media analysts have criticized the advertising supplements because these are written by journalists based on PR material offered by advertisers that could provide one-sided or distorted information to readers. But, on the other hand, analysts acknowledge that Korean newspapers were facing an issue of economic survival and they may not care much about editorial independence in such a situation.

In a case study done of the *Korean Financial Review* by Kim (in George 2008), editorial staff at the paper has insisted that advertising supplements are designed not to provide 'news' but information to the readers. They said that many of the readers 'appreciate useful information given' on credit cards, digital cameras, health, real estate and so on. They argue what they do is provide 'company-related information' that is provided by the advertisers. The stories are sometimes selected not by the editorial team but by their advertising section. However, many journalists have said that they practise editorial judgement by selecting the material from that provided to them and rejecting 'exaggerated and unfounded parts'.

Chequebook Journalism—The Australian Experience

A controversial issue in Australia for a long time has been what is called CBJ, where commercial television channels, in particular, pay tens of thousands of dollars to people for interviews. This has been widely criticized by the journalism academia as a scourge that goes against everything the craft is supposed to stand for—that is emphasized in journalism courses.

In April 2016, this practice came to the limelight when a group of journalists from Channel 9 TV's '60 Minutes' programme, and its 'talent', were detained by Lebanese authorities.[8] The three journalists had gone to Lebanon with an Australian mother whose children had been abducted by the Lebanese father and they were trying to bring them back to Australia. They were later released with a guarantee from the government that she would be able to negotiate the release with the father.

This created a big debate in Australia about the ethics of CBJ, which has been a long-standing practice in Australian journalism. Australian convicted drug smuggler Schapelle Corby who was jailed in the Indonesian island of Bali for nine years is believed to have made millions of dollars upon her return for having given her story exclusively to a television channel and associated media outlets; TV personality Kerri-Anne Kennerley signed a deal for AUD350,000 to tell

---

[8] http://www.news.com.au/finance/business/media/chequebook-journalism-nature-of-the-beast-or-crime-against-truth/news-story/901ecae7e175e3f835ed37c9961c6fc7 (accessed on 14 June 2019).

the emotional story of her partner's spine injury after a freak accident and how she is coping with the trauma; a family tragedy like this could earn victims AUD10,000 to pour out to television and the same could be earned by celebrities opening to the media their weddings or birth of a child.

Australia's two commercial television networks—Channel 9 and Channel 7—have been in a bitter rating war for years. One of the biggest CBJ story of recent years is the deal struck by Channel 9 network for two miners who were stuck underground for two weeks to tell their story exclusively to Channel 9 and their associated media outlets. The deal is believed to have netted the two miners a sum of AUD2.6 million. The mine collapse occurred on 25 April 2006 in Beaconsfield in Tasmania state. Of the 17 people who were in the mine at the time, 14 escaped following the collapse, 1 was killed and the remaining 2 were found alive using a remote-controlled device. These two miners were rescued on 9 May 2006, two weeks after being trapped nearly a kilometre below the surface. When they finally saw the light of the day, they came out to the glare of TV cameras but were quickly whisked away by ambulance.

The Channel 9 deal included the two miners appearing on a two-hour live TV show. They and their families were barred from giving any interviews to other media outlets. A 30-second TV commercial on the time slot is normally between AUD75,000 and AUD50,000 but for this show it was doubled and station ran 24 minutes of advertisement during the show netting them an estimated AUD4.5 million. In addition, their stories were published in the network parent company's popular magazines.[9]

Science Writer and Philosopher Tim Dean in an opinion piece published in the ABC television website[10] argued that

---

[9] http://lib.oup.com.au/he/media_journalism/bainbridge2e/bainbridge1e_case05.pdf (accessed on 14 June 2019).

[10] http://www.abc.net.au/news/2015-01-20/dean-chequebook-journalism-and-the-sydney-siege/6025600 (accessed on 14 June 2019).

if we're taking a moral perspective on the issue of survivors selling their stories, we should really shift the focus away from the survivors and on to the parties offering them money in the first place. If there's a moral failing in this situation, it's with cheque-book journalism. Paying money for a story doesn't improve the quality of that story. If anything, it corrupts. Whipping out the cheque book only guarantees access to a source and blocks that source from other outlets. That also encourages sources to hold out before telling their story.

On 16 December 2014, an Iranian-born Australian man raided an upmarket café in the Sydney business district and held 10 hostages at gunpoint for 16 hours. During the rescue attempt, two were killed. Only two of the hostages spoke to the media and the others did not give their personal accounts of the tragedy to the media for almost a month because Channel 7 has signed a number of them to appear on their Sunday night programme and the *Australian Women's Weekly* has signed up one of the women hostages for an exclusive feature. The delay was believed to be because of an intense media bidding war for their stories and they were believed to have been paid anything between AUD10,000 and 100,000 each.[11]

Dean argues:

There's certainly nothing legally problematic about them doing so. (But) it taints the source's testimony, as they might feel inclined to embellish their story in order to justify their payment. Conversely, it suppresses the winning media outlet from interrogating them objectively in case they reveal any aspects that undermine the 'value' of their source. Cheque book journalism also favours the wealthy established media players and prevents smaller or niche outlets from having an opportunity to apply proper scrutiny to a story. Not least, cheque book journalism creates a market for information that titillates rather than informs.

---

[11] https://www.theguardian.com/australia-news/2015/jan/15/lindt-cafe-siege-survivors-sign-tv-deal-with-channel-nines-60-minutes (accessed on 14 June 2019).

In response to this type of criticism of CBJ, television news executives who are involved in the practice have argued that every time you pay for such a story you are getting a news story which otherwise would not be covered and you also get raw emotions.

Influencer Marketing and Journalism

An article in the *Forbes* magazine (Hall 2016) titled 'The Influencer Marketing Gold Rush Is Coming: Are You Prepared?' perhaps reflects a new threat faced by journalism's editorial independence and revenue raising, especially at a time when full-time jobs in the journalism profession are declining and freelancing is increasing. The article pointed out that budgets are shifting towards what is called 'earned media' (comments earned from advertising ambush). 'Companies want distribution options that won't be blocked and that they know can reach the right audiences. This leads me to believe that we're about to see an influx of marketing dollars into influencer marketing programmes', predicts Hall.

This is what has been happening in Singapore's blogosphere for a while where popular bloggers—some rumoured to be earning five-figure revenue monthly—have created a career writing about commercial products or services. The IM scene in Singapore is very vibrant but sometimes plagued with controversy. But as long as they keep out of the MSM exposure, they do fine.

IM is about 'product context and expertise through an inspirational person', says blogger Amber.[12]

> For earned influencer marketing, brands work with influencers who do unpaid brand endorsement. Alternatively, they might already have an existing relationship with the brand before the promotional activity. In this case, brands in Singapore usually simply sponsor the influencers some products without monetary compensation, with the hope that they blog or Instagram about it.

---

[12] https://ambercreative.sg/influencermarketing/ (accessed on 14 June 2019).

For paid IM, influencers usually already have a huge following. This means that they have agents to negotiate contracts on their behalf. 'Regardless of the type of influencer marketing, the idea is for brands, agencies and influencers to work out a win-win-win situation', says Amber.

In 2014, a controversy erupted in Singapore when a hugely popular blogger XiaXue exposed how major telecom company Singtel through an influence marketing agent Gushcloud instructed its influencers to bad-mouth Singtel's competitors in its blogs. This led to the Advertising Standards Authority of Singapore to issue new ethical guidelines in August 2016 that include the following: disclosures of commercial relationships; paid reviews, testimonials and endorsements have to be clearly indicated and reviews that are disguised as being from impartial sources are not permitted.

'Mr Brown' is another popular Singapore blogger, and his 13 September 2017 blog[13] from Apple's San Jose headquarters attending a new product launch is interesting reading to analyse the thin line between product endorsements and independent journalism. One assumes that he was sponsored by Apple to make the trip to San Jose, which is a common practice in the journalism trade. If you are a foreign correspondent working for a news agency that operates on a shoestring budget, you know what that is all about.[14]

In the blog piece, he gives his opinion about the iPhone 8 and iPhone X, the prices, special features and 'wow' how gimmicky the products are. He even discusses whether you should buy it via a telecom or directly. He writes about the iPhone X which is 'not a jump, but a leap in iPhone design'. He adds, 'face ID is very cool tech too. I know other smartphones have had Face Recognition before, the implementation of it isn't as sophisticated as the iPhone X's. It recognizes you with or without your glasses, or if change your hair'.

---

[13] http://www.mrbrown.com/blog/ (accessed on 14 June 2019).
[14] The author had many such experiences when working for IPS news agency as a foreign correspondent between 1991 and 1997.

The article is very well written and in a style that would encourage young Singaporeans to read and it includes good pictures too. For journalistic style, I would give him an 'A' grade, but what about any discussion of values, whether you really need it and what for? Is it just to show off to your friend that you have got the newest iPhone? Would you bring in social values into your article and question the ethics of forking out over 1,000 dollars for a new phone when you already have one that is as good as new and satisfy your needs?

But 'Mr Brown' knows the market he is writing for (and also the needs of his sponsors); it is for young Singaporeans in a society that could be described as 'post-modern', who have been conditioned from their childhood to leave politics to the politicians except every five years when you have to come out and vote. And religion is a private affair and the media usually does not discuss its ethical, philosophical and social values. Thus, production endorsement journalism goes largely unchallenged.

Is this the new journalism of today? Are we wasting our time teaching youngsters about 'watchdog' journalism and journalists' code of ethics in journalism courses?

This is a good point to conclude this chapter and go to the next to explore whether the 'fake news' hysteria, particularly in the USA, is an attempt to stifle free flow of information—a principle held very dear by the West—or an attempt to protect community harmony—a principle long espoused by the East.

CHAPTER 9

Fake News Hysteria
Attempt to Stifle Alternative Views?

> Times have changed. It used to be that we had gatekeepers. We had the ABC. They went to the news agent and got their paper and paid their money. Now news comes to us via text message or email or Twitter or Facebook. The design of it is very complicated. We don't know what is what, which is the mainstream media, which is a blogger or a friend sharing a rumour. It is very difficult to make sense of all of this. So, as citizens of information and consumers of information, we have to learn how to be critical of the information that we consume and journalists have got an important role to play in helping audiences navigate the news ecosystem. But as users we have to take responsibility for checking what we are receiving and, crucially, what we share ourselves.
> —Claire Wardle, Head of First Draft

Claire Wardle, a former research director of the Tow Center of the Columbia Journalism School, was speaking in a debate on fake news and MSM on government-funded ABC,[1] which has been regularly criticized by the conservative side of politics in Australia as having a left-wing bias.

---

[1] http://www.abc.net.au/news/2017-03-20/q&a-on-fake-news-and-the-role-of-the-media/8370756 (accessed on 14 June 2019).

Speaking on the same panel was Wadah Khanfar, former director general of the Al Jazeera network, who argued that mainstream journalists have to look at their own bias as well.

> We need to engage with the public in educating and also telling them exactly how they should read up, how they should define our biases and look up what mistakes we do. I think we, as journalists, have higher ethical role to play in educating the public on how to figure out our own biases before we even start with telling them your Facebook is full of nonsense ... we sometimes are actually giving them a bad role model on how to do news and how to spread it and how to analyze it and contextualize it.

Guerrilla War on Social Media

Former political editor of the BBC Nick Robinson writing in *The Guardian*[2] said that there is a 'guerrilla war' being fought on social media 'day after day and hour after hour' to convince people not to believe 'the news' dished out by the BBC. 'They share a certainty—fuelled by living in a social media bubble—that we reporters and presenters are at best craven, obeying some diktat from our bosses or the government, or at worst nakedly biased', he added, calling such attacks as a 'torrent of half-facts and opinion, prejudice and propaganda, which risks overwhelming us all'. Referring to the common complaints by BBC's critics that they say we don't hear 'people like me', Robinson argues that the BBC should confidently tell them 'that they will hear people with whom they'll disagree'.

One of the social media Robinson referred to was the left-leaning Canary, whose Director Drew Rose[3] hit back telling him that BBC is certainly facing a 'guerrilla war' against it, but not the war he thinks it is. 'For years now, swaths of the population have been ignored or otherwise failed by the established media. We're fighting to serve those

---

[2] https://www.theguardian.com/commentisfree/2017/sep/27/mainstream-news-win-back-trust-dissident-voices (accessed on 14 June 2019).

[3] https://www.theguardian.com/media/2017/sep/28/alternative-news-sites-attack-nick-robinsons-claim-of-guerilla-war-on-bbc (accessed on 14 June 2019).

people. We're doing that by helping to build a more diverse media operating outside of the establishment', he explained.

Ash Sarkar, a senior editor at Novara Media, another left-wing site mentioned by Robinson, agreed with Rose that the BBC cannot understand criticisms against it. She argued:

> It's that since 2003, exacerbated by the financial crisis, our political classes—whether that's establishment political media, or the centre-left and the centre-right in parliament—have been trying to assure us that they are still responsible custodians of power, which after a disastrous intervention in the Middle East and a financial calamity, people aren't feeling any more.

Pointing out that the voting patterns in recent British elections, including Brexit vote, have shown that majority of voters tend to ignore the MSM news agenda, Robinson, however, believes that if the MSM is to win back the trust, it needs to pay attention to dissident voices or, in other words, 'people they'll disagree' with. In Britain, after Labour leader Jeremy Corbyn nearly won the 2017 general elections—when the MSM had written him off for a long time—and following closely on the media's inability to predict the Brexit and Trump victories, peoples' faith in the MSM hit rock bottom.

If Robinson wants BBC to broadcast voices of dissent, what about a video clip of Ishmahil Blagrove, a film-maker and a veteran of the Hyde Park speakers corner, who said just after the British general elections, in a YouTube clip that went viral.

> For two years, you've hounded and demonized Jeremy Corbyn. You said he was unelectable. You created that narrative and people believed your bullshit for a while. But what this election has done is shown that people are immune. They're wearing bulletproof vests to you and the other billionaires, the media owners and Rupert Murdoch.[4] (Box 9.1).

---

[4] https://www.youtube.com/watch?v=xfCR1VYPRmQ (accessed on 14 June 2019).

Box 9.1: Britain: Media Delegitimizing Jeremy Corbyn

As media and communication scholars we have been troubled by the problematic way in which the British media has systematically attacked Jeremy Corbyn ever since he came to national prominence in the summer of 2015. At the same time, we also acknowledge that the media needs to fulfill an important watchdog role in a democracy. Indeed, we expect and value our media to be critical and to ask difficult and probing questions of those in positions of power. Jeremy Corbyn is an unconventional party leader in a British context, more leftwing than previous leaders of the Labour Party, contesting the neoliberal common sense and promoting an anti-austerity and anti-war agenda. The question we pose here is to what extent this warranted the acerbic and overtly aggressive media reaction he has consistently received over the last year? Is it acceptable for the media to delegitimise to such an extent a legitimate democratic actor who is the leader of the main opposition party in British politics?

—Nick Couldry and Bart Cammaerts of London School of Economics (LSE), Department of Media and Communications in a Foreword to the Report 'Journalistic Representations of Jeremy Corbyn in the British Press: From Watchdog to Attackdog'

The aforementioned study was undertaken by the LSE's Department of Media and Communications, which set out to empirically analyse the nature of the media representation of Jeremy Corbyn in eight British newspapers from 1 September to 1 November 2015. First, it distinguished between critical reporting and antagonistic reporting. Second, it aimed to demonstrate and assess the ways in which the British media systematically delegitimized Jeremy Corbyn as a political leader. The overall conclusion of this report was that the UK journalism played an 'attack dog' rather than a 'watchdog' role. How? This is a brief summary of the study's final report published in July 2016.

The report first looked at the overall tone of the articles—whether it is positive or negative towards Corbyn—but since this judgement could be too subjective, three other elements were considered as specific forms of delegitimization of Corbyn

- through lack of voice or misrepresentation/distortion
- through scorn, ridicule and personal attacks
- through association

It is through a combination of these three elements feeding each other that, the researchers argue, it has detrimental consequences for democratic life in the UK.

Overall Tone

In assessing the overall tone of the articles, two criteria were used—antagonistic tone and critical tone. The former includes being scathing, disingenuous, insulting or mocking, while the latter—though legitimate journalism practice in a democracy—includes not being measured and even-handed. The researchers' statistical analysis found a co-relationship between the political leanings of newspapers and its coverage tone about Corbyn.

Delegitimization through Lack of Voice or Misrepresentation/Distortion

An important way in which Corbyn was delegitimized in the press was in the way his own voice was used in such a fashion that the report/reporters took an antagonistic stance towards him. His voice was not only largely ignored in the reports but his voice when taken was misrepresented or taken out of context. In 56 per cent of the reports analysed, Corbyn himself was absent as a source on reporting about him. In many reports, especially in the Right-wing press, members of the Conservative Party were often used as source in critiquing Corbyn.

Delegitimization through Scorn, Ridicule and Personal Attacks

On this topic, the report says: Much of the newspaper coverage of Corbyn, simply put, ridicules the new Labour leader. Three in ten (30%) news stories, editorials, commentaries, features or letters to the editor mock the leader of the opposition or scoff at his ideas, policies, history, his personal life and, alarmingly, even his looks. Such attacks included him portrayed as a clown-like figure and since he is bearded and dresses casually, he was often sneered in the press for this.

Delegitimization through Association

The report said on this count: A final—and arguable most harmful—way in which Corbyn was delegitimized is through subtle and less subtle forms of association. Many journalists and commentators described his political ideas as loony, unrealistic or outdated and highly unlikely to deliver an election verdict. He was also positioned as unpatriotic and hating Britain. He was also portrayed as someone sympathetic or having links with Hamas, IRA, Hezbollah, Iran and various terrorist groups.

Conclusions

The report concluded that the newspapers' overreaction to Corbyn's elevation to the leadership of the Labour Party is because he is a

(Continued)

(Continued)

> politician, who refuses to play the part that the British establishment has carved out for political leaders in a position of authority. Some have argued that as a result he deserves the negative coverage he gets. The authors argue that the degree of viciousness and antagonism with which the majority of the British newspapers have treated Corbyn is 'deemed to be highly problematic from a democratic perspective'. They add that the high degree of media power needs to be accompanied by a high degree of media and democratic responsibility.

Source: Cammaerts, DeCillia, Magalhaes and Jienez-Martinez (2016).

Trump's 'Fake News' Awards

On 17 January 2018, President Donald Trump made the highly anticipated 2017 Fake News Awards. All the 10 awards he announced went to leading US news networks with CNN getting 4 of them, *NYT* 2 and ABC, *Time*, *Washington Post* and *Newsweek* 1 each. These were all related to negative news about the Trump presidency (Box 9.2).

> ### Box 9.2: Mainstream Grabs Trumps' 'Fake News' Awards[5]
>
> 1. Paul Krugman of the *NYT* for claiming on the day of President Trump's victory that the economy would never recover.[6]
> 2. ABC News' Brian Ross for sending markets in a downward spiral with a false report.[7]
> 3. CNN for falsely reporting that candidate Donald Trump and his son Donald J. Trump Jr. had access to hacked documents from WikiLeaks.
> 4. *Time* for a false report that President Trump removed a bust of Martin Luther King Jr. from the oval office.

[5] https://gop.com/the-highly-anticipated-2017-fake-news-awards/ (accessed on 14 June 2019).

[6] https://www.nytimes.com/interactive/projects/cp/opinion/election-night-2016/paul-krugman-the-economic-fallout (accessed on 14 June 2019).

[7] https://www.washingtonpost.com/news/arts-and-entertainment/wp/2017/12/03/abc-news-apologizes-for-serious-error-in-trump-report-suspends-brian-ross-for-four-weeks/?noredirect=on&utm_term=.8cfcad54e2fb (accessed on 14 June 2019).

5. *Washington Post* for falsely reporting that the president's 'massive sold-out' rally in Pensacola, Florida, was empty. The reporter showed picture of empty arena hours before crowd started pouring in.
6. CNN for falsely editing a video to make it appear that President Trump defiantly overfed fish during a visit with the Japanese prime minister.
7. CNN for falsely reporting about Anthony Scaramucci's meeting with a Russian, but retracted it due to a 'significant breakdown in process'. This resulted in three CNN journalists resigning as a result.
8. *Newsweek* for falsely reporting that Polish First Lady Agata Kornhauser-Duda did not shake President Trump's hand.
9. CNN falsely reporting that former FBI Director James Comey would dispute President Trump's claim that he was told he is not under investigation.
10. The *NYT* falsely claiming on the front page that the Trump administration had hidden a climate report.

It is clear that what he sees as 'fake news' are also opinions that are critical of him, especially the first two are clearly in that category. There was a mix reaction to the awards with most of the MSM seeing it as an attempt to undermine the 'freedom of the media', while his supporters saw it as an exposure of the media's dishonesty and bias against Trump.

Former presidential candidate and Republican Senator John Cain, in an op-ed piece published in *The Washington Post*[8] on the eve of President Trump's announcement, argued that by bestowing 'fake news awards' on reporters and news outlets whose coverage he disagrees with, he is undermining the free press America holds very dear and promotes around the globe. 'Whether Trump knows it or not, these efforts are being closely watched by foreign leaders who are already using his words as cover as they silence and shutter one of the key pillars of democracy', warned Senator Cain.

---

[8] https://www.washingtonpost.com/opinions/mr-president-stop-attacking-the-press/2018/01/16/9438c0ac-faf0-11e7-a46b-a3614530bd87_story.html?utm_term=.0926298443b9 (accessed on 14 June 2019).

'The phrase "fake news"—granted legitimacy by an American president—is being used by autocrats to silence reporters, undermine political opponents, stave off media scrutiny and mislead citizens', he added, pointing out that the Committee to Protect Journalists has documented 21 cases in 2017 in which journalists were jailed on 'fake news' charges. 'Trump's attempts to undermine the free press also make it more difficult to hold repressive governments accountable', he noted. 'For decades, dissidents and human rights advocates have relied on independent investigations into government corruption to further their fight for freedom. But constant cries of "fake news" undercut this type of reporting and strip activists of one of their most powerful tools of dissent.'

Fake News or the Fear of the Alternative

Since President Trump labelled the CNN as 'fake news' in his first news conference as president-elect, the word 'fake news' has shot up to top of the agenda on any discussions about the role of the news media in society.

Kirsten Han,[9] editor-in-chief of New Naratif, a Singaporean alternative news portal, noted:

> Suddenly, the term was everywhere, applied to situations ranging from malicious and petty to valid and worrying. While Trump gleefully labeled any news coverage he didn't like as 'fake news', governments elsewhere grappled with the spread of misinformation online, and how it distorted people's worldviews and affected communities.

Referring to the Singapore government's strategy of confronting the threat from 'fake news' with a media literacy campaign promoted by the government, she warned that by treating people merely as consumers of the media will promote a narrow focus on cyber wellness and civility online 'while neglecting their role as active producers in an era

---

[9] https://newnaratif.com/journalism/learning-media-literacy-singapore/ (accessed on 14 June 2019).

where smartphones and gadgetry make it easy to snap photos, shoot videos and author posts'.

It is this technology that has broken the back of what we call the MSM. These new 'active producers' could be compared to the 'indie music' producers of the 1980s, who armed with new technology to produce music video clips on the cheap, embarked on a campaign to break the back of the mainstream music industry—both locally and internationally—controlled by a very few by using the new medium of video. These new news producers—one may call them 'citizen journalists'—have made news a 24-hour cycle challenging the MSM to keep space with them. Speaking to a group of local university students, Warren Fernandez, editor of Singapore's *Straits Times* reflected on this dilemma:

> There is this big tension between wanting to be accurate, fair, balanced ... and wanting to be fast. Because you can't take forever to verify, the vacuum would be filled. I tell (our reporters) that we want to be first with the accurate news. If it means that we take a bit longer to verify, so be it. For a news organisation, you trade on trust and reputation. And as soon as you tarnish your reputation, you've lost your currency to trade.

As we have been discussing in this book, this reputation is being increasingly tarnished by alternative news sources that have questioned the accuracy of the MSM. This accuracy could be based on the subjectivity of the news report as discussed in Chapter 4. This is where the very term 'fake news' is open to different interpretations and challenges.

Fake news by definition is a system of information that misleads people/society, misrepresents reality and causes damage to the communication system itself. It could also lead to a culture of mistrust, hatred, cynicism and confusion in the society leading to social disharmony and conflict (see examples given in Box 9.3).

Box 9.3: The Real Fake News

These examples from different countries are given to illustrate how 'fake news' may be defined.

The USA: 'Pope Francis Shocks World, Endorses Donald Trump for President'—the story was first published by a site called WTOE 5 and it was picked up by over 960,000 Facebook engagements by the time of the November 2016 US presidential elections according to BuzzFeed.[10]

The USA: 'FBI Agent Suspected in Hillary Email Leaks Found Dead in Apartment Murder-Suicide'—the article, which generated some 567,000 Facebook engagements, according to BuzzFeed, was originally published by the 'Denver Guardian' just three days before the presidential election. The site has since been deleted, and it was found out that there was no such newspaper, but there is *Denver Post* which had nothing to do with the story. It was also found that the contact address listed for Denver Guardian was a vacant car park.

Malaysia: Hundreds of people crowded a supermarket in the town of Johor in southern Malaysia after hearing—through WhatsApp voice message that went viral—that Johor's Crown Prince Tunku Ismail Sultan Ibrahim was coming over to pay for their groceries. The prince had a few days earlier forked out over 1 million Malaysian Ringgits (about US$300,000) on groceries for shoppers at another supermarket in town. Supermarket had to make public announcements to say that the news was 'fake'. It also complained that angry shoppers left their trolleys full of goods they had loaded with—some damaged—for shop staff to clean up later. It has cost the supermarket quite a lot of money.

India: 'Fatwa in Saudi Arabia that men can eat their wives if hungry'—the 'story' carried by *India Today*'s Hindi channel had its origins in a satirical column by a Moroccan blogger.[11]

Australia: In April 2017, on Anzac Day, the day Australia celebrates its war heroes, Dr Anne Aly, Australia's first female Muslim MP, attended a dawn service in Ballajura in her electorate, laid a wreath and made a speech. But rumours began circulating online that she had refused to lay a wreath at a dawn service at Wanneroo RSL—a war veterans club in her electorate—after Kim Vuga, founder of the Love Australia or Leave Party, posted a message on her Facebook page. She received this news from a friend who was at the service. It is true Dr Aly did not lay a wreath at the service as she was attending another local service taking place at the same time—as mentioned earlier—but

---

[10] https://www.cnbc.com/2016/12/30/read-all-about-it-the-biggest-fake-news-stories-of-2016.html (accessed on 14 June 2019).

[11] https://www.altnews.in/top-fake-news-stories-circulated-indian-media-2017/ (accessed on 14 June 2019).

> Vuga's Facebook message led people to flood Dr Aly's Facebook Page with abusive comments.
> These are just a handful of examples of what could constitute a 'fake news' story and how it could generate confusion, chaos, hatred or frustrations.

Singapore's Media Literacy Council defines 'fake news' as

> different types of misinformation, often circulated as deceptive headlines, questionable theories, articles, tweets, and other sources of information that cast doubt around an issue (which) often mimics real news and is sometimes created with the intention of generating revenue through advertising that depends on viewer clicks.[12]

But fake news is not a new phenomenon. Rumours of celebrity deaths, contaminated food products, sexual exploits of politicians or sporting personalities, autism-causing vaccines and climate change denial have been spread via various communication channels—including sometimes MSM—even before the Internet age. From everyday gossip to conspiracy theories, the exchange of unverified information is as old as language and the printed word itself.

James Carson[13] of UK's *The Telegraph* also observes that fake news has existed for a long time but it was not called such. 'Fueled by mass communication, propaganda grew in scale and persuasive power during the turmoil of the 20th centuries in a series of major ideological struggles', he argues. What has changed today is that it is not prohibitively expensive to set up a mass circulating system for the dissemination of fake news (Box 9.4).

---

[12] https://www.todayonline.com/singapore/big-read-era-fake-news-truth-may-not-always-be-out-there (accessed on 14 June 2019).

[13] http://www.telegraph.co.uk/technology/0/fake-news-origins-grew-2016/ (accessed on 14 June 2019).

Box 9.4: What Is Fake News? Its Origins and How It Grew

In the First World War, the British government used propaganda very effectively in motivating the population against Germany, which was frequently depicted as 'The Hun'. The Nazi party used the growing mass media to build a power base and then consolidate power in Germany during the 1930s, using racial stereotyping to encourage discrimination against Jews.

In the ensuing Second World War, the propaganda machines were used relentlessly by all sides across the media spectrum. It even took hold in lighter forms of entertainment: Donald Duck woke up in a dystopian caricatured Nazi world in an effort to sell more US war bonds.[14]

This sort of propaganda was largely funded and controlled by governments, but the blatant bias it carried waned as the ideological struggles became less apparent. Added to that, as populations became more used to mass communication, they could more easily see through it.

The rising trend of fake news during 2016 was very different to largely state-controlled analogue modes of the 20th-century propaganda. What we saw often here were small groups of people taking advantage of social media interaction and algorithms through creating hyperbolic articles around a major political event.

Before the Internet, publishing fake news and gaining an audience that could be monetized was nearly impossible for three reasons:

1. *Distribution and cost:* Distributing information on any kind of scale needed a prohibitively expensive logistics operation.
2. *Audiences and trust:* Building a large audience took much longer and because it was expensive to acquire and built on trust of information, publishing fake news would be damaging to reputation and thus have economic consequences.
3. *Law and regulation:* Because it was expensive to distribute information, there were far fewer players. These abided by media law and could be regulated. Publishing fake news would likely end up with the publisher being sued or losing the license to publish.

But this gate of information exchange was unlocked around 2007, with the beginnings of the social media revolution. The creation of social networks like Facebook and Twitter allowed people to exchange information on a much greater scale than ever before, while publishing platforms like WordPress allowed anyone to create a dynamic website with ease. In short, the aforementioned barriers to creating fake news were undone.

Source: The Telegraph (2017).

---

[14] https://www.youtube.com/watch?time_continue=3&v=kzH1iaKVsBM (accessed on 14 June 2019).

The fact that cheaper and thus more affordable technology has made it possible to set up a diversity of media outlets that could have a global reach should have been nirvana for those who advocated the libertarian free media model of communication. Now we have more players who are privately owned and can be the 'watchdog' for the wrongdoings and abuse of power by governments as well as others.

Initially, the Internet and the social media were seen as a welcomed tool by the West to open up closed societies such as in China and other Asian and African countries, and in the Arab world. But, as we have discussed in the previous chapters, it seemed to have backfired on the West, especially on its ruling classes. Thus, they seem to have a common cause with the ruling classes elsewhere, especially the authoritarian ones. Stalin and Mao in their new reincarnations should be delightfully watching the deeds of Comrade Trump and his allies.

So why are the same people (or countries) who advocated this model going hysteric now? They are now arguing that the rise of what we call 'social media' has accelerated the spread of falsehoods. They also argue that it has facilitated echo chambers, where like-minded people validate each other's views and provide encouragement to act on them. Earlier, when people came into streets—mobilized by the telephone or word of mouth—to demonstrate against governments, it was seen as a healthy sign of a vibrant democracy. If it is now happening via the Internet, why is there such a fuss?

Can we blame the problem entirely on the new digital media age and are we trying to kill the messenger? For example, the hysteria created by the MSM of Russian interference in the US elections has put on the back burner the question of why people were susceptible to those messages. The socio-economic problems plaguing America are not being addressed, and so are questions of funding of election campaigns, which has made it impossible for minor party candidates that would appeal to these disgruntled voters to be heard in the MSM or be elected to Congress.

'Fourth Estate' Failure Giving Rise to a 'Fifth Estate'

It is a tragedy of our times that the 'fake news' hysteria is giving ammunition to authoritative governments everywhere to tighten media freedoms further.

The 2017 Digital News Report by Reuters Institute[15] found that, in the UK, the growth of social media has exposed people to alternative viewpoints and a 'more emotive form of news' which is making politicians concerned. The Conservative Election Manifesto (of 2017) has promised to crackdown on social media and search engines that failed to crackdown on 'extremist' propaganda and adult material. The study has found that 41 per cent of respondents depend on social media for news and 43 per cent don't trust the mainstream news media. The 2017 Grenfell building fire[16] in London has also added to peoples' distrust of the media because it has not investigated and reported on breaches of fire safety in such buildings, which turned out to be widespread.

Thailand's *The Nation* in an editorial[17] argued that the rise of the social media has been the doing of the MSM, as 'any user of the networks will acknowledge that the modern media platforms are full of misinformation and overly self-righteous people'. As the editorial points out, the US elections exposed the shortcomings of the 'Fourth Estate' when they sacrificed their reputation for perceptiveness by confidently predicting a Hillary Clinton victory and getting humiliated in the process. 'Democratic societies have always looked to the Fourth Estate for ideological (read: moral) guidance and they in turn have reflected public sentiment. Now there is a Fifth Estate, quicker to inform, more accessible, more widely shared and more trusted.'

---

[15] http://www.digitalnewsreport.org/survey/2017/united-kingdom-2017/ (accessed on 14 June 2019).

[16] A 24-storey building in London's North Kensington caught fire in July 2017 requiring 40 fire engines and more than 200 firefighters to fight the blaze. It destroyed 151 homes and killed 71 people (Wikipedia/BBC).

[17] http://www.nationmultimedia.com/news/opinion/today_editorial/30303578 (accessed on 14 June 2019).

While the 'fake news' claims dominate media discourse across the world, what this discourse tends to gloss over is the fact that this has existed in the public domain for generations, such as in gossip- and rumour-mongering. The difference is that these used to be transmitted via verbal conversations by people when socializing such as sipping tea or coffee or at bars, meeting up in the streets or conversations seated on a culvert and so on. In Asia, there were many forms of popular culture that conveyed news—some of which would be 'fake news' in today's terminology—there were the people who went with a drum from village to village in South Asia giving out news (as well as gossip) some in poetry or song; even puppetry could be used and later cartoons also played such a role in conveying certain ideas; so was street theatre. Now that transmission is happening via cyberspace.

In an article distributed across Asia by the Asia News Network (ANN; Asia News Network 2017), it warned about a fake news epidemic sweeping across Asia and gave a few recent examples of stories that were transmitted via social media to illustrate it, such as a story during a flood in Bangkok which said it would have contaminated the city's water supplies; child kidnappers in the Indian state of Jharkhand that resulted in mob 'justice' killing seven suspected kidnappers and a resurgence of communists in Jakarta that resulted in mobs disrupting a legal meeting.

But such rumour-mongering (that was what it used to be called) is not something new. However, articles like these are setting up the stage for governments to repress voices that are beginning to be heard—voices that are authentic and come from the grass roots traditionally ignored by MSM—that are not controlled by the Confucius tradition of respecting authority.

ANN's editor Shefali Rekhi[18] argued (in a commentary published by Singapore's *Straits Times*) that all stakeholders—media platform providers, users and governments—need to play a part to tackle the problem. 'A growing number of such instances, coupled with the lack of adequate regulation, damaging consequences for legacy media, and

---

[18] http://www.straitstimes.com/asia/all-stakeholders-have-part-to-play-experts (accessed on 14 June 2019).

repercussions on efforts to build informed societies, is stoking debate anew on tackling the issue', noted Rekhi.

But are more regulations the solution? Quoted in the same article was Nanyang Technological University communications lecturer Edson C. Tandoc, who noted that societies have long confronted rumours. 'But fake news has found an ideal platform in social media, which allows the quick spread of erroneous information outside the control of institutions', he noted, adding:

> Fake news also thrives in social networks as users depend on other users not only for their information supply, but also for verification. An increasing mistrust in traditional media is being replaced by dependence on popularity ratings online, so that a post that gets viral is accorded more attention, and most likely, more credibility.

Thailand's *The Nation* in an editorial published on 30 October 2017[19] argues that journalism and activism should also have its place in the form of alternative media.

> The proliferation of so-called alternative media has confused a lot of people about the concept of journalism. Activists who fight for certain causes and who tend to always have conflicts of interest in the things they want to communicate with the public, have found fresh channels for their operation, thanks to online broadcasting being 'democratised' by advanced technologies. The development is good, as long as people who matter can draw a clear line between journalism and activism....
> The general definition of alternative media describes operations designed to serve 'smaller' people, not corporates, influential organisations, or politicians in power ... Alternative media have emerged because of the general perception that the mainstream media tend to protect the status quo and always have conflicts of interest.

In neighbouring Malaysia, for almost two decades now, an alternative news source—*Malaysiakini*—using the open-access Internet has

---

[19] http://www.nationmultimedia.com/detail/opinion/30330358 (accessed on 14 June 2019).

knocked on the door of the mainstream. In the process, they have had to face many threats to its existence (Box 9.5).

> ### Box 9.5: When the Alternative Challenges the Mainstream—Malaysiakini
>
> For a casual observer, Malaysia's media scene may look vibrant and diverse with privately owned newspapers, magazines, radio and television, plus web-based media. Except for the latter, most of the other 'private' media are owned by business cronies of the ruling coalition which has been in power ever since Malaysia gained independence in 1957 until their shock defeat in 2018, in which alternative news outlets like Malaysiakini played a big role.
>
> Malaysia's first online news portal Malaysiakini.com went online in November 1999 at the height of the country's 'Reformasi' movement following the sacking of Deputy Prime Minister Anwar Ibrahim. It exploited an opportunity because Prime Minister Dr Mahathir Mohamad has given an undertaking—to attract foreign investments to his Multimedia Super Corridor project—that the Internet will not be censored.
>
> Malaysiakini is one of the major success stories of independent media in Asia. It is the most popular news website in Malaysia with around 37 million views monthly (according to Alexa rankings) and about 20,000 subscribers. It has about 40 editorial staff and publishes in Malay, Chinese, Tamil and English.
>
> Because of Malaysia's crony system of media ownership, co-founder and news director Steven Gan[20] says that initially they wanted to offer something different to the pro-government news Malaysians receive. 'We tried to offer something different, knowing there was a lot of censorship of political news (and) those journalists who wanted to be independent had difficulties, because their owners still relied on government for contracts and what's not', he explained. Since co-founder Prem Chandran and him have worked for *The Sun* newspaper owned by leading businessman Winston Tan, who was one of Dr Mahathir's cronies, they knew the situation well.
>
> > We do see there was censorship of news on daily basis (because) he earned a lot of money from gaming, property.... Most Chinese newspapers from Sarawak are owned by logging companies.... (Tan) owned a big business empire and he owned the media not to make money but to buy influence.

(Continued)

[20] Interview with the author recorded in Kuala Lumpur, 26 November 2016.

(Continued)

> Gan admits that without Dr Mahathir's pledge not to censor the Internet, they would not have succeeded. He gave this interesting background to how they survived during those difficult first years:
>
>> We give a voice to practically everybody ... if government wants to talk to us we have no problem with it. When we first began government did not want to talk to us ... it was a bad decision and that allowed opposition to move into Internet and use it successfully. After 2008 election, when ruling government lost ground they started to worry about Internet media. Until then they thought because they controlled mainstream they can get to the voters ... without realising that quite a lot of the voters were no longer relying on mainstream media they rely on Internet media. (So) after 2008 we got the press card. There was a change in government policy...when Dr Mahathir was around it was hostile attacks on Malaysiakini we were called traitors, computers taken away, police raids .... when (his successor) Badawi came there was a shift, change on government policy towards Internet media, no attacks they left us alone ... we had few years of peace ... but we were still kicked out of press conferences. After Badawi came I think there was a discussion in government about engaging Internet media. I received a phone call immediately after 2008 election for a lunch with minister. First thing he asked was what can we do for you. I said first thing you can do is give us a press tag ... within a month we got it.
>
> About 90 per cent of the funding for Malaysiakini comes from subscriptions and advertisements. It has recently built a brand new three-storey office in a suburb of Kuala Lumpur, for which they raised money by selling a brick to its supporters—very similar system to how Buddhist monasteries raise money for buildings. Initially when Malaysiakini was launched, they were supported with a grant of US$100,000 by SEAPA, which got funding from George Soros's Open Society Foundations and later they also did a deal with a foreign investor based in the Czech Republic, which is believed to have links to Soros's foundation. Thus, up to this day, when the government does not like any reporting done by Malaysiakini, they are accused of getting funds from Soros—a hated figure in Malaysia for his alleged role in the Asian financial crisis of 1997. Malaysiakini went for a subscription-based model after noting that even though there are many free-to-air TV networks in the USA, Cable TV still thrives. Thus, the secret is you need to offer something different which the people want, according to the co-founder and CEO Chandran. Their subscription is about US$40 a year.

> Gan says that they do not need foreign funding anymore. 'These represent no more than five to ten per cent of our income. We do it only if we think it is something that we would not want to spend our own money on', explained Gan, pointing out how the dynamics of their interaction with foreign agencies (with funds) has changed:
>
> They come to us to see how they can partner with us. A US NGO that gets a huge amount of money from US government, wanted to do training and we tell them that if you want to do training you have to hire local Malaysians or Asians ... their concept of training is bringing their journalists and we say that is stupid, lot of things they bring along doesn't really fit Asian requirements. Prem once told them that if you don't want to do that, forget about that, we will not be on board. We can tell them because we don't need their funding ... of course they want Malaysiakini because of its prestige ... we know the hidden agendas, Prem and me have been there for a long time and we know.

When reading all this debate about how the MSM got the Brexit and Trump vote wrong, and why social media has triumphed, my mind always goes back to 2004 Indian elections. In January that year, I travelled across North India for a month where there were billboards everywhere with the slogan 'India is Shining'. These were election billboards put up by the ruling BJP in preparation for the May general elections that year. The media—television and newspaper—news was full of glowing reports about how well India is doing under the Vajpayee-led BJP government where the Indian economy was said to be booming, relations with Pakistan were improving and India has just had a bumper harvest. So the media was predicting a landslide victory for the BJP come May. But it lost the elections in what the media called a 'shocking verdict'. The Congress Party snatched victory through the vast rural and marginalized voters who obviously did not see a 'shining India'.

The Hoot[21] in an election post-mortem editorial made some interesting observations about how the MSM got the story wrong. With

---

[21] http://www.thehoot.org/media-watch/media-practice/the-media-and-the-verdict-of-election-2004-1143 (accessed on 14 June 2019).

television playing a greater role in the elections, it noted that the TV channels perhaps filled too much airtime with party spokespersons who are 'motivated (but) not representative'. They also went after celebrity candidates, while ignoring the vast number of non-celebrity candidates, because in advertising-led coverage, the contest had to sell with the cable and satellite voter. It also pointed out that in a country where 81 per cent of the rural households don't have a TV set, the media has overestimated its influence. 'So while TV may give a lot of coverage at election time, millions of voters will not see any of it', noted Hoot.

This brings us to the simple question—how do you reach the population with news and messages, be it election time or not? We are perhaps in a strategic communication rather than mass communication age. This is where alternative media strategies could be as important as so-called MSM strategies. This was well illustrated in President Duterte's successful election campaign in the Philippines in 2016 (Box 9.6), which his opponents alleged was based on the spread of 'fake news' via the Internet. President Duterte has—like President Trump—publicly expressed his disdain for the MSM. Having won the elections, his 'cybertroopers' have not disbanded, they continue the fight because the 60 per cent vote he got on election day is only 40 per cent of the registered voters and he has to win over many of the rest to govern effectively for six years.

Box 9.6: The Philippines: Duterte's Cybertroopers Smarter than Corporate Media

In the Philippines, the electoral victory of Rodrigo Duterte, an underdog who did not come from the political establishment or the elites of Manila, surprised political 'experts' in Manila and across the region. With meagre financial resources but committed grass-roots support, he fought a successful campaign that would not have been possible before the Internet era.

In the Philippines, with a population of 100 million, there were an estimated 47 million active Facebook accounts as of 2015. With almost 100 per cent literacy rate covering both the urban and rural areas, in the 2016 presidential elections, the Philippines perhaps gave the world a new template in electioneering, especially when an underdog from a marginalized area of the country entered the race for the country's top job.

Facebook recorded about 22 million users during the campaign, interacting and actively talking about, and debating over the elections with friends and their respective connections. Yet most political campaigners belittled the ability of social media to sway voters and influence voting—some political camps said it was just all noise with little power for conversion—but they were all forced to consume some Filipino 'toddy' on the night of the elections as Rodrigo Duterte, a long-time mayor from Davao, in one of the most marginalized islands in the country—Mindanao—swept to the presidency on a landslide national vote.

With almost all of the national media based in the capital Manila—a three-hour flight from Davao—Mindanao has always been marginalized in the Philippines media. They usually attracted attention because of the Islamic insurgency in the island, when some clash occurred between the army and the terrorists or they kidnaped a foreigner for ransom money. Thus, how Mayor Duterte transformed its main city Davao over a period of 23 years from a crime-ridden dangerous area to one of the safest cities in the Philippines with a low incidence of drug trafficking that infected most of the Philippines was largely unknown to the rest of the Philippines. When he announced his bid for the country's top job, no one—except his die-hard fans in Davao—expected him to win the race. The fact that he was able to do it, in spite of the Philippines MSM focusing on his tough guy image and threat to kill drug addicts, is due to an imaginative social media campaign spearheaded by well-trained Filipino 'cybertroopers' that in fact used the MSM's negative imaging to its advantage.

It is widely agreed in the country now that the social media campaign was a crucial factor in Duterte's victory and it was run with a shoestring budget. Heading it was a former political activist and ex-MSM sales executive Nic Gabunada, who had a meagre budget of 10 million pesos (US$195,000) and 500 committed volunteers who tapped into their own networks.

In an interview with the Philippines news portal Rappler, he explained how it was done.[22] There was a huge array of Duterte supporters that were scattered and once the Mayor announced his presidential bid in December 2015 he had to organize them into four groups—the overseas Filipino workers (OFWs running into tens of millions who could vote from overseas), Luzon (the large northern island that includes Manila), Visayas (central parts of the Philippines islands)

(Continued)

[22] https://www.rappler.com/newsbreak/rich-media/134979-rodrigo-duterte-social-media-campaign-nic-gabunada (accessed on 17 June 2019).

(Continued)

and Mindanao. These groups were handled by another group of people, aside from the influencers they had tapped from the areas. They were the ones in charge of making sure that the plans push through.

'Every day of their lives they talked to these people, discussed whatever the new findings, and provided them the so-called message of the week', Gabunada explained. The 'message of the week' usually came in the form of hashtags to be trended on Twitter or posted in the comments section of social media posts. 'During a certain point in the campaign when we wanted [them] to reiterate their support [for] Duterte, we popularized or made it a point the hashtag #DutertePaRin would trend on the Internet', he said.

There was a feeling that they had to stick with Duterte until he won the elections and at times they were also involved in negative campaigning as tit for tat, when he was attacked by other candidates (usually in the MSM). 'We were able to amplify in the sense that each one of the volunteers was handling groups with members of around 300 to 6,000', he explained to Rappler. 'I think the biggest group had 800,000 members'.

Jay Jaboneta, who at one stage was working in the new media office set up by the outgoing President Aquino when he came to power six years before, listed 10 takeaways from Duterte's campaign in an article on Rappler.[23] These were the following:

1. The most successful digital strategies for the campaign were things that helped create a movement around the mayor—it created an advocacy around Mayor Rodrigo R. Duterte. These activities included, but were not limited to, building a sizable base on Facebook, including proliferation of Facebook pages and groups talking about the candidate; building an e-mail database; sending high-quality and engaging e-mails and other materials.
2. The Duterte campaign built a team from various volunteer groups who probably numbered in the thousands at the end of the campaign. Many of the most talented people in their individual professions became part of this team.
3. More so than any other campaign in the Philippines' history, the Duterte campaign was a data-driven operation. A simple and concise digital strategy was developed to be at the heart of the campaign. Virality of content became one of the key goals.
4. The campaign's recognition of the value of maximizing social media led to a critical decision of making the team an important part of the overall campaign—having the same priority as the field

---

[23] https://www.rappler.com/move-ph/133035-lessons-duterte-digital-campaign (accessed on 17 June 2019).

operations, and finance and other units. The campaign was open to crowdsourcing content from the start.
5. The campaign used a simple measure of success: the value of higher engagement on Facebook over the lifetime of the campaign. The campaign boosted content that was resonating with supporters and voters.
6. What made Duterte's campaign materials special? The volunteers and supporters were given the creative leeway to design it on the basis of their own interpretation of the campaign narrative and it then allowed the messaging to be strategically aligned with what voters cared for at the moment.
7. There was strong coordination between the digital and field teams. Facebook allowed faster communication between different supporters and groups supporting Mayor Duterte.
8. Thousands of online/digital content were created by volunteers and supporters themselves—this included hundreds of songs composed and created by various musicians for the candidate.
9. The team curated content that was coming out from the volunteers and supporters, and segregated it on the basis of the target market such as Facebook videos and image memes and the team allowed supporters to co-manage the campaign.
10. It has to be mentioned that the way the candidate conducted himself allowed his supporters to create content about him and about his campaign. In the end, the candidate allowed the people to see him as the authentic candidate compared to his rivals.

Source: Rappler.com

Is 'Fake News' Stifling Democracy?

Fake news is one of the most overused and badly defined terms in the modern political and media vocabulary. With Pope Francis declaring the spreading of fake news a sin, Donald Trump continuing to label traditional media as 'fakes', and Russia engaging in disinformation efforts in and about the European Union, there is more confusion than clarity regarding deliberate misinformation. Political elites and media can't agree exactly what fake news is, nor how to deal with it. Researchers argue about whether fake news is content of purely political or commercial origin, whether satire can be considered as fake news, and even whether this term should be banned. Still, there is a consensus about common features that distinguish fake news from other types of biased or untrue information. First, this content poses as news and has all elements of 'traditional' news content. Second, it spreads misinformation. Third, this distribution of misinformation is deliberate. The University of Westminster defines fake news as 'a serious and complex problem that has complex societal causes and threatens to undermine democracy'. (Komlach, 2018)

Under new 'cybersecurity' laws, China has recently fined its biggest Internet company for hosting fake news; Malaysian government has set up a 'fact-checking' website and has shut down over 3,000 'fake news' accounts since the beginning of 2017; two notable 'de-bunking' websites have been set up in India; under questionable legislation, Indonesia's National Police's cyber division and the Ministry of Communication and Technology have been monitoring social media websites and blocking some sites they suspect of transmitting fake news; Vietnam has imposed sanctions on those found to be disseminating false news using fake accounts. Such repressive measures have even spread to Europe where Germany has passed legislation that could impose fines of up to €50 million on social media companies, if they don't delete comments the government deem to be illegal, racist or slanderous within 24 hours. The Czech Republic has set up a Centre Against Terrorism and Hybrid Threats ostensibly to fight fake news after falsehood disseminated via social media on migrants raised social tension. All these points towards 'fake news' becoming the reason to tighten screws on free speech.

Cyberspace Administration of China has introduced rules that came effective from October 2017[24] to regulate Internet chat groups and information released from online public accounts. Under the law, service providers of online group chats are required to clarify and identify users and ensure that users' personal information is not leaked. They must also find safety flaws and loopholes that create risks and provide remedial measures for them on time. The Administration also suggests that service providers build a credit rating and blacklist system to strengthen management and supervision of group chats.

---

[24] http://www.straitstimes.com/asia/east-asia/regulating-chat-groups-news-reporting (accessed on 17 June 2019).

In the pre-Internet days, people used to exchange such information and viewpoints through letters sent through the postal system or through telephone calls usually made through private telephone connections on government-owned telecom systems. What China's new laws are doing tend to be similar to government agencies opening and readings peoples' letters before delivering it or phone tapping their lines. This was considered in the Western libertarian tradition as akin to censorship and infringement of peoples' privacy. China sees this law as building stronger journalistic professionalism to strengthen the management and social responsibility of news providers, but others could argue that this is an excuse to tighten an authoritative media system's controls.

One may ask when did peoples' private conversations via chat lines become public media? So are we seeing the beginning of a clampdown on the nascent social media revolution across the world and would China's model become the norm for other countries?

There is no doubt that the very nature of multiparty democracy and the way elections are conducted to elect peoples' representatives are being questioned around the world. The hysterics built around the 'fake news' phenomenon could further dampen peoples' confidence in democracy. The way governments are moving to introduce new legislations to address the issue is worrisome.

Facebook—The Villain or Saviour of Democracy

When the so-called Arab Spring began in Tunisia in December 2010, the events unfolding in the region were reported in a triumphant celebratory mood by the Western media focusing on Arab youth's clamour for freedom and democracy, and the role social media—Facebook and Twitter in particular—were playing in it. A documentary broadcast by the BBC[25] in September 2011 under the heading 'How Facebook Changed the World' reported the events in a

---

[25] https://www.youtube.com/watch?v=lnPR90dJ3Gk&t=16s (accessed on 17 June 2019).

celebratory mood looking at the way Arab youth are going about using the new tools at its disposal to bring democracy to their region.

'This year the Arab world erupted as a generation of young people no longer prepared to suffer in silence, rose up against the hated despots who rule their countries', said reporter Mishal Husain in introducing the programme. 'Weapons of the activists of the so-called Arab Spring weren't guns and bombs, but the internet and mobile phones. For the first time in history, world's changing events were recorded hour by hour by the man and woman on the streets'.

'Unique filmed record now exists charting the downfall of tyrants in Tunisia, Egypt and Libya, and exposing the unimaginable brutality of embattled regimes in other parts of the Arab world', she added. In the rest of the 25-minute programme, Husain travelled across the region tracking down the people behind these images, thus meeting those who led the revolts and showing the unique footage they shot about how they are trying to bring some positive change—democracy of course—to the Arab world. It was a fascinating programme about the power of Facebook, Twitter and the Internet to change the social and political order in the world. BBC was very upbeat about its potential to do good.

But today, these movements are spreading in Europe where young people are rising up against the power of big business—including banks—who are accused of exploiting the people and making cost of living unbearable. They too are asking for governments to be accountable to the people. They too are using the Facebook, Twitter, WhatsApp to mobilize people to come to the streets to protest.

The Western media that reported the Arab Spring uprising in a celebratory mood hailing the young people as 'brave fighters for freedom' are now reporting about the social movements in Europe such as the 'Yellow Jacket' movement in France—that erupted in late 2018 and is threatening to spread across Europe—as 'trouble makers', 'anarchists' or even 'terrorists'. The media calls it 'riots' not peoples' uprisings and Facebook is being blamed for helping to destabilize governments and societies in Europe.

'The Yellow Jackets movement is what happens when you point Facebook's traffic hose at France's small towns', argued Ryan Broderick of BuzzFeed News.[26]

> This week, protesters scaled the Arc de Triomphe, burned cars, and clashed with police in the third consecutive weekend of riots in France. More than 300 people were arrested in Paris last weekend alone, and 37,000 law enforcement officers have been deployed around the country to restore order. The 'Gilets Jaunes' or 'Yellow Jackets' protests have only gotten more violent since they began last month. Three people have died, hundreds more have been injured. To hear the protesters tell it, they're marching through the streets to fight back against rising fuel prices and the high cost of living in the country. Beyond that, though, it's an ideological free-for-all.

This is how Broderick began his report and he went on:

> But what's happening right now in France isn't happening in a vacuum. The Yellow Jackets movement—named for the protesters' brightly colored safety vests—is a beast born almost entirely from Facebook. And it's only getting more popular. Recent polls indicate the majority of France now supports the protesters. The Yellow Jackets communicate almost entirely on small, decentralized Facebook pages. They coordinate via memes and viral videos. Whatever gets shared the most becomes part of their platform.

It is also fascinating to see how Facebook and WhatsApp are able to mobilize people in communities to protest against what they see as injustices, but the tone of the report is more about a threat to European societies rather than its potential to make governments more accountable to the people.

Broderick makes this interesting observation in the article about how a petition begun by a 32-year-old woman from Paris, Priscillia

---

[26] https://www.buzzfeednews.com/article/ryanhatesthis/france-paris-yellow-jackets-facebook?utm_source=Daily%2BLab%2Bemail%2Blist&utm_campaign=b312a90c28-dailylabemail3&utm_medium=email&utm_term=0_d68264fd5e-b312a90c28-396175385 (accessed on 17 June 2019).

Ludosky, went on Change.org calling for a drop in fuel prices at the pump, and it gathered momentum with social media linking up with the traditional media:

> In less than two weeks, what you end up with is this: A Change.org petition with fewer than 1,500 subscribers gets talked about on a local radio station. The radio appearance is written up by a local news site. The article is shared to a local Facebook page. Thanks to an algorithm change that is now emphasizing local discussion, the article dominates the conversation in a small town. Two men from the same suburb then turn the petition into a Facebook event. A duplicate petition goes viral within the local Facebook groups. Then a daily newspaper writes up the original petition. This second article about the petition also goes viral. So does the original petition. And then the rest of French media follows. Ludosky's petition now has over a million signatures.

For Broderick, the 'Anger Groups' that have cropped up across Europe using Facebook for mobilizing 'have always been huge hubs for fake news and general fringe-internet nonsense'. He discusses at length about what he refers to as 'fake news' peddled by these movements. 'The newfound national attention is making things even worse', he argues.

Thus, one is entitled to ask, why is it that Facebook is a saviour when it comes to Arab youth using it for mobilizing against injustices, but a villain when European youth do the same and the information the latter shares becomes 'fake news' and a threat to society?

Biggest Fake News Stories of the 21st Century

If we accept the fact that 'fake news' is about misrepresentation and misleading, the biggest 'fake news' stories of the 21st century were not in the social media, but in the mainstream. In lectures at universities in Asia, I often ask students what they think are the three biggest 'fake news' stories in the 21st century. Most students from Southeast Asia and China usually show a sense of cluelessness. But those in India are able to come up with at least one example, the first three I will list as follows.

Iraq's 'Weapons of Mass Destruction'

One that will top the list is 'Iraq's WMD' that became the excuse to invade Iraq in 2003. Most of the Western media cheered the USA and UK in invading Iraq holding up this 'fake news' as evidence why action should be taken sooner rather than later.

US and UK's justification for going to war against UN Secretary General Kofi Annan's view that it was not an UN-sanctioned war is based on a 93-page classified CIA document that was declassified in 2016. It says there was a lack of 'specific information' about Saddam Hussein having WMD,[27] but that was not what Bush administration officials told the media to sell the war to the American people. The report also provides details of some of the suspect intelligence regarding Saddam's military training Al-Qaeda militants.

In an excellent opinion piece in London's *Guardian*, Jeff Sparrows (2017) argued that today's preoccupation with 'fake news' could be traced to the stench of the 2003 Iraq War. He argues that if you wonder how Trump can say barefaced lies and get away with it, you need to look into 2002–2003 period when President George W. Bush, UK Prime Minister Tony Blair and Australian Prime Minister John Howard were able to 'get away with the duplicity with which they maneuvered us into the Iraq charnel house'.

He points out that on 8 September 2002, *NYT* ran a story about Iraq stepping up its quest to acquire nuclear weapons, which helped the Bush administration to 'launder talking points', lending a liberal imprimatur to unverified (and totally untrue) claims. 'When the key members of the Bush administration launched a publicity blitz to make the war happen, they were able to quote the *NYT* as evidence: in effect, reacting to newspaper revelations for which they themselves were responsible', notes Sparrows.

He points out a commentary by a well-known Australian journalist Greg Sheridan who argued that no one believes that Iraq has no

---

[27] https://news.vice.com/article/the-ciajust-declassified-the-document-that supposedlyjustified-the-iraq-invasion (accessed on 17 June 2019).

WMD. Pointing out that the Bush administration rhetoric painted the American media that did not support his war as treason, which Trump is also trying to do through the intimidation using fake news tag, Sparrows argued:

> He was certainly right about that. In 2002 and 2003, journalistic 'seriousness' over Iraq was defined by participation in the feedback loop between the pro-war reporters and the pro-war politicians, who leaned upon each other like drunks at closing time, repeating and amplifying the (largely untrue) claims of the Bush and Blair administrations.

Toppling Saddam's Statue—Iraqis 'Welcoming' US Troops?

The next ranked fake news should be the greatest untold story of the Iraq War—its 'ending'—which remains to be told, that is, who was behind the toppling of Saddam's statue in Baghdad?

It was by all accounts a staged event, where the US troops provided cover for militiamen of Ahmed Chalabi's Iraqi National Congress to perform the ritual, which could be beamed around the world as the 'defining moment of the war', where the American liberators were greeted by the grateful Iraqis.

Australian ABC television's Media Watch programme[28] (14 April 2003) showed a zoomed-out view of the square, which was basically deserted except for those few Iraqis who were pounding the statue for the close-up angles of American television cameras whose reporters claimed that thousands were 'celebrating the liberation'.

Stopping Gaddafi's 'Imminent Attack on Benghazi'

The third biggest 'fake news' story of the 21st century must be Libya's Muammar Gaddafi's 'imminent attacks on civilian population in

---

[28] http://www.abc.net.au/mediawatch/transcripts/s832042.htm (accessed on 17 June 2019).

Benghazi' which led to a UN Security Council resolution in 2011 that created a 'no-fly zone' supposedly to protect this civilian population. This ultimately led to NATO bombing civilian populations to overthrow Gaddafi.

> Five months into the bombing campaign, it is no longer possible to believe the initial official version of the events and the massacres attributed to the 'Gaddafi regime'. Moreover, it is now essential to take into account Libya's legal and diplomatic rebuttal, highlighting the crimes against peace committed by television propaganda, the war crimes perpetrated by NATO military forces, and the crimes against humanity sponsored by political leaders of the Atlantic Alliance.
> Just under half of Europeans still support the war against Libya. Their position is based on erroneous information. They still believe, in fact, that in February the 'Gaddafi regime' crushed the protests in Benghazi with brutal force and bombed civilian districts in Tripoli, while the Colonel himself was warning of 'rivers of blood' if his compatriots continued to challenge his authority.
> During my two months' investigation on the ground, I was able to verify that these accusations were pure propaganda intoxication, designed by the NATO powers to create the conditions for war, and relayed around the world by their television media, in particular Al-Jazeera, CNN, BBC and France 24. (Meyssan 2011)

Thierry Meyssan, a French writer and peace activist, wrote the aforementioned comments while the attacks against the Gaddafi regime was in full swing in Libya. He noted:

> The difference between those in the West who believe that Gaddafi is a tyrant who fired on his own people, and those in Libya who believe that he is a hero of the anti-imperialist struggle, is that the former live in an illusion created by TV propaganda, whereas the others are exposed to the concrete reality on the ground.

It is interesting that in the propaganda campaign carried out by the Western MSM (and Al Jazeera media) to build Western public support for the war to overthrow Gaddafi, there was no discussion about the tens of thousands of Libyan killed by NATO bombings in areas where Gaddafi supporters were concentrated in, especially taking into account that UN Security Council approval was obtained for a 'no-fly zone' to protect civilians in Benghazi (that were under anti-Gaddafi forces) from being killed by air raids from Libyan Air Force. Once the approval was obtained, NATO bombed civilian targets at will (outside Benghazi) and the Western media reported it as 'striking Gaddafi's military structure'.

In March 2011, London's *Guardian* even went to the extent of writing about how the 'Gaddafi-controlled media is waging propaganda war'[29] describing how they refer to rebels in Benghazi as 'rats' and how they use 'crude' cartoons in the propaganda campaign. There was no mention about the counter propaganda in the Western media. On 2 August 2011, Reuters ran a report about how Libya's warring parties have increased their propaganda war with a lull in fighting. It said that Gaddafi loyalists are trying to play on 'fears among Libyans that western-backed rebels will tip the country deeper into chaos'.

Looking at Libya today, one could see how true this fear has been, where the country has no real government and there is utter chaos in the country.

Target Myanmar—Rohingya Propaganda

The latest target in such 'fake news' campaigns in the international media against a sovereign non-Western country is Myanmar. Video clips and photos are being provided by some unnamed activist group which is then flashed in the media across the world as 'evidence' of 'genocide' against the Rohingya minority in Myanmar (a similar campaign against Sri Lanka was discussed in Chapter 7). Any rebuttal the government would provide is dismissed as propaganda. It is no wonder that when Myanmar's de facto leader Aung San Suu Kyi spoke for the first time about the Rohingya issue, she said that what

---

[29] https://www.theguardian.com/world/2011/mar/17/gaddafi-controlled-media-propaganda-war-libya (accessed on 17 June 2019).

we are seeing around the world is an 'iceberg of misinformation'[30] about her country.

Just before she spoke, she's spoken on the phone to Turkish President Recep Tayyip Erdogan who has been particularly critical of Myanmar's treatment of the Rohingya, dubbing it a 'genocide', and she's believed to have complained about his Deputy Prime Minister Mehmet Simsek posting fake pictures of alleged genocide in Myanmar on his Twitter account[31] calling on the international community to act. It has been shared 1,600 times and attracted more than 1,200 likes. He later retracted it and issued an apology.[32] The photograph was alleged to have been taken in Rwanda in 1994. Images shared by Simsek prompted allegations on Twitter that reports of human rights abuses against Rohingya people are fake, and there were also images being shared which claimed to prove that Rohingya militants are being trained in Bangladesh.[33]

On 7 December 2016, UK's *Daily Mail* published an article online with the headline: 'Heartbreaking Images Show Rohingya Toddler Tortured with a Stun Gun by Laughing Burmese Soldier' as Burma continues crackdown on the country's Muslim minority.[34] The article featured horrifying images of a toddler being attacked by a man with an electric prod, but it was soon revealed by Cambodian sources that this video was in fact shot in Cambodia and the child was not a Rohingya boy as the UK newspaper claimed. This attracted outrage among people in Myanmar, who tweeted about the fake story and the Myanmar government threatened to take legal action against the

---

[30] http://indianexpress.com/article/world/aung-san-suu-kyi-slams-iceberg-of-misinformation-over-rohingya-4831598/ (accessed on 17 June 2019).

[31] https://www.irrawaddy.com/news/burma/turkish-deputy-pm-denounced-misleading-twitter-pictures-rakhine-conflict.html (accessed on 17 June 2019).

[32] https://twitter.com/memetsimsek/status/903652812986482688?lang=en (accessed on 17 June 2019).

[33] https://www.theguardian.com/global-development/2017/sep/05/fake-news-images-add-fuel-to-fire-in-myanmar-after-more-than-400-deaths (accessed on 17 June 2019).

[34] http://archive.is/IJlIW (accessed on 17 June 2019).

newspaper. The *Daily Mail* took down the item later but without an apology.

Singapore's Channel News Asia reported[35] that a Dutchman was charged by a Cambodian court over the disturbing videos that appeared to show his Vietnamese boyfriend torturing the naked toddler with a stun gun. The footage shows the two-year-old screaming and crying as a man prods different parts of his body with the stun gun and later shoves an object down his throat.

Disinformation, Fake News and Strategic Communication

It is a huge task to discuss various 'fake news' stories in the social media, but in the context of the moves to define and ban 'fake news' from public platforms, it is important to understand the role propaganda has traditionally played in the media and to guard us against the 'fake news' hysteria stifling further freedom of expression—be it in the West or elsewhere.

Recently, there has been intense concern around the world whether this 'fake news' hysteria will lead us into a Third World War. Propaganda war on Syria gives a good insight into how it is shaping up.

In an interview in February 2017 held in Damascus, an American journalist from Yahoo News grilled Syria's President Bashar al-Assad with a barrage of questions surrounding allegations of human rights abuses and war crimes against the Syrian government in a tense interview that at times saw Assad putting the questions back to the reporter and catch him off guard with his sharp responses. He pointed out a number of times what he is referring to as reliable sources are based on unverified facts (fake news). The video and the transcript of the interview were released for the world to hear by the Syrian Arab News Agency via the Middle East Observer and YouTube.[36]

---

[35] http://www.channelnewsasia.com/news/asiapacific/dutchman-charged-in-cambodian-child-torture-case-7660724 (accessed on 17 June 2019).

[36] http://middleeastobserver.net/video-syrias-assad-us-reporter-battle-over-human-rights-violationswar-crimes-english-subs/ (accessed on 17 June 2019).

Singaporean strategic communications expert Viswa Sadasivam[37] argues that 'fake news' has always existed in the mainstream and alternative media, but we didn't call it such:

> Fake news always existed accept that we didn't call it fake news, we called it disinformation. (It) is incorrect information propagated with the aim of deceiving. Militaries use this in psychological warfare … in lying and propagating untruth … governments use a lot of disinformation quite often to propagate information to people outside their own country … some governments use this information to lie to their own people. Governments have always done this using various means some subtle some blatant … it did not constitute fake news because the news itself was not completely fake. There was a certain amount of strategic ambiguity embedded into the news. So that there was an exit clause … if caught they can exit, its fuzzy enough. What you see as fake news propagated in social media is that which is less deeply considered … like the way it used to be by political regimes using the mainstream media. This is ranging from mischief to pork fun … in a serious way at incumbent regimes.
>
> What is challenging is that at one stage fake news was in the domain of incredible aspects of the media. In the US there's a lot of tabloids and you read what is there with a pinch of salt … because you know there's a lot of fake news … say Elvis was seen walking the streets of Manhattan … that kind of stuff. People read it because it is bizarre. Today fake news is actually hard to detect because its entering mainstream … even major news agencies have not been able to find that some news they disseminate are fake news. That is what I'm afraid of—you cannot find the truth anymore … no matter how you try you cannot fight fake news … sophistication with which stories can be faked or moving visuals could be doctored … its going to be more and more sophisticated which means harder to detect.
>
> It (media) has to go back to some level of disciplined curated media. You need to reverse the migration (to social media) and have more people trust the mainstream media and go back to the mainstream media … that will only happen if governments that have

---

[37] Interview with the author in Singapore, 24 April 2017.

been using the mainstream media only for their (propaganda) purpose realize that they are shooting themselves on the foot. They need to give space for true journalism to grow in mainstream media space.

As I complete writing this book at the end of 2018, there is intense debate in the international media about 'fake news', Russians trolls on social media sites, the need to regulate Facebook and other social media tools and so on. It looks like we are looking straight into an upheaval, disruption and revolution. These words, though not necessarily said as such, seem to be what is behind the minds of those who are advocating control. The words we now associate with the Internet's impact on traditional storytelling and the very people who hailed it as a beginning of a bold new era of FOE and democracy are now asking for it to be controlled because they have lost control of the media, it seems. The very people who spread a gospel of 'libertarian media' arguing that the people are logical and they could work out what is good or bad, are now saying, a 'free media' needs to be controlled otherwise 'foreign agents' will undermine their democracy. Thinkers on Capitol Hill and Kremlin seem to be on the same wavelength now—something unimaginable until 9 November 2016 (when Trump won the Presidency).

The Beacon of Hope Fading

Ever since President Trump came to office, the White House correspondents have faced such a barrage of criticisms and harassment from their president that German Deutsche Welle Radio's Global Media Forum was convinced that the White House Correspondents' Association (WHCA) deserved the 2017 'Freedom of Speech' Award.[38]

In an acceptance speech, WHCA's President Jeff Mason said that he and his colleagues would 'never have sought or expected' such an

---

[38] http://www.dw.com/en/white-house-correspondents-win-dws-freedom-of-speech-award/av-39320282 (accessed on 17 June 2019).

award. Quoting the first amendment of the US Constitution, Mason said:

> [I]f there is anything I have learned in the last eleven months of leading the correspondents' association, it is that we cannot take those rights or the law that guarantees them for granted. We must remain vigilant against any attempt to curtail the freedom of the press and any attempt to undermine the important work journalists do. We must also correct mistakes when we make them and report truthfully to guard against actual made-up or fake news, which does indeed exist and is dangerous to a functioning democracy.[39]

Just a few days after Mason's speech, President Trump got the fillip he needed when CNN accepted the resignation of three senior journalists over a story about alleged Russian involvement in his presidential campaign and transitional team, when the story was retracted by CNN for lack of validated facts (AP 2017). The retracted story was about a supposed investigation into a pre-inaugural meeting between an associate of President Trump and the head of a Russian investment fund. Trump soon grabbed the opportunity and tweeted: 'Wow, CNN had to retract big story on "Russia," with three employees forced to resign. What about all the other phony stories they do? FAKE NEWS!'[40]

A day later, during a press briefing, White House Deputy Press Secretary Sarah H. Sanders scolded reporters over the use of unnamed sources and complained about 'the constant barrage of fake news' aimed at the administration. 'If we make the slightest mistake, if the slightest word is off, it's just an absolute tirade from a lot of people in this room', she said. 'But news outlets get to go on day after day and cite unnamed sources' (Stableford 2017).

---

[39] http://www.dw.com/en/freedom-of-speech-laureate-mason-even-in-strong-established-democracies-reporters-rights-must-be-fought-for/a-39319715 (accessed on 17 June 2019).
[40] https://twitter.com/realdonaldtrump/status/879648931172556802?lang=en (accessed on 17 June 2019).

The comments set off a heated argument between a newspaper reporter in the White House press pool, Brian Karem, and Sanders. 'Come on—this administration has done this as well', he told her. 'If any one of us doesn't get it right, the audience has the opportunity to turn off the channel or not read us. You have been elected to serve four years at least—there's no option other than that'.

'We're in here asking you questions', Karem continued.

You're here to provide the answers and what you just did is inflammatory to people all over the country who look at it and say, 'See, once again, the president's right, and everybody else out here is fake media'. And everybody in this room is trying to do their job.

'I disagree completely', Sanders shot back. 'I think if anything's been inflamed, it's often the dishonesty that takes place in the news media. And I think it's outrageous for you to accuse me of inflaming a story when I was simply trying to respond to [a] question'.

Karem, who has worked for a Washington (DC)-based newspaper since 2004, said he's been alarmed by the administration's treatment of the press. 'We've been called the enemy of the people from that White House. We've been told that we're fake news. We are bullied and browbeaten every day', he told MSNBC in an interview. 'For the government to sit there and undermine what is essentially checks and balances in the system, it's disheartening', he said. 'It's unnerving. I can't take it anymore. It's nuts' (Stableford 2017).

Web 2.0: The Panacea

If the 'fourth estate' theory of the media as watchdog has been undermined with the expansion of neoliberal economic models into the media arena, the advent of the Web 2.0 communication model may well provide an alternative.

Samuel Freedman, professor of journalism at the Columbia University, agrees that the advent of the Internet has opened up avenues for peoples' voices to be heard. Yet, he argues, the concept of

'Citizen Journalist' thrown up by this technology has thrown a serious challenge to the profession of journalism (Profita 2006).

> To its proponents, citizen journalism represents a democratization of media, a shattering of the power of the unelected elite, a blow against the empire of Big Brother. Citizen journalism does not merely challenge the notion of professionalism in journalism but completely circumvents it. It is journalism according to the ethos of indie rock 'n' roll: Do It Yourself. For precisely such reasons, I despair over the movement's current cachet. However wrapped in idealism, citizen journalism forms part of a larger attempt to degrade, even to disenfranchise journalism as practiced by trained professionals. I appreciate the access that citizen journalism provides to first-hand accounts of major events. Yet I recognize those accounts are less journalism than the raw material, generated by amateurs, that a trained, skilled journalist should know how to weigh, analyze, describe, and explain. (Freedman cited in Profita 2006)

This freedom of professional journalist to independently weigh, analyse, describe and explain is at the root of the 'free media' thesis. But it has been unravelling in the past two decades as the traditional media institutions have been transforming into big businesses with mergers making them hostage to big corporations. The Libertarian Media Function Theory worked as long as media companies only owned media, but now they own entertainment companies, film studios and sports franchises—even large arms manufacturers such as GE and Westinghouse have large stakes in the media. And so are oil companies and huge financial institutions. At the same time, the new digital media technologies and the Internet have been providing platforms that could be utilized to democratize the media and make it more accountable to the people.

As Professor Biplab Loho Choudhury,[41] head of the Centre for Journalism and Mass Communication at Visva-Bharati University observes:

---

[41] https://www.youtube.com/watch?v=EVjX-8_7AvU (accessed on 17 June 2019).

From 2000 onwards we have found on the wheel of the world wide web, and on the platform of new media technology (which is a result of) a huge creation of audience matchmaking software development. The social media has grown strong. The result is you are neither in the centre (and) you are neither in the periphery. You start sending message, say in WhatsApp group to your friends, each of them have equal chance to send you a message and they also have a very cool chance to send message to all of you, already a new message he or she can send. So mass communication, we are finding, achieved within one platform one-to-one interpersonal communication, then one-to-many group communication and from many to many communication. This is actually making the shift in the concept of communication and media.

Yet, just when the doors are opening for a more 'free media', it could be bolted again with the challenge posed to 'web-neutrality' by the Trump administration[42] and the hysteria on 'fake news' promoted by MSM and authoritative governments.

Thus, in this book we have been examining and exploring ways of how to navigate through many bottlenecks thrown up by neoliberalist economics that have made news a commodity and media a manufacturer of consent. As we have discussed in this chapter, 'fake news' is a complex issue, especially when it is confused with the peoples' freedom of speech to express an opinion. In the final chapter, we will examine some new ways of thinking, especially drawn from Eastern philosophy, to develop a new generation of communicators with ethical considerations.

---

[42] https://www.reuters.com/article/uk-usa-internet/u-s-fcc-faces-tough-questions-from-court-on-net-neutrality-repeal-idUSKCN1PQ5CA (accessed on 17 June 2019).

CHAPTER 10

Fighting the Gloom with New Thinking

Filipino communication scholar Crispin C. Maslog (Masterton 1996: 140) argued two decades ago that Asian journalists have absorbed the Western values of journalism uncritically and become more popish than the Pope.

> Journalism as we know it came to Asia from the West and the journalism values that came with it were understandably Western: objectivity, press freedom from government control, and the news values of conflict, prominence, proximity, timeliness, consequence, human interest, oddity and, of course, sex. In the beginning we Asians, especially Filipinos, practiced Western-style journalism with a vengeance. With our early colonial mentality we accepted these Western journalism values without question.... We have been more popish than the Pope in defending these inherited values, the synthesis of which seems to be 'make war, not love'. According to these Western principles, a reporter tries to fashion a clear, concise straight news story with the Who, What, Where, When, Why, and How, and arranges the facts in their descending order of importance and interest. This is to enable busy readers to grasp the essentials of the stories immediately and to allow editors to cut stories from the bottom up. The reporters' job is to hold a mirror to an event and show its surface. Explaining why it occurred and

what should be done about it is the job of the editorial writers and columnists. We seem determine to give the audience what they want, regardless of what they need.

In the 1960s, Sri Lankan journalist Tarzie Vittachi and many others countered this tradition of journalism through the Press Foundation of Asia (PFA). They coined what came to be known as 'development journalism' and in a pioneering training course designed in 1968, this approach was described by Vittachi (cited by Maslog in Masterton 1996: 141) thus:

> They (the participants) decided they would no longer regard themselves as economic writers but as development journalists who should now consciously serve as part of the efforts for their nations to develop their resources and not merely as recorders of economic events.

Jose Luna Castro (cited by Maslog in Masterton 1996: 143), former president of the Asian Institute of Journalism, makes this link between the media and the community it serves.

> One of the most remarkable developments in journalism is the realization that traditional news—about fires, accidents, floods, famine, violence and sex—does not fill the bill of giving readers a multidimensional view of the world. ...We must admit that absence of news about the basic, plodding and undramatic efforts to improve the quality of life among the people and to modernize the environment, results in the presentation by the media of a lop-sided view of the world. There is something perverse about a situation where the ordinary citizen knows more about the scandals of the neighbourhood than the communal or municipal efforts to build a road or a dam in the community ... the gradual transformation of a village to a progressive community should be reported more systematically.

If you are critical of the adversarial role of journalism, does it mean that negative news, such as stories of graft and corruption in government or anywhere else, should not be reported because it may hamper development? On the contrary, no, as Maslog argues, we may need to develop a new formula where the media is an agent of change, not a provocateur of violence. This may need an examination of the economic model of the media that is dependent on the mass media becoming a successful 'seller' rather than a 'giver' of what people need.

Thus, while looking at changing news values, we also need to look at the economic model of the news media. Can the media serve the people while making an economic profit from it? As Batra argued in Chapter 3, any media model has to be economically viable. We would discuss in this chapter different approaches to reporting, especially from an Asian context, keeping in mind that it needs to be an economically viable model.

Another World Is Possible

'With the emergence of new media genres and communication technologies, the era of Western-centric form of journalism education is under scrutiny', argues Professor Yusuf Kalyango,[1] director of the Institute for International Journalism at the Ohio University, who observes that, over past decades, traditional journalism education took place through the prevailing Western (European and North American) lens. 'Even to-date, there are still efforts from institutions such as UNESCO that are advancing a universal homogenization of journalism education with a Western dominance in the so-called journalistic values and knowledge systems', he adds. Thus, Professor Kalyango believes that in the light of how globalization is changing information societies (netizens, bloggers, etc.) as well as media ecology, this state of affairs needs to change and journalism education needs to be de-Westernized.

It is hoped that this book offers material for assisting such an effort. Professor Kalyango, who was born in Uganda, argues further that

> although journalism in various societies embodies the traditions of public service, education, and advocacy, digital, satellite technology

---

[1] Presentation to a workshop on 'De-Westernising Journalism and Communication Theory' held at the World Journalism Education Conference in Auckland, New Zealand in July 2016. The author was part of this workshop.

has triggered many implications for both, in all societies for mass communication, media, and journalism. This new shift away from the traditional norm of universalizing journalism makes it necessary to shake up certainties grounded in a narrow set of cases and analytical perspectives, and to break away from the universalism to provincialism or localism of journalism curriculum.

Western journalism tradition of adversarial journalism designed to be watchdog of government's abuse of power would need some reformation in the midst of new media tools and social media. That role by itself should not be defining the role of journalism. Mindful communication—which is rooted in Buddhist philosophy—needs to be considered to craft a role for the media to be more a builder of community harmony rather than its destabilizer.

Pipope Panitchpakdi[2] believes that news has to be critical. But being critical doesn't have to be confrontational, he argues.

> Being critical is looking at it objectively but the approach of doing it doesn't have to be negative. We have to find a concept of finding a solution to journalism. It may be quite suitable (to find a new) discourse, more than words (to) have an ongoing dialogue as a news piece.

At the same time, he admits that people like bad news as long as it happened to someone else and they can warn themselves and family not to fall into same trap, or it is some kind of entertainment.

In an interview in the mid-1980s in Sydney, this is how the then Editor-in-Chief of Reuters news agency Michael Ruepka[3] described news values:

> News worthiness for me is information someone needs for his business and everyday life. Say a member of public should know to take the right sort of attitude towards his government or right sort

---

[2] Interview with the author in Bangkok, April 2017.
[3] I recorded this interview with him for a university radio programme I was producing at the time.

of attitude in voting or form his opinion intelligently in what is happening around him. Or, its information, which is important for him, to be aware of things around him. Events that may not have direct relevance to his life but in general important.

But, he added that because Reuters is in the business of collecting and selling news, to whoever it is needed, and is prepared to pay for it, they need to gear their reports to that market. Thus, what they cover tends to be news of exception. As pointed out in the preface, he described this type of news as 'someone falling under a bus'.

This tradition of news of exception as a saleable commodity is what is driving the corporate media takeover of the news industry today as we have discussed in this book. It has become easier for entertainment companies to take over news outlets and make money out of it, because this news of exception is usually entertaining with a little bit of tweaking. Dixit (1997) notes that as the public service role of the media is being undermined, 'it is not a coincidence that news business is being taken over by conglomerates that also owns entertainment empires' such as Time Warner and Disney. Thus, he says:

> Fewer and fewer people today control the information we get, and they are setting the agenda for the rest of us—how we should behave, what we should buy, which credit card we must use, what we should wear, what movies we can't afford to miss, what we should eat, what we should smoke. They are saying to us Saddam Hussein is a crook, free trade is good. It is Ok for five per cent of the world's population to consume half its resources.

I often ask my students in Asia why do you spend, for example, 300 dollars for a shoe or 400 dollars for a handbag that has a branded name? They say, it is because the product is of good quality and long-lasting and they think it is 'cool' and 'the right thing to do' to have those products. When I ask them 'if you know that it is worth just a fraction of what you pay, if you consider the costs of material and labour that have gone to produce it, would you still buy it?' They say 'because others buy we will buy'. Then I point out that it is the media you consume that says so, and that media is dependent on their advertising for survival. So they need to convince (brainwash) you to believe in what you just said—it is for their mutual survival. 'Would you still buy it?' Some react 'hmmm...' and look up. Yet, some others would say, 'that is Communist thinking'.

It is this system of brainwashing that could be counter-attacked today with the arrival of Facebook, Twitter, Instagram, etc. (as discussed in Chapter 9). Until then, the entry cost to the global communication system was so steep that only big companies could enter it. Their business model is now threatened and threatened very seriously.

From Propaganda to Community News

As discussed in Chapter 2, Noam Chomsky (1991: 12) argued that the American media constitutes the most awesome propaganda system in the world, where it manipulates people to 'manufacture consent'. He says that social sciences best describe this process, where the media shapes perceptions, selects events, offers interpretations and so on 'in conformity with the needs of the power centres in society, which are basically the state and the corporate world'. He also argues that this propaganda system is very good in using adversarial style of reporting to obscure what is happening in the world (which has been discussed in length in this book).

Adversarial journalism as the pall-bearer of libertarian media model is increasingly coming under scrutiny. Editor of Indian media watchdog website The Hoot, Sevanti Ninan,[4] cites Arnab Goswami's style of TV journalism as a clear example of entertainment-oriented adversarial news that the audience likes, but may obscure the realities of Indian power centres (his news style was discussed in Chapter 3). It's successful (because) he decides what I should be angry about today and he does that, shouts at everybody and people love it, she notes. 'They don't stop to think that this is a performance which it is actually, but public see it as (asking for) accountability (from public officials)'.

---

[4] Interview with the author in Delhi, 9 December 2016.

Panitchpakdi argues that reforming the news industry need not be seen as repressing negativity in news. 'It should not be that bad news by itself is negative', he argues.

> But it's the approaching and explaining of that news. If news has the value of bringing positive change I will call that positive news. Even if it's reporting on a bad situation say floods for example. …it's bad news if you report people are being flooded government did not go and help. But if you show why help from the government was so delayed and why the floods did take place it could have positive impact. Its multi-conditions, and (the challenge is) if news can maintain that complexity, and at the same time have good narratives.

Singaporean strategic communication specialist Viswa Sadasivan[5] believes that the adversarial style of journalism is going to be increasingly unpopular. 'Universal values of integrity, constant search for the truth which can sometimes be very elusive, and very importantly the model fiber that encourage to express what you believe in—these are ethos that are universal, these ethos should be promulgated', he argues. 'It is wrong to assume that young people today do not believe in these values…. Disillusionment you see in young people, rejecting what is establishment, what is mainstream media is (because of) a lot of crap that they see.'

Sadasivan sees a danger for 'freedom' aspects of the media in that there is no curation and it is fertile ground for manipulation 'like what you saw (with) Arab Spring. You can have organized syndicates, organized government regimes employing these powerful platform to reach out to young people who are seeking for something to believe in and manipulating these minds, using the same platforms that they have come to trust. That for me is grossly unethical. Problem right now is we don't have an antidote for it', he laments.

The waves of political manifestations and social movements that occurred between 2009 and 2012 were often labelled by the global media as social media revolutions, Facebook revolutions or Twitter revolutions, definitions that reveal a techno-determinist vision and that underestimate the different political and social contexts in which

---

[5] Interview with the author in Singapore, 24 April 2017.

each of these protests took place. In addition, the role of non-traditional media in mobilizing peoples' uprising is not new.

In the 1970s, it was the audio cassette that quickly spread the word of Ayatollah Khomeini and played an important role in the uprising that toppled the Shah of Iran in 1979. In 1968, the communication technologies that most supported the French students' movements that brought Paris to a virtual close-down were radio, graffiti and mimeographs. In 1971, when the Marxist rebellion by the JVP (*Janata Vimukthi Peramuna* [People's Liberation Front]) almost toppled the Sri Lankan government, it was called the 'poster revolution' because they mobilized the youth via a nationwide wall poster campaign—the only media available to them at the time. Throughout the 1980s, American pop stars like Stevie Wonder and Jamaican Reggae idols like Bob Marley and Peter Tosh played a big role in raising the consciousness of a whole generation of youth, especially in the West, about the evils of Apartheid in South Africa, which led to the release of Nelson Mandela and Black majority rule in the 1990s. In the mid-1980s, it was the Catholic Church's community-based radio that mobilized the people in the Philippines for the 'people power' revolution that toppled President Marcos; and in 2001 the 'peoples' power' that brought down President Estrada was powered by text messages transmitted on mobile phones. In the 1970s, community street theatre is believed to have played an important role in mobilizing the Bengali masses for liberating the country from East Pakistan rule and birth of Bangladesh. As technology improved, in Genoa in 2001, a mix of the Internet, mailing lists, mobile phones and web radio contributed to the mobilization for street protests against G8. Since then, Internet-based social media networks have played a major role in international mobilizations for protests against corporate globalization.

The Economist on 4 November 2017 had the heading 'Once Considered a Boon to Democracy, Social Media Have Started to Look Like Its Nemesis' in an article that argued fake news spread around the world has created a political problem to many governments. *The Economist* noted:

> Governments simply do not know how to deal with this—except, that is, for those that embrace it. In the Philippines President Rodrigo

Duterte relies on a 'keyboard army' to disseminate false narratives. His counterpart in South Africa, Jacob Zuma, also benefits from the protection of trolls. And then there is Russia, which has both a long history of disinformation campaigns and a domestic political culture largely untroubled by concerns of truth. It has taken to the dark side of social media like a rat to a drainpipe, not just for internal use, but for export, too. Vladimir Putin's regime has used social media as part of surreptitious campaigns in its neighbours, including Ukraine, in France and Germany, in America and elsewhere.[6]

It would have been better if *The Economist* was also able to understand how the West does the same, such as manipulating young minds in triggering the Arab Spring, the promotion of R2P via global media propaganda and creation of information/activist NGOs—'dollar chasing democracy vendors'—as discussed in Chapter 5. The libertarian free media model tells us that the news media as an institution mirrors the interest of the 'public'. But, as we have discussed in this book, as the media becomes commercialized this 'public service' role is being diluted and manipulates the public to serve these commercial interests.

Philippines media system can be described as motivated by what I call PPPP. That is profit, propaganda, privilege, power. Those are the motives why there are media outfits in the country, most of them anyway. And I was asked if I would like to change the system what would I replace it with. I said if I was to replace the system, I would have to bulldoze the whole system, and set up one where the controllership of the media is in the hands of people who really represent the community and the country.
—Louie Tabing, Founder of Tambuli Community Radio, the Philippines[7]

What Tabing argues is that the most important 'P'—the People—is missing in our media structure. Asia is today in the process of building trade routes, tourism circuits and regional community-building

---

[6] https://www.economist.com/news/briefing/21730870-economy-based-attention-easily-gamed-once-considered-boon-democracy-social-media (accessed on 17 June 2019).
[7] Personal interview with the author in Manila, October, 2004.

through economic, cultural and trading partnerships. While rapid economic and technological progress is shifting the world's centre of gravity towards Asia, can Asia also develop a communication infrastructure that may provide a better model than the adversarial journalism model? When we look at the way Asia's progress is reported today, some form of bulldozing may be necessary to create a media infrastructure that puts the media in the hands of the people, rather than surrendering to commercial interests.

While Asians are building (or trying to build) systems of cooperation and peaceful coexistence, the Western media keeps focusing on conflicts mainly imagined or potential than real, in South China Sea, Indian Ocean and the Korean peninsula. While China is offering money to build ports, railways, bridges and highways, the USA calling it the 'pivot to Asia' is offering missile defences, gunboats and fighter jets to the Asian nations. Thus, the contrast in how Asia and the West see the region is starkly evident today. Is the adversarial model of journalism to be blamed for it?

Asia needs to learn the lessons of the Arab Spring and should not allow foreign media and social media activists/trainer to turn a peaceful Asia into an arena of conflict, chaos and turmoil as what we see in the Middle East today. Thus, it is very important that the Asian media looks for a different model of journalism and, to do so, to look seriously at the ancient philosophies of Asia that offer much wisdom in creating communities that could live in harmony while, at the same time, acknowledging its cultural and social diversities. The way Indian culture and religion spread across Asia is a good lesson in peaceful interaction, which the young people of Asia tend to be ignorant of today.

Building Links Not Conquest

In a keynote address to a Mekong–Ganga Cooperation (MGC) meeting in Bangkok,[8] Professor Ram Madhav, the director of India

---

[8] https://www.indepthnews.net/index.php/the-world/asia-pacific/1798-ganga-initiative-brings-culture-into-new-asian-trade-routes (accessed on 17 June 2019).

Foundation, argued that 'soft power' which is promoted by big powers these days is an imposition of one's cultural practices on others without using military means and is not a suitable option for Asia. 'We must seriously revisit the soft power theory', he argued, noting that it is a Western concept. 'The Ganga–Mekong cultural flows (in ancient times) were interplay of cultures', he said, referring to how Hindu and Buddhist thoughts spread across Asia through the Ganges and Mekong river routes. 'The history of India has shown how culture has helped to prosper others.'

Pointing out that Indians have been travelling as far as China since at least the 1st century BCE (Before Common Era) marrying princesses and establishing communities influenced by the Hindu and Buddhist philosophies, Professor Madhav said: 'From Cambodia to Bali, Indian influence was not seen as colonizing.' Though Indians saw the region as greater India or further India, 'traders, monks and travellers did not come across "savages" in the lands they encountered; they came across people living in similar civilized societies like them'. Professor Madhav argued further that people in these regions saw the Indian infiltration as 'offering a framework from India which could be used to develop their own societies ... India did not colonize or occupy their lands'.

The Asian media needs to develop similar mindsets today and this cannot be learned from the West. The way China's peaceful rise as an economic super power is reported by the adversarial reporting culture of the Western media is a good example of why we need to look for a different model of journalism. The Western media sees China's investments on building 'New Silk Routes' as a 'debt trap', whereas for Asia, it could be seen as a welcome initiative to build infrastructure in the region—such as roads, railways, ports and bridges for Asia to trade and interact with each other and prosper together.

The ASEAN Economic Community (AEC) has come into force at the beginning of 2016 that would transform the Southeast Asian 10-member ASEAN bloc into a region with free movement of goods, services, investment, skilled labour and freer flow of capital. The AEC envisages a single market and production base, a highly competitive economic region, a region of equitable economic development and a region fully integrated into the global economy. In South Asia, the regional body SAARC has been handicapped because of the fierce rivalry between India and Pakistan created by the division of India. To overcome this, the countries bordering the Bay of Bengal—that includes India—are developing a regional organization Bay of Bengal Initiative for Multi-Sectoral Technical and Economic Cooperation (BIMSTEC) to accelerate economic and cultural links in the region. India has also launched the MGC grouping consisting of India and five nations that border the Mekong River to promote economic and cultural cooperation on the basis of its ancient Hindu–Buddhist links.

Meanwhile, a re-emerging China is investing heavily in building new connectivity across the Asian and Eurasian regions to rekindle the great trade and cultural roots of the past. The building of the Silk Route Economic Belt and 21st-century Maritime Silk Route, a multi-trillion dollar project, which China calls BRI, is bound to change the world and transfer the centre of gravity of the world economic system back to Asia.

Li Hong,[9] China's permanent representative to the United Nations Economic and Social Commission for Asia and the Pacific (UNESCAP), says:

> BRI identified seamless connectivity as the driving force for economic re-balancing, establishing the connections of the east–west economic centres to release a great geographical and resources potential. BRI encourages and calls for the broadest possible joint action for building cross-border infrastructure networks with a view to facilitating the flow of goods and raising the efficiency for resources allocation and extending the value chain to more remote regions. BRI embraces its partners to carry on the connectivity agenda in line with their national priorities, and it supports the implementation of the multilateral connectivity arrangement such as the Asia Highway Network Agreement, the Tran-Asia Railway Agreement, by providing political support, investment guidance, cross-border facilitation etc. There is no hidden agenda.

[9] https://www.indepthnews.net/index.php/opinion/1132-enriching-the-belt-and-broadening-the-road (accessed on 17 June 2019).

To achieve these goals, the media in Asia needs to play an important role in facilitating and promoting regional integration and not focus on and/or promote conflict. It needs to look at the region not as a collection of economic entities but as societies with a great shared cultural heritage and a long history of cultural and economic interaction. Looking at Asia through this context, rather than a repression of religious freedom, China's crackdown on underground Christian evangelical churches could be seen differently. Thus, it needs to be mindful of peoples' need for social harmony and their longing for heritage protection after centuries of European cultural repression. This is why when the Indian Prime Minister Narendra Modi visited China in May 2015 he proposed to Chinese President Xi Jinping to bring in cultural links to the new trade routes that are being developed. Modi called it the 'Indic-Buddhist Civilization' links. The Indian-initiated MGC is an example—and perhaps a future template—for developing such cooperation across Asia.

To develop these trade and cultural links, the Asian media needs to play a crucial supporting—not adversarial—role. Along with technical training in the use of journalistic tools, they also need education in Asian cultural studies, history and ancient trading infrastructures, so that Asian media practitioners could utilize these knowledge to analyse and promote the 21st-century links. This may also need a new look at the aspects of training journalists to look at the issues from a regional perspective with less emphasis on conflicts and greater efforts to build an infrastructure of cultural knowledge and better community bonding. In doing so, there may need to be new thinking on how to report on economic, business, environment and development issues, where Asia's needs, its priorities, its historical experiences and its cultural knowledge are taken into account.

Especially in building cultural knowledge, the idea of secularism needs to be reviewed. In the West, secularism usually means separating religion from the state or, in other words, at an individual level, have no loyalty to a religion. In the eastern way of thinking, secularism is respecting all religions, especially its positive aspects. This may have evolved from the fact that in India, for centuries, there have been various philosophers with different perspectives on life and spirituality that existed side by side. They debated with each other freely, whereas in the European Renaissance, the success of the European modernization project is attributed to separating the Church from the State.

Thus, new communication methodologies need to be built in to share and respect each other's cultures, not to reject them and accept a modernity where you have no cultural identity. While teaching international communications and journalism to Asian students in Singapore and Thailand—my classes have included students from other Asian countries as well, particularly China—I find it very unfortunate that young Asians hardly know anything about their history, cultural expressions or even the religion. I often point out to them, how can we look at Asia-focused journalism if you do not know your past and your culture, in order to plan your future different to what the West has prescribed to us?

Asia's Historic Contributions to Mass Communication

Mass communication courses taught in universities across Asia are usually based on Eurocentric concepts of communication with a heavy focus on individual rights, FOE and dissent—the so-called 'fourth estate' principle (as discussed in Chapters 1 and 2). In the Asian region where the protection and promotion of community and social harmony plays an important role in political and social discourse, media practitioners focusing on individual rights over community harmony sometimes create unnecessary conflicts that could be avoided by more sensitive and mindful communication strategies that would have the same result of opening up public and community space for more FOE.

A major reason why Westerners and Asians often disagree on the concept of FOE is that the international narrative on the issue is driven by a belief that democracy was born in Europe. People across the globe believe that democracy and the mass media were European innovations. It is supposed to be common knowledge that democracy originated in ancient Greece in the 5th century BCE, but we are kept in ignorance of the peoples' assemblies that existed in Vedic societies in India much before that, known as 'samitis' and 'sabhas' (Misra 2000).

The Vedic period (1500–500 BCE) was the earliest period where Hindu scriptures, the Vedas, were composed. It was the time Indo-Aryans settled into North India and societies were formed along with the formation of Hindu religious traditions. The societies formed had a chief called *rajan* whose powers were restricted by peoples' councils called 'sabha' and 'samiti', which were responsible for the governance of the societies. The *rajan* was actually elected or approved by these bodies. The 'sabha' are believed to be meetings of the community leaders/elders, while the 'samiti' was more like a peoples' village council. Singh (1998) notes that the two assemblies formed an essential feature of the government in the ancient Vedic societies as described in ancient Hindu texts the Vedas.

> Although it is difficult to distinguish between a 'sabha' and 'samiti' it appears that 'samiti' was the august assembly of a larger group of people for the discharge of tribal (i.e. political) business and was presided over by the king, while the 'sabha', a more select body, was less popular and political in character than a 'samiti'. Although the functions and the powers of 'sabha' and 'samiti' cannot be exactly defined, numerous passages referring to them clearly indicates that both these Assemblies exercised considerable authority and must have acted as healthy checks on the power of the king. (Singh 1998: 8)

Isn't it what we today assign as the role of national assemblies, city halls and village councils in modern democracies? Even in contemporary India, it is the parliament (sabha) elected by the people who elect the president. The village-level panchayats are the modern-day replicas of the 'samiti'.

And when it comes to mass media, we teach in universities across the world—including Asia—that it originated with the Gutenberg Bible printed in movable type in the 15th century in Germany. Again, we ignore the fact that six centuries earlier the Chinese printed the Buddhist Diamond Sutra on the block type (Morgon 2012). In fact, it was the Chinese who invented paper and printing, and after the Tripitaka[10] was written at Aluvihare in Sri Lanka in the 1st century BCE, it was the written/printed word that spread Buddhism across Asia.

Buddhist role in the development of print technology across Asia, especially in China and Korea between 1 and 7 century CE is well documented. As Mair (1994) notes, Buddhism was probably the most important factor in the development of printing in China as the demand for its texts increased. Not only Buddhism influenced the spread of printing but also, as a result, the printed word helped to influence the society at large in adopting the norms of Buddhist thought. In the last two decades of the 11th century CE, more Korean Tripitaka woodblocks have been carved than for Chinese texts, and Korea's zealous attempt to acquire Buddhists texts has inspired a printing boom.

If the origins of the mass media are about spreading knowledge via the printed text, shouldn't this be the beginning of the mass media? Why is Asia's role in these developments not acknowledged in our mass communication textbooks?

Why I'm bringing up the aforementioned points about the birth of democracy and mass media here is because it is important that the minds of both Asian academics and students need to be de-colonized for them to embrace aspects of Asian philosophical thought in developing new models of journalism and communication. Otherwise they will blindly believe the Western description of these ancient wisdom as 'mythology'.

Balancing of Communication Theory

Eurocentrism, argues Amin (1989: 90), is not properly speaking a social theory. 'It is rather a prejudice that distorts social theories. It draws from its storehouse of components, retaining one or rejecting another according to the ideological needs of the moment.' He points

---

[10] Tripitaka are three categories of Buddhist texts what are called the Buddhist cannon. It consists of Buddha's sermons (*sutra*), codes of conduct for monks (*vinaya*) and Buddhist psychology (*abhidhamma*).

out that the 'myth of Greek ancestry' performs an essential function in the European construct. So is the choice of Christianity as the basis of Europeaness that creates a thorny question for social theory because Christianity was not born in Europe. The dominant ideology and culture of the capitalist system as European is also problematic, he argues, because trading systems existed in the East and elsewhere before the European Renaissance period. Thus, he notes 'Eurocentrism is a relatively modern construct'.

In the past two decades, as mass communication departments and schools across Asia grew, there has been an increasing debate about de-Westernizing communication theory—at least that was taught in Asian institutions. I would prefer to call this 'balancing' rather than 'de-Westernization', because we are not going to reject Western theory outright, but balance it away from the Eurocentrism it is hinged onto. Accompanying this attempt has also been a debate on 'Asian values' in journalism (see Xiaoge, 2005).

It is imperative that Asian scholars take a fresh look at the FOE theories in the context of recent developments globally where the West see it as their right to 'protect' people under threat using human rights as a cover (as discussed in Chapter 6). Communication theories need to be formulated using Asian philosophical principles of communicating mindfully to promote harmony through cooperative communication models (see Seneviratne, 2018).

McQuail (2000) argues that to expose Eurocentric bias in Western media, communication researchers need to come up with a set of sub-questions, such as tracing the sources of Western media bias, and forms and levels of expression and solutions to solving such bias. 'It is hard to ignore the fact that most media theorizing has been done by "Western" scholars, living in and observing the media of their own countries and inevitably influenced by their own familiar social cultural context and its typical values' (McQuail 2000: 6).

From Negativity to Positive Approach

Gunaratne, Pearson and Senarath (2015) make the point that a Western approach to journalism is more concerned with a negative rather than a positive approach and generally means the immunity of the communication outlets from government control or censorship either directly through laws and regulation or indirectly through economics and political pressures.

Gunaratne et al. (2015: 5) espouses a 'mindful journalism' path based on Buddhist principles to overcome this negativity and bias. 'The aim of mindful journalism is not profit making', they argue, 'but truthful reporting without institutional restraints that might defile the clarity of the trained journalist's mind'.

In their book *Mindful Journalism and News Ethics in the Digital Era*, Gunaratne et al. (2015: 18) described the theory of mindful journalism on the basis of the Buddhist Four Noble Truths, thus:

> Mindful Journalism requires the journalist to understand the reasons for sorrow/unhappiness, and to desist from using his/her craft to increase desire (tanha) and clinging (upadana). We extracted this principle from the first and the second truths. The mindful journalist must distinguish between pleasure and happiness to understand the reality that cyclic existence (samsara) means suffering (dukha) that one can avoid only by attaining Nibbana or enlightenment. Pleasure is physical and short-lived whereas happiness is mental and long-lasting. The mindful journalist must not mislead the people that lasting happiness is attainable without purifying their minds from defilements. Enlightenment means eradication of all fetters—the mental state of supreme bliss or Nibbana. S/he should understand the reasons for the existence of unhappiness (dukha), and desist from using journalism to knowingly promote attachment (upadana) and desire (tanha).

There are two principles based on Asian traditional thinking that an Asian theory of media function could offer an alternative, that is, taking into account the idea that things are impermanent and subject to change, thus being mindful of this change and being able to understand, acknowledge and analyse it to assist people and society to adjust to these changes. The other, which naturally leads from the first, is that social harmony is paramount and journalism should play a more positive role rather than an adversarial role in assisting to manage, particularly the economic and social impermanence of societies/ communities.

Asia's philosophies are very much focused on how you guide the mind in the communication process to be mindful of what you are doing. UNESCO's own preamble can give us some food for thought. It declares that 'since wars begin in the minds of men, it is in the minds of men that the defences of peace must be constructed'.

Mindful Communication

Developing mindfulness is at the very heart of Buddhist teachings. Known as 'Vipassana', which means to see things as they really are, it is one of India's most ancient techniques of meditation. It was rediscovered by Gautama Buddha more than 2,500 years ago and was taught by him as a universal remedy for universal ills (art of living). Vipassana (mindfulness) is a way of self-transformation through self-observation.

Developing mindfulness has become a global movement today. This is a practice that could be cultivated to train our minds to practise mindful journalism in a secular setting. However, we need to be careful about the secularization of mindfulness. Buddhism teaches that mindfulness needs to be accompanied by the gathering of wisdom (*panna*) and that should result in the development of compassion and loving kindness in one's mind and actions. Thus, as the 'fourth estate' model of journalism says, the journalist has to be the friend of the people to protect them from governments' abuse of power, developing this wisdom and compassion should help in that process. This 'friend' also needs to have a compassionate mindset.

Burmese-Indian meditation master S. N. Goenka, who introduced Vipassana Meditation to the West in the 1980s, explains this attitude thus:

> Being sensitive to the suffering of others does not mean that you must become sad yourself. Instead you should remain calm and balanced, so that you could act to alleviate their suffering. (Hart 2012: 19)

It is this principle that could be applied to developing curriculum for journalism training. Mindfulness training for journalists should be seen in the context of training oneself to gather knowledge and wisdom to gain a deeper understanding of the issues you are reporting about and how to communicate with (rather than to) the society/community to improve their lives. One may argue that investigative journalism does that. Yes, but can we offer a more philosophical and ethical guide for that practice?

Dukka Path to Investigative Reporting

Each Noble Truth	Meanings	Duties to Deal with It
1. *Dukha*	Suffering, dissatisfaction	To comprehension of suffering. To know location of the problem
2. *Samudaya*	The cause or origin of dissatisfaction or suffering	To eradicate the cause of suffering. To diagnose of the origin
3. *Nirodha*	The cessation or extinction of suffering	To realize the cessation of suffering. To envision the solution
4. *Magga*	The path leading to the cessation of dissatisfaction or suffering	To follow the right path through actual practices

In the Buddhist philosophy, it is argued that the peoples' inability to understand and cope with impermanence leads to *dukka*—unhappiness or dissatisfaction. The path to understand it and eradicate or manage it is contained in the 'Four Noble Truths'. You do not need to be a Buddhist to adopt this path.

Let's apply it to journalism in a secular manner. What is the cause of underdevelopment? It is poverty. What is poverty? It is *dukha* (suffering). So we have to be mindful of this suffering. In order to understand it in a non-judgemental way, we need to approach the investigative journalism path with a compassionate mind willing to listen deeply to the people. This is where mindfulness training will play a part. Unfortunately in the West, in order to secularize mindfulness, this part of the training has been taken out. This is the wrong approach as compassion and loving kindness are very much part and parcel of practising any religion.

We need to investigate what are the origins of poverty? Is it wrong government policies? Is it exploitation of the poor by the more powerful such as in bonded labour or in sweatshops? Is it discrimination based on stereotypes or religious beliefs such as India's caste system or marginalization of migrants in Western societies? Is it unjust economic and trade regimes? Is it corruption—which is the ultimate manifestation of greed or craving (which are poisons in the Buddhist as well as other religious teachings)? We need to find out the views of the people suffering under poverty about these issues.

So what should we do or advocate for the eradication of poverty? What is the solution? Adversarial journalist would now begin to point fingers at corruption, bad governance, 'despotic' rulers, greedy business people, etc. Yes, that may be the reasons, but we need to find solutions and our communication methodology could adopt the eightfold *magga* (path) principles enshrined in the fourth of the Four Nobel Truths.

The role of a reporter is to understand all these, be mindful of the situation on the ground and set about to encourage or advocate policies that will lead to the eradication of poverty and suffering. This involves you practising compassion and loving kindness in your activities.

The Noble Eightfold Path has advocated eight steps to eradicate suffering. These are the *panna* or wisdom dimensions of Buddhist teachings. It includes right understanding, right thought, right speech, right action, right livelihood, right effort and right mindfulness.

First, we need to understand how poverty is created and continues to exist. We cannot just dismiss it—because we are comfortable—and say 'oh these people are lazy, uneducated or drug addicts'—if that is so, we need to think and investigate why that is so. That leads to the right thought. Once we understand through right thoughts, our new *panna* (wisdom) will lead us as a communicator to right speech and right action.

That communication would not be merely directed at the people who are suffering under poverty but also to those who are making them to suffer, such as unsympathetic or corrupt governing systems or those nasty, greedy business people who exploit the poor.

A lesson we have learned in the 21st century is that 'regime change' is not the answer, it brings more chaos and suffering as we have seen in the Arab Spring that has become an 'Arab Winter' today.

How can we make governments honest and business people compassionate and less greedy? Should development communication (reporting) involve encouraging, promoting and investing in social businesses rather than in stock markets? Thus, should we pay more attention to reporting about social business models and some of the success stories? Some micro-credit projects on the Grameen Bank model could be reported in this context, but we also need to be mindful of the exploitation of the poor involved in some of these projects run by NGOs.

So such right speech (reporting) could lead to right action—rather than overthrowing governments to bring in a better lot—who may turn out more corrupt. Peoples' pressure based on *panna* (wisdom cultivated by mindful reporting) should force governments to change policy.

Mindful reporting also needs to be communicated to the poor opportunities available (not encourage them to go to the streets and demonstrate which may not achieve anything in some societies, other than give them more *dukha* when they get arrested or violently attacked or even killed)—after we have understood their problems—communicating mindfully the sustainable development options may motive these people to take positive action to improve their livelihood rather than waste their time taking part in demonstrations and rallies.

In devising our mindful communication strategy, we need to communicate to eradicate what Thai Buddhist social activist Sulak Sivaraksa calls the 'structural violence' of our economic systems. We need to be mindful of the fact (as discussed already in this book) that much of our global media networks, as well as local ones, are owned and/or controlled by arms manufacturers, oil companies and large business conglomerates. It is in their interest to have a large reservoir of poor living under poverty to be exploited for cheap labour to feed the consumerist appetite of the rich.

We need to bring development rights (as discussed in Chapter 6) —spiced with development of compassion and loving kindness—to the forefront of the global human rights agenda. Peoples' right to be freed of unjust economic sanctions should be a top priority in such reporting, especially of international affairs. Development communication/reporting needs to promote a compassionate mindset among global leaders as well.

As we have discussed in Chapter 7, development reporters must be acutely aware of the unjust 'free' trade agreements that are negotiated behind close doors, which could make essential medicines unaffordable for a majority of the world's people, take away the rights of governments elected by the people to device their development policies and other deals that will make the rich richer and even drive the middle classes to poverty. These are the 'structural violence' of the evolving global development model based on 'free' trade, which development communicators have to address. After all, the East India Company came to Asia to promote 'free' trade and ended up colonizing and plundering Asia's resources—both natural and human.

We should not point fingers only at the West. We rightly condemn slavery practised by the Europeans 300 years ago or the apartheid system in South Africa until very recently, but today we have a system of modern-day slavery that is practised mainly by Asians and Arabs. That is called 'labour migration', and recruitment agents treat human being as commodities. This is what Sivaraksa calls 'structural violence'.

Another issue we need to mindfully investigate is the global banking system and the way they give out loans that may drive people into more poverty in the name of development. Banks like the Asian Development Bank (ADB) and the WB are giving loans to governments to provide 'clean' drinking water to the poor, when, in fact, they are helping to take away a freely available resource from the people to give to companies to profit from it. When farmers across Asia protest about it, if we are not mindful of what is happening on the ground, we don't listen to the farmers with compassion, what we read in the media is as follows: farmers as troublemakers; 'mobs' disturbing public order as reflected by the report that appeared on the front page of Singapore's *Straits Times* (Tang 2000, sucidial Farm Policy), with the heading 'Mob Overshadows ADB Meeting'. These farmers were protesting during an ADB meeting in Thailand over a loan given to the Thai government to privatize their water supplies in the name of providing 'clean drinking water' to the people.

Today, we often hear of farmer suicides in India and other parts of Asia. Let me refer to you an article, which I did over 20 years ago and it was widely published across Asia and even in Africa.

I was in Australia at the time and I read a one-paragraph news clip in the local newspaper about 11 rice farmers committing suicide in Sri Lanka. I knew at the time that Sri Lanka has just signed into a SAP with the IMF that had forced the government to cut subsidies, especially to their rice farmers. These SAPs have been singled out by Sivaraksa as root causes of 'structural violence'.

I did this story for IPS from Sri Lanka by visiting the area and listening deeply to the concerns of the rice farmers. I even attended a Sunday morning meeting of a rice farmers association where they discussed their problems. When I met them, my fears were justified. Because of the SAP, the government had cut fertility subsidies, stopped low-interest loans from state banks and closed paddy purchasing centres in most rural area—these centres purchased paddy at a government-guaranteed price.

As a result, the farmers were thrown into the arms of unscrupulous businessmen, who were moneylenders, paddy purchasers and fertilizers providers, often all in one—they lent money at higher interest rates than the state banks—who were not lending anymore at the low rates—and just before the harvesting season they flooded the market with rice and brought down the price of paddy. Thus, the businessmen were making money at both ends and driving the rice farmers into poverty and ultimately, when they could not pay the debts and feed the family, to commit suicide.

Such suicides are still happening across Asia and other parts of the world. Recently, there were some reported suicides in Sri Lanka too—often governments blamed it on drug pushers. Even worse, mischievous journalists or politicians could turn this into a religious conflict because many traders in Sri Lanka are Muslims and farmers are Buddhists. But it has nothing to do with religious identities.

Mindfulness is a training in being non-judgemental in the spirit of free inquiry. Guided by the philosophical principles, Gunaratne (in Gunaratne et al. 2015: 5) argues that mindful journalism could establish a set of norms that perceptive human beings could use to compare and contrast with the traits of 'commodity-oriented news' served in a hurry with all its warts or defilements. 'Mindful journalism requires no written code of ethics, but only a set of guidelines acceptable to most people in the world'.

Gunaratne believes that at a time when the moral fabric of mainstream journalism is losing its relevance, mindful journalism could provide a logical moral framework to fill that gap. The benefits that it could bring to both the journalist and sources—as well as society in a broader sense—is an effective truth-seeking and truth-telling mechanism.

Putting Mindful Communication to Practice

An article published in the *Bangkok Post* provides a good example of what mindful reporting of Asia's 'conflict-driven' (according to adversarial reporting) societies could look like and how such reporting could lead to solving conflicts rather than adding fuel to it.

The article by Johanna Son,[11] titled 'Looking for "ASEAN Way" in Rohingya Crisis' is a good piece of mindful reporting on the Rohingya issue in Myanmar. This is a far cry from the Buddhist bashing, hectoring style of journalism from the Western media that is reproduced in the regional media outlets.

Being Asian herself, the journalist is mindful to the fact that hectoring type of journalism (as done by the Western media) has led to anti-foreign sentiments and xenophobia building up in the country and that is not conducive to finding a solution to a serious socio-economic and political crisis. She also points out that it will push Myanmar into instability at a crucial time of nation building.

Her article reflects the 'mindful critically appreciative' style of journalism that a growing number of Asian communication scholars are now advocating. A number of us who are Asian communication scholars are trying to introduce these skills into Asian journalism programmes.

Son's article reflects the values we are trying to inculcate into young Asian communicators: to be mindful and critically appreciative of the socio-economic and cultural sensitivities of the issues you cover and contribute towards understanding the complexities and nuances of working out a solution. Her article does not talk about a Buddhist–Muslim conflict but looks at the deeper issues that underline peoples' concerns from all sides.

She refers to the legitimate concerns of Myanmar people about the involvement of foreign-born fighters in the Arakan Rohingya Salvation Army, which attacked police posts in Myanmar's Western Rakhine state in August 2017—an issue the Western media prefers to ignore or dismiss as Myanmar army (or Buddhist) propaganda. She

---

[11] https://www.pressreader.com/thailand/bangkok-post/20180326/281732680030208 (accessed on 18 June 2019).

also acknowledges the 'massive military response' and the refugee crisis created.

The article points out the socio-economic problems of Rakhine state where 78 per cent of the people (Rohingyas as well as Buddhists) live in poverty, and how ASEAN has facilitated study tours to Indonesia for both Rakhine (Buddhists) and Rohingya (Muslim) leaders to see how multicultural and multiracial issues are tackled there. It also talks about how (Muslim majority) Indonesia is working with (Buddhist majority) Myanmar in building hospitals and schools to help alleviate poverty in the region. While there is reference to indifferences to refugees and some criticism of ASEAN policy, yet the article looks for solutions through cooperation rather than blaming someone or calling for 'war crimes' investigations.

It is a welcome sign that the article does not use words such as 'war crimes', 'crimes against humanity' and 'genocide'—words that are adopted by the Western media and their human rights NGOs in a hypocritical manner (as discussed in Chapter 6). The article also points out that it will take years to resolve the problem and most Rohingyas may never return to Myanmar as part of a deal. The issue of statelessness and a lack of refugee policy in ASEAN are also touched upon.

The complex issues raised in the article reflect the journalist's deeper understanding of the region and nuances of its political dealings. The subtle message in the article is that this is a political issue with national security implications, and it is not necessarily a religious issue or it should not be treated as merely a religious conflict and hold one party responsible for it.

Perhaps the Asian media could go further towards helping to resolve the crisis by discussing issues such as whether Muslim Malaysia could help out by taking Rohingya refugees and settling them there as Malaysia faces a huge labour problem and currently imports thousands of Bangladeshis, Indians, Sri Lankans, Indonesians and Filipinos on migrant labour visas. Sometime ago, the Malaysian PM and Islamist groups showed great concern for the plight of Rohingyas fleeing Myanmar. Would they now make a positive contribution to help resolve the conflict? It is worth discussing this in the Asian media from a socio-economic and immigration policy (as opposed to refugee) perspective.

Also, Australia has expressed human rights concerns about the Rohingya refugee flow. They have huge tracks of ideal land in Queensland and Northern Territory around Darwin where Rohingyas could be settled and trained to become farmers of tropical produce. Who knows in time to come they may contribute to making Australia the bread basket of Southeast Asia. Indochinese refugees who settled in Australia in the 1980s are now running large farms that export tropical vegetables and fruits to Asia.

More articles like these are needed in the Asian media to wean us away from the adversarial tradition of Western journalism. Also, that major socio-economic changes happening in the region could be done in an orderly and peaceful manner—without creating religious or ethnic conflicts. Asian media needs encouragement to get into this practice of mindful journalism and contribute to encouraging cooperation and resolving problems without creating social chaos.

Communicating for Sustainable Development

SDGs have become the new buzzword in international development thinking. But can we achieve these goals if we deny that the current development model is the biggest obstacle to it? How can we report the impacts on communities through the peoples' voices without it leading to socio-economic conflicts and instability? Such reporting needs to lead to better development policies both at national/local level and internationally.

Climatic change is today a major fad in development or environmental reporting. Yet its impacts at local level such as devastating typhoons or floods or droughts cannot be reported just as events, but processes with a global dimensions.

Let's look at a couple of examples.

Devastating Typhoons in the South Pacific

Pointing out that three tiny South Pacific nations—Kiribati, Tuvalu and Marshall islands—are 'destined to slip below the waves altogether', Fijian Prime Minister Josaia Bainimarama, in a keynote speech at the UNESCAP annual meeting in May 2016, appealed to the international community to help Fiji and the other South Pacific island states to build resilience to the impact of climatic change, which he described as the 'terror of the extreme weather events'.[12] He told ministers and senior officials from over 65 countries in the Asia-Pacific region that the industrial nations 'must use a portion of the wealth they have derived from the carbon emissions of their industries to assist those of us who aren't as wealthy as they are and are bearing the brunt of the crisis they created'.

Just three months earlier, the biggest cyclone ever to hit landfall in the Southern Hemisphere slammed into the Fiji Islands with wind speed of over 300 km/hour, killing 44 people and destroying over 40,000 homes and 229 schools. The WB has estimated the total cost of damage at around US$1.4 billion. 'A single extreme weather event scoring a direct hit on us could devastate our economies for many years to come ... and reverse all the development gains that we have worked so hard to achieve', noted Bainimarama, adding a sobering message that the SDGs will have no meaning in the South Pacific without concerted assistance from the international community to help the small vulnerable island nations to weather these threats.

Such help does not involve international disaster relief agencies descending on their countries under the glare of television cameras to provide reconstruction assistance after a disaster has struck. The Fijian leader, as well as many other ministers from the region, pointed out that what they need are material to build houses and other infrastructure, which could withstand future cyclones. Perhaps, if one were to report from the human-centric perspective of the people on the ground

---

[12] https://kalingasen.wordpress.com/2016/05/21/south-pacific-seeks-action-to-solve-climate-terror-not-of-its-making/ (accessed on 18 June 2019).

(living in the communities) this is also what they would say. They do not want to run into shelters every time a typhoon hits them waiting for foreigners to bring them relief supplies. They would prefer to be able to lock themselves up inside their houses for a few hours or days in the knowledge that the structure of the house will withstand the onslaught of the winds and the storms.

Farmer Suicides in India

Climatic change has been linked to 60,000 farmer suicides in India in the past three decades, according to a study by the University of California. The report by *South China Morning Post* [13] focuses on the despair in the farming belts of India and a protest by Tamil Nadu farmers who brought skulls and bones of dead farmers to Delhi. It pointed out that in 2016 the Indian government had launched a US$1.3 billion insurance scheme to protect against crop failures and the governments of Punjab and Uttar Pradesh had passed farm debt waivers at 'enormous cost to the public purse to appease the demands of the agricultural sector, which commands strong political sway'.

However, a report from ThinkProgress[14] two years later gave a more people-focused perspective on the same issue. Farmer suicides are doubly devastating because they mark the death of a breadwinner and often mean the loss of a season of crops as well. The report further said quoting prominent environmental activist Dr Vandana Shiva that genetically modified seeds, specifically those sold by the agricultural giant Monsanto, are driving farmers to lose control of their own farming practices. She claimed that Monsanto's proprietary policies— which forbid farmers from planting, selling or even accidentally growing seeds from Monsanto's patented crops—push farmers to the brink. Shiva refers to the seeds as 'suicide seeds'. However, Monsanto argues that its crops require less pesticide purchase and less loss of yield—meaning that farmers who opted for its genetically modified

---

[13] http://www.scmp.com/news/asia/south-asia/article/2104987/climate-change-linked-60000-farmer-suicides-india-over-last (accessed on 18 June 2019).
[14] https://thinkprogress.org/behind-indias-epidemic-of-farmer-suicides-fa820ad674f3/ (accessed on 18 June 2019).

seeds would be more successful than those who use traditional seeds. But Shiva has countered, claiming that Monsanto drove up the price of seeds 8,000 per cent, and that 'the high costs of purchased seed and chemicals have created a debt trap'.

Unfortunately, the article does not go as far as going into the farms and speaking to farmers to find out who is right and what policies the governments may need to adopt to alleviate the suffering of farmers.

Compensation for Slum Dwellers in Phnom Penh

In recent years, 'land grabbing' for so-called development has been a hot issue in Cambodia, with many of the city poor forced to flee their homes in slum settlements when the folk-lifters come in. From time to time, the foreign media, in particular, has reported about the issue focusing on the battles fought between the poor and the police.

June 2015 report by Radio Free Asia (RFA)[15] is an example of the type of reports that have been done by foreign media on the issue. It shows the demolition squads at work, people protesting and throwing stones at the police, local residents complaining about lack of compensation given to them, while a government officials defends it, saying what was given is more than enough for them to repair the houses, after some of their land was taken for a sewerage and water system to be installed.

The RFA report was done basically from the peoples' viewpoint, but it was still in the framework of an adversarial report. The question here is how can the news media take the necessary extra step to create a communication platform between the people and the government so that these issues could be ironed out before the fork-lifters are sent? When there is an authoritarian government and the people are too poor to fight back, it is not that easy to create such a communication flow. But the adversarial style of journalism can only expose the problem, and sometimes it could add fuel to it.

---

[15] https://www.youtube.com/watch?v=JG8hbcYxVOQ (accessed on 18 June 2019).

Nepali journalist Dixit (1997) points out the problem we face in reporting such events.

> Traditional journalism schools teach you to look for the counterpoint to make stories interesting. They tell us it is controversy, the disagreement, that gives the story its tension. Most reportage therefore sounds like a quarrel, opposites pitted against each other, even when the point of argument may be minor and the two sides are in overall agreement. The technique of press interviews is to provoke the head of the Olympics drug testing committee to make a nasty remark, and play that back to the chief swimming coach of the Chinese team, and ask him to comment. The next day the headline is readymade: 'China Blasts Olympic Committee'. Conflict is the adrenaline of the macho media. But this kind of 'on the one hand this, on the other hand that' reporting can be an obstacle in spreading clarity about global problems'.

Three Types of Objectivity—The Sainath Formula

Award-winning Indian journalist P. Sainath[16] argues that there are three types of objectivity—one is desirable, another is genuine and the other is a fraud. He describes the three as follows:

> The first kind of objectivity is the objectivity of the pure sciences. Now, that is admirable, desirable, but not replicable in journalism. Because, say, suppose someone claims they have created cold fusion ... a thousand scientists across the country, across the world, are able to replicate those conditions in a lab and check the veracity of the claim. You and I can't do that as journalists. Our labs are entirely different.... The laboratory is the laboratory of daily life and human beings are incredibly different from chemical compounds. The objectivity of the pure sciences, where something can be verified, checked, and examined, that is very desirable and it's admirable but it's not replicable beyond a certain degree in the social sciences and in journalism.

[16] https://psainath.org/sitting-down-with-p-sainath/ (accessed on 18 June 2019).

The second thing is the doctrine of objectivity, which I consider a fraud and really ends up giving the last word to authority and the powerful. Incidentally, all this doctrine of balance and two sides goes out the window when the major interests of the newspaper or the channel or the country it represents are threatened. There is a difference between objectivity and the doctrine of objectivity. The doctrine of objectivity, which is the gift you guys give the world, is a fraud. It defends the powerful. It always weakens the arguments against power.

[We] have tried for a third kind of objectivity that I am very supportive of, which is your personal objectivity, the honesty with which you deal with a subject. The first thing about being honest is to accept that our value systems have an impact on us. Now, the day that we accept that journalism is a very subjective art is the day we begin striving for objectivity. Now, if I start with the myth that I am objective then you will be actually committing a serious disservice to your readers, or viewers, or listeners. If you start from the point of view that we all have our deep subjectivities, we all are affected by our sensitivities and our socialization then you know what to look out for. You know the biases and the prejudices to watch out for when you write.

Such subjective reporting values, in crafting what you believe is the truth, were discussed in Chapter 4. What we are doing here is bringing in the compassion and delusion aspects of Eastern philosophy.

Another interesting angle to pursue in terms of mindful journalism as a follow-up to the farmers protests about the ADB loan would be to look at the links between farmers' poverty and prostitution in Thailand. The Southeast Asian Buddhist kingdom has a worldwide fame—or rather a shame—for its well-established prostitution, sex trade and human trafficking trade.

Puntarigvivat (2013: 214–215) argues that the structure of the world economic system makes it difficult for Thai farmers to sustain their families through agriculture. 'In the Thai local tradition, especially in the north, parents prefer the birth of a daughter to that of a son', he notes.

Usually both a Thai son and daughter hold to traditional values of filial piety, but a daughter is especially valued because she can do more for her parents ... it's easier for women to find a 'job' than men because they can quickly become prostitutes (in the massage parlours) earning more money than factory workers. This has led to poor rural families to send their daughters to towns and cities for 'jobs' to support their family.

Another area that could benefit from human-centric reporting is tourism. This is an industry that is highly labour-oriented service industry, and it is also an industry where there is a high degree of people-to-people contact. Often, reports on tourism will focus on the economic data, exploitation of tourists or on prostitution and other vices associated with the industry. But there is growing trend in Asia, particularly in the Mekong region of community-based tourism. This area needs a lot of human-centric reporting to ensure that community-based tourism really assists the community to be self-reliant and they are consulted in planning tourism projects and programmes.

Recently, Channel News Asia's Desmond Ng[17] did an interesting investigative report about how China's BRI project has created a tourism boom in Cambodia's coastal town of Sihanoukville. In two years, Sihanoukville has seen nearly three dozen Chinese-run casinos spring up with another 70 under construction. Thus, this coastal town has been reshaped into a casino hub—with tourism numbers, foreign investment and the economy all booming. But when Ng spoke to the local people, he found that not everyone is happy with the rapid development. Restaurant owners lamented how their businesses have suffered, as Chinese tourists and investors prefer to dine in the newly opened Chinese-run restaurants. Some family-run restaurant owners have been evicted from their premises by landlords, who prefer to rent the building to Chinese investors. It has also invited an influx of Chinese-organized crime networks. On the other hand, locals say that industrial parks set up by Chinese investors are creating jobs for locals.

---

[17] https://www.channelnewsasia.com/news/cnainsider/china-belt-road-casino-boom-sihanoukville-cambodia-phnom-penh-10846730 (accessed on 18 June 2019).

Thus, the report gives a different perspective to development that you may get if you only spoke to the government officials and Chinese investors, and mined data provided by official sources.

People-centric Journalism Is Not about Using People for Propaganda

The article 'Children, Media and Political Agendas' written by Malaysian Islamic scholar Dr Chandra Muzaffar, who is also the president of the International Movement for a JUST World, reflects a mindful journalism strategy (Box 10.1). He focuses on the *dukka* of children caught up in the terrible conflicts in the Middle East and the need to address these issues divorced from political agendas.

Box 10.1: Children, Media and Political Agendas

The image of five-year-old Omran Daqneesh rescued from the rubble in the aftermath of a devastating airstrike in Aleppo on 17 August 2016 has reverberated around the globe. Every major media outlet—from the *NYT* and *The Wall Street Journal* to the BBC and Al Jazeera—has highlighted the picture. It shows a little boy 'sitting in an ambulance after the attack, his face, arms and legs caked in blood and dust...' It has become 'a symbol for the suffering of children in Syria's brutal five-year conflict'.

However, Chinese State broadcaster, CCTV, has suggested that 'the video may have been partially staged and criticized the way it was used to stir pro-rebel sympathies'. The footage of Omran was released by a group called the White Helmets, which, it is alleged, is closely linked to the British military. The author of the footage Mahmoud Rslan, who describes himself as a war journalist and activist, has ties to the Harakat Nour al-Din al-Zenki, a rebel group which in July circulated a video showing the beheading of a 12-year-old Palestinian boy. It is said that the group had also conducted kidnappings and torture of journalists, aid workers and civilians in Aleppo. It was considered a 'moderate' rebel group by the USA and received weapons from it.

It is significant that initially segments of the Western media blamed the airstrike that injured Omran upon the Russian air force. Russian authorities not only denied the baseless allegation but also accused the Western media of 'cynical use of this tragedy in anti-Russian propaganda material'. They argued that 'the damage shown in the footage published by world media outlets indicates a blast less powerful than

---

(Continued)

(Continued)

> that produced by an aerial bomb, considering that some of the glass in nearby buildings was not shattered'. They instead suggested 'that it may have been caused by a mortar shell ...'
>
> The cynical manipulation of tragedies in the Syrian conflict has occurred on numerous occasions. One other example that also featured a small boy was the case of three-year-old Aylan Kurdi who was drowned off a Turkish beach on 2 September 2015 as he and his family sought to cross the Mediterranean to reach Europe. The media had hoped that the infant's death would expose the cruelty of the Bashar Al-Assad government in Damascus and persuade the Western public to endorse direct, active US-led military intervention in Syria aimed at ousting Bashar. It did not happen. Instead, Europe was forced to reappraise its stance towards refugees and compelled to accommodate a portion of them.
>
> The media's biased attitude and its utter lack of moral responsibility becomes even more blatant when one considers what happened in Iraq two decades ago.
>
> As a result of Anglo-American sanctions imposed through the UN Security Council, as many as 576,000 Iraqi children may have died in the 1990s. Was this stark fact projected through the principal media channels at that time as a way of igniting the world's conscience so that young lives would not be snuffed out because of the desire of the powerful to control Iraqi oil and strengthen Israel's position in the region? Did anyone see the victims of these inhuman sanctions on the front page of the *Financial Times* or through some special programme on CNN?
>
> The examples we have provided illustrate a crucial point about the media. When the major media outlets dramatize a particular event, especially in relation to children and ignore or downplay other episodes, they are advancing the political agenda of some powerful actor. We should not be deceived. We would do well to remember the words of John Pilger, one of the most honest journalists of our time, 'It is not enough for journalists to see themselves as mere messengers without understanding the hidden agendas and myths that surround it.'

Source: Chandra Muzaffar (JUST Features, Kuala Lumpur, Malaysia, 29 August 2016).
Note: This is an edited version of the original article.

This is exactly the path mindful journalist must tread. There would be many follow-up stories to Dr Muzaffar's article, if one were to visit the conflict areas. In Chapter 4, there was a discussion about an article I did from Baghdad in 1994 on the impact of UN-led economic sanctions on the children of Iraq after visiting a children hospital in the Iraqi capital and speaking to doctors and people working there. At that time, no one was talking about mindful journalism, but now I realize that this is what I practised at the time. There are many such stories to be told from Syria, Iraq, Yemen, Libya, etc., today. If written with *panna* (wisdom) and *metta* (compassion), the plight of the children in the Middle East could move the world, as long as it is not used for propaganda because it attracts denial from the other side, and the real issue of the suffering of the people gets drowned out.

In an interview with me in Kuala Lumpur, Dr Muzaffar[18] argued that there are major lessons Southeast Asia has to learn from the conflicts in the Middle East.

> Major lesson Southeast Asia can learn is to preserve independence don't get into a situation you become beholden not only to governments of the West but also NGOs ... you have to be careful how the media in our region report about the people here and elsewhere... most of the time Malaysia learns about what happens in Vietnam or elsewhere in Asia through Western news agencies (about) why your neighbor is in a mess and so on, always through their lenses. This is something, which is not healthy at all, we have to develop our own mechanism, and part of this situation is that we have to blame ourselves. We have not given enough support to indigenous attempt to develop news networks or support such initiatives—to interact with one another. I think it is partly because of our own selfish interests. Because governments don't want independent media to develop (also) partly because of moneyed interests, they don't see the value of this. Our foundations, billionaires, etc., also our own civil society groups, because they are very enamoured with the West. We need to put the blame on intellectuals in universities who don't see the role of the media in articulating regional interactions.

What Is Different—East versus West Battle

One is entitled to ask what would differentiate the path discussed in this chapter, from the existing ones. Is this an exercise in East versus

---

[18] Interview with the author in Kuala Lumpur, 25 November 2016.

West battle? It is certainly not and challenging the West is not trying to create conflict. Using an Eastern metaphor, this is an exercise in developing *panna* (wisdom) to gain insights and be enlightened to the diversity of perspectives available for communicating in today's information-rich society.

Today, we are at an age where the West is going gaga in adopting mindfulness to improve its health services and stressful lifestyles. Mindfulness is at the root of the ancient Asian philosophical approach to a healthy enlightened lifestyle, which the Buddha taught over 2,500 years ago. But the Asians have forgotten it, perhaps as a result of 500 years of European colonization and indoctrination that makes them feel inferior in the face of 'wisdom' from the West. The late Malaysian scholar Dr Syed Alatas explained it well in devising his theories on the 'Captive Mind' (Alatas 2000).

Imperialism is defined, in the political and historical sense of the word, as the subjugation of one people by another for the advantage of the dominant one. There are many ways this could be done. But the theory of the 'Captive Mind' deals with intellectual imperialism. In pure imperialism, the imperial country regard its colonies as sources of raw material and as markets for its industrial goods sometimes manufactured from raw material taken from the colonies. Alatas argues that intellectual imperialism also takes a similar form.

> Data is from this region (Asia), raw data on certain topics are collected in this region, processed and manufactured in England in the form of books or articles, and then sold here. On the whole, people of this region including their scholars were used mainly as informants. We are continuously bombarded by foreign publications. I am not using the term 'foreign' in a judgmental way, but I'm merely referring to the origin of things. Most of our own history was written by scholars from abroad. They came here, gathered the raw intellectual materials, went back, published their books, and exported the finished product back to the country of fieldwork. (Alatas 2000: 25)

Thus, Alatas argues that the imperial powers practise this imperialism by capturing your mind in the way you think. It leads to many traits such as tutelage (you know less than them), conformity (you conform to their academic theories and methodologies) and subordination (secondary role you are required to play). 'Intellectual imperialism conditions the mental attitude of those who have been caught in its web', argues Alatas (2000: 30). 'Apart from encouraging docility, it stifles creativity.'

Be it Asian communication scholars uncritically adopting theories of communication that have been framed and developed in a Western social context; or Thai media reporting uncritically in their front page how local football fans turned up in their thousands to welcome the British football champions Leicester City to Bangkok because it is owned by a Thai tycoon; or Asian media carrying pictures and reports from Western media sources of President Obama being mobbed by Vietnamese youth in Ho Chi Minh City without asking the question 'why couldn't Obama apologize for American war crimes in Vietnam such as using napalm bombs (chemical weapons)' dropped not that far from the city; all these point to what one may call the impact of Intellectual and cultural imperialism on the Asian mindset.

'Middle Path' Journalism

Addressing a Forum in Geneva in 2011 to mark the 25th anniversary of the UN Declaration on the 'Right to Development', Nobel Economics laureate Joseph Stiglitz[19] noted, referring to the US and European economic crisis of 2008:

> Today we know that the gross domestic product—known as GDP—is not a good measure of success of development. For instance, in the last three decades, the GDP per capita in the United States increased while income per capita for the majority of Americans decreased.

As a result, while the GDP may increase, the well-being of citizens may go down. As we see in 'Occupy Wall Street' movement, markets have failed a very large portion of citizens, he added.

---

[19] https://www.ohchr.org/EN/NewsEvents/Pages/PeopleAtTheCentre.aspx (accessed on 18 June 2019).

'Political leaders seem to have forgotten that health care, education, housing and a fair administration of justice are not commodities for sale to the few but rather rights to which all are entitled without discrimination', added UNHRC Chief Navi Pillay, speaking at the same event. 'Anything we do in the name of economic policy or development should be designed to advance these rights, and, at the very least, should do nothing to undermine their realization.'

Mindful journalism drawing from the Asian philosophical traditions could be adopted to craft a model of journalism that could address the aforementioned concern. Rather than listening to economists from the IMF or the WB, we should listen to the leaders of Bhutan or the ideas that were espoused by the late King Bhumibol Adulyadej of Thailand at the height of the Asian economic crisis in 1997. Bhutan, which has a Gross National Happiness (GNH) Index,[20] aims to gauge the happiness and well-being of its people and give equal importance to non-economic aspects of their well-being. The Sufficiency Economy[21] is a philosophy developed by the Thai King through his royal remarks over three decades. It adopts a Buddhist approach to economics emphasizing the middle path, a way of thinking, in which, no one lives too extravagantly or too thriftily. It encourages people to live in a way where they consume only what they really need, choose products carefully and consider their impact on others and the planet. Further afield, Ecuador and Bolivia have also framed their constitutions around the idea of *buen vivir*[22] (living well), which calls for sustainable development, peace and harmony, according to a social development report prepared by the UNHRC in 2012.

Bhutanese scholar Dorji Wangchuk (2016) argues that middle path journalism based on Buddhist philosophical roots could be a useful paradigm to practise journalism to serve the community. He argues:

[20] https://www.grossnationalhappiness.com/ (accessed on 18 June 2019).
[21] http://hdr.undp.org/sites/default/files/thailand_2007_en.pdf (accessed on 18 June 2019).
[22] Eduardo Gudynas, a leading scholar on *buen vivir*, talks about the limits of capitalism, consuming less and developing a sense of the collective (see https://www.theguardian.com/sustainable-business/blog/buen-vivir-philosophy-south-america-eduardo-gudynas [accessed on 18 June 2019]).

Although the concept is still a work in progress, middle-path journalism could be defined as a human-centric model that takes into account the Values and Vision of a country in the practice of media and communication. Middle Path journalism strives to avoid the extremes by finding the delicate balance (the middle-path) in the practice and use of all forms of media as well as in the consumption and analysis of media contents.[23] Middle path journalism is thus anchored in two concepts—Values and Vision. Values are a set of principles or standards of human behaviour that determines one's judgment and belief of what is important in life within one's place in society. Vision, on the other hand, is the long-term stated goal of a nation that provides the strategic direction of what it to be achieved collectively—and as a nation.

Finding an Economically Viable Model

When one looks at economically viable news media models, what I would call the Murdoch and Lee models stand out.

Rupert Murdoch-owned News Corporation's famous news formula includes what Arsenault and Castells (2008) call the 'Four S'—scare headlines, sex, scandals and sensation. This formula has helped many of his acquisitions—some of which were losing money before he purchased them—to make money. In turn, many other local rivals have followed suit, with India providing a good example with Murdoch's foray into the country in the 1990s with the purchase of Star TV generating a news media, especially on television, that thrives on 'infotainment'. Arnab Goswami's success (as discussed in Chapter 3) is a good example. The audiences this model attracts—perhaps to be entertained rather than be informed—have given such media enormous power to shape the public political agenda. As Arsenault and Castells (2008) argue, 'the perception that Murdoch wields influence over public opinion is a critical battering ram through which NewsCorp has obtained political and regulatory favors'.

---

[23] Media is to be understood as any form of mediated communication in traditional media, social media and in the new technological platforms.

The small island state of Singapore has had a remarkable history in the past five decades while it transformed from a 'Third World' fishing port to one of the world's richest and most modern nations. Without any natural resources to exploit, Singapore achieved this success by mobilizing its human resources. Its founding father Lee Kuan Yew has often said that the media played a great role in this endeavour. But his media model was not the 'fourth estate' model. For him, the media was one of the three institutions in Singapore he had to control, the other two being the Treasury and the Armed Forces.

'The mass media can help to present Singapore's problems simply and clearly, and then explain how if they support certain programmes and policies, these problems can be solved', he told the International Press Institute (IPI) meeting in 1971 after they had criticized his media model.

> More important, we want the mass media to reinforce, not undermine, the cultural values and social attitudes being inculcated in our schools and universities.... The freedom of the press must be subordinated to the integrity of Singapore and the primacy of purpose of an elected government. (Cheong 2015)

This is also the model communist countries adopted, where the media's main role is to explain the policies of the Communist Party to the people. Most of the MSM in Singapore is owned by the government, but it is run on a commercial structure with government subsidies and tight editorial controls.

Both Murdoch and Lee models are certainly not the media the Libertarian Media Function Theory prescribed as a 'free media' model. Perhaps the middle path journalism what Wangchuck described earlier as a 'human-centric model that takes into account the Values and Vision of a country' could be practised to a certain extent in Lee's model but not necessarily in Murdoch's sensationalism and entertainment-driven model.

As former Singaporean newspaper editor B. N. Balji argued in Chapter 2, for independent media to be established, you need philanthropy journalism. Identifying people who are willing to spend money because they think this is good for the future of the community and country. As pointed out in Chapter 9, *Malaysiakini* offers a possible model, and newspapers like London's *Guardian* and America's *Huffington Post* are also showing us that through a combination of reader and advertiser-supported revenue streams, high-quality independent news media could be established using cyberspace as its delivery system. Yet the latter two already had a brand name when they embarked on this strategy.

Another latest trend is what is called 'crowd sourcing journalism' but critics argue that this may be a ruse by media companies that are losing advertising revenue to social media and are unable to employ as many journalists as they wish to, to get contents for free.

GuardianWitness is part of *The Guardian*'s open journalism initiative that was introduced in 2013, based around diversity and plurality. Its origins appear to be based on a report the company published in 2011 on how to sustain journalism and the newspaper. *The Guardian* decided that user-generated content would be the future for the news organization. At GuardianWitness, *Guardian* journalists request and review content from the public and the best pieces feature on the *Guardian*'s website.

News is about 'Interpretative Storytelling' and if crowdsourcing is the future of journalism, then the question will arise 'who is a journalist?' Until and unless a viable economic model is found that enables 'independent interpretative storytelling' to be told without fear or favour, the profession of journalism, as we know it today, is on very shaky grounds. Human-centric 'middle path' journalism that respects values and provides a vision for the country/community to live harmoniously may be the way to go, but it needs a viable economic model.

'We are in an era when we have more communication tools than ever before in order to reach out to people across the globe', argues Geary (Quinn 2013: 14).

> Those people across the globe are reaching out to their friends and other people around the world to talk about stories. Bringing the two worlds together and collaborating creates greater, richer, more interesting stories. We become better journalists and we do better journalism as a result when we bring those two worlds together.

Bringing these two worlds together is an important role media needs to play today, in order to counter the 'clash of civilizations' narratives of both mainstream and social media, as we have discussed in this book. The challenge is to find the economic model that could sustain such media. Unfortunately, with a paucity of such media, many minds are beginning to decrease its aperture as economic insecurities and loss of privileges begin to bite in.

Indian novelist and activist Arundhati Roy (2004: 45) whose mother is a Malayali (Indian) Syrian Christian argues:

> After the September 11th terrorist strikes in New York and Washington, the mainstream media's blatant performance as the US government's mouthpiece, its display of vengeful patriotism, its willingness to publish Pentagon press handouts as news, and its explicit censorship of dissenting opinion became the butt of some pretty black humour in the rest of the world.
> Then the New York Stock Exchange crashed, bankrupt airline companies appealed to the government for financial bailouts, and there was talk of circumventing patent laws in order to manufacture drugs to fight the anthrax scare (much more important and urgent of course than the production of generics to fight AIDS in Africa).
> Suddenly, it began to seem as though the twin myths of Free Speech and Free Market might come crashing down alongside the Twin Towers of the World Trade Centre.
> But of course that never happened. The myths live on.

Let's find ways to debunk this myth. This book was about the 'myth of the free media', and thus I had to be critical of the existing media models in order to examine the myths. In this chapter, I have tried to suggest some new thinking and pathways to train and practise a new form of journalism—perhaps we should not call it journalism, rather let us call the new journalist a 'communicator' because the word journalist is too tainted with the notion of adversarial reporting and watchdog journalism that has become a lapdog for powerful interests.

APPENDIX A

Obama's Final Asian Tour 'Unpivots' US War Crimes in Asia

Bangkok (IDN | Lotus News Features): President Barack Obama's 'pivot to Asia' policy that realigned US' relationship to Asia is largely regarded favourably in this region. Yet his farewell visit to Asia 'unpivoted' a darker side of America's involvement in Asia—of horrendous war crimes committed by the USA in Laos in the 1960s and 1970s for which Washington is yet to be held accountable.

Laos, the tiny landlocked country in Southeast Asia inhabited by 6.9 million people, is one of the most heavily bombed countries in the world, per capita, following the Vietnam War. The dangerous unexploded ordnance (UXO) left behind is a sad legacy of the war that continues to be a threat to the lives of rural populations and a hindrance to the use of land for agriculture and development.

Between 1964 and 1973, a secret CIA-led operation to cut supplies to the Viet Cong resulted in 2 million tons of ordinance being dropped on Laos—more than the combined total dropped on both Japan and Germany during the Second World War. This includes more than 270 million anti-personnel sub-munitions released from cluster bombs.

Speaking at the National Cultural Centre in Laos, while announcing a grant of $90 million for landmine clearance operations in the country, President Obama came very close to apologizing for his country's war crime.

'For those years in the 1960s and 70s America's intervention in Laos was a secret to the American people who were separated by vast distances and a Pacific Ocean—and there was no Internet and information didn't flow as easily', he said, adding, 'for the people of Laos obviously this war was no secret'.

The money will be provided over the next three years and will be spent on surveying Laos for some 80 million unexploded cluster bombs dropped during the war. Obama told his audience that the USA has an obligation to help Laos clear the munitions that remain in the ground after bombing raids that have devastated large parts of the country.

'Villages and entire valleys were obliterated. Ancient plains were devastated. Countless civilians were killed. That conflict was another reminder that whatever the cause, whatever our intentions, war inflicts a terrible toll, especially on innocent men, women and children', Obama said, stopping short of offering a formal apology for the US actions.

He added:

Many of the bombs dropped never exploded. Over the years thousands of Lao people have been killed or injured, farmers tending fields, children playing. The wounds, a missing leg or arm, last a lifetime. That's why I've dramatically increased our funding to remove these unexploded bombs.

As *Vientiane Times* pointed out, about 580,000 secret bombing missions were carried out over Laos. A quarter of all villages in Laos are contaminated with UXO, the impact of which is particularly visible in many of the poorest districts.

Although the Indo-China war ended more than three decades ago, the bombs killed and injured about 50,000 people as a result of UXO incidents between 1964 and 2008, with many being women and children.

Explaining the effect of the atrocious actions, Somsack Pongkhao wrote in the *Vientiane Times*: the bombs that remain continue to have a major impact on the safety and livelihoods of rural people, diminishing their ability to cultivate crops and killing and maiming those who take the risk of working on contaminated land.

'Unexploded ordnance has a significant effect on social and economic development as a whole, increasing the cost of the construction of schools, hospitals and roads throughout Laos, due to the need to carry out clearance activities before work can begin.'

It is ironic that while the US Administration goes around the world, often asking the UNHRC and the International Court of Justice, to demand from countries in Asia, Africa and the Middle East to account for war crimes, it took almost 50 years to acknowledge its heinous actions in Laos.

Yet, as former American war correspondent in Laos and Vietnam Robert Scheer argued in an interview with The Real News Network, Obama used his visit for a charm offensive rather than accounting for one of the most horrendous war crime in history. 'If you don't take ownership for your own atrocities, you first of all have no authority to condemn atrocities anywhere in the world and you don't learn the lessons of history,' he argues.

'It was one of the most brutal uncivilized, vicious attacks on a people that we've seen in human history and the president is lying. It's a bald-faced lie to say oh people couldn't get the information because we didn't have the Internet', notes Scheer who has witnessed the atrocities, and documented and reported the same.

'There were plenty of journalists. They couldn't get mainstream media to cover the story in any effective way. But the most important thing was that the US government was very effective in lying about what it was doing.'

While these war crimes were well documented, Scheer notes that the USA never took ownership or responsibility for what it did. It was only in 2012 that Hillary Clinton went there as Secretary of State.

'This was a war against peasants. People who were using oxen to till their fields. Who barely knew what a pencil was and you went to war with them to destroy them, to demoralize them, and it had nothing to do with them', says Scheer. 'It had to do with China, it had to do with the Soviet Union, it had to do with some crazy ideas about the Cold War.'

By offering $90 million to clear mines, President Obama made it to look like an altruistic gesture to the Laotian people and the uncritical MSM assisted the process.

Even New Zealand, which was a US ally during the Vietnam War, chipped in with Prime Minister John Key, who was also attending the East Asia Summit in Vientiane that Obama attended, announcing a grant of $7.2 million to the United Nations Development Programme's (UNDP) UXO clearing operations.

The UNDP is headed by New Zealand's former Prime Minister Helen Clark who is also one of the candidates for the post of the UN secretary general.

Prime Minister Key said at a ceremony at the UXO Training Centre in Laos:

> New Zealand has a strong legacy of supporting UXO clearance around the world, including for the past 20 years in Laos, and this funding will make a real difference to the safety and economic prospects of the people here. We are proud to stand alongside the people and the government of Laos to continue this important work.

But no journalist present there asked him why couldn't New Zealand stand with the Lao people 60 years ago to stop the US atrocities or whether they were part of the bombing campaign?

Meanwhile, at a side event to the ASEAN Summit, from 6 to 8 September in the Lao capital, Prime Minister Thongloun Sisoulith and UN Secretary General Ban Ki-moon inaugurated Laos's own national SDG 18 on UXO. It says: 'Make lives safe from UXO; Remove the UXO obstacle to national development'.

Source: IDN (11 September 2016).

APPENDIX B

Rounding Up Coca-Colonization
Will the UN Human Rights Council Stand Up for the People?

Regulatory capture and the influence of powerful TNC in lobbying the policymakers towards their own advantage is no secret. Putting profits before people and planet is their ordinary course of business.

Now that the first draft of a legally binding treaty in International Human Rights Law has been submitted to the UNHRC, will they have the courage to stand up for the people against powerful TNC?

The draft was submitted on 16 July 2018 to the UNHRC and it should be in the agenda of the ongoing thrice yearly meeting of the council.

On 10 August 2018, a jury in Superior Court of California (San Francisco) has given a groundbreaking verdict by awarding US$290 million as compensation payable by Monsanto Corporation to DeWayne Johnson (46), groundskeeper dying of cancer. Jurors took into consideration the failure of Monsanto Corporation production of weed killer Roundup—which contains its main chemical ingredient glyphosate—to warn Johnson and other users about the possibility of cancer creating properties that are used in its weed-killing herbicide.

Bayer, the German chemical company which now owns Monsanto Corporation, has gone to media and stresses that their chemicals including Roundup are not harmful to users and is planning to appeal against the verdict given by the jury in California.

Methyl isocyanate leak in the Union Carbide factory in Bhopal, India, in 1984 took almost 3,787 lives. The Government of India estimated that the total causalities of the tragedy were around 15,000 human beings plus livestock. Toxic material remains, even after 30 years, many of those who were exposed to the gas have given birth to physically and mentally disabled children.

Business & Human Rights Resource Centre website reports that still a sum approximately to the tune of US$330 million is yet to be distributed to the victims to date, out of the Indian Supreme Court approved settlement as compensation payment of US$470 million in 1989.

In an interview after the California judgement, a senior official of Monsanto reveals that there are over 800 scientific researches done and which confirms that glyphosate does not create cancer and it is safe to use. Quite the contrary, the World Health Organization (WHO) warns that glyphosate may cause cancer among the users of the herbicide. But the USA and EU do not subscribe to WHO warnings.

UN's International Agency for Research on Cancer (IARC) declared in March 2015 that glyphosate probably raises the risk of cancer in people exposed. Accordingly, UN IARC claims glyphosate as a probable human carcinogen, a substance capable of causing disease in living tissue.

At the 26th session of the UNHRC, in July 2014, a resolution was adopted for the introduction of a legally binding instrument on TNC and other business enterprises (OBE) with respect of human rights.

The main focus of the proposed treaty was emphasizing that TNCs and OBEs have a responsibility to respect human rights, and civil society actors have a significant and legitimate role in promoting corporate social responsibility and in preventing, mitigating and seeking remedy for the adverse human rights impacts of TNC's and OBEs.

What is interesting to note is the original resolution put forward by Ecuador in 2014 was adopted after a vote of 20 in favour and 14 voting against it. Many human rights champion nations such as France, Germany, Ireland, Italy, Japan, the UK and the USA voted against the motion. In spite of their objections, the resolution was passed with the support of countries including China, India, Indonesia, Russia, South Africa and Vietnam.

The writer is the regional director responsible for the Finance Sector of UNI Global Union, Asia & Pacific Organization, Singapore.

Source: Jayasri Priyalal (IDN [21 September 2018]).

References

Alatas, S. Y. 2000. 'Intellectual Imperialism: Definition, Traits, and Problems.' *Southeast Asian Journal of Social Science* 28 (1): 23–45.
AMIC. 2000. *Media and Human Rights in Asia: An AMIC Compilation.* Nanyang Link: AMIC.
Amin, Samir. 1989. 'Eurocentrism.' *Monthly Review Press*, p. 152. New York.
AP. 2017, 27 June. *CNN Accepts Resignation of Three Involved in Retracted Story.* Available at https://www.yahoo.com/news/cnn-retracts-story-supposed-russian-175206933.html (accessed on 24 May 2019).
Arsenault, A. and M. Castells. 2008. 'Switching Power: Rupert Murdoch and the Global Business of Media Politics.' *Media Culture and Society* 23 (4): 488–513.
Asia News Network. 2017, 30 October. 'Fake News Epidemic Sweeps through Asia.' Bangkok: Asia News Network.
Balaji, J. 2011, 21 October. '"Paid News" Claims First Political Scalp as EC Disqualifies MLA.' *The Hindu.* Available at https://www.thehindu.com/news/national/paid-news-claims-first-political-scalp-as-ec-disqualifies-mla/article2556366.ece (accessed on 14 June 2019).
Balogh, S. 2017, 7 July. 'Too Many Anglo-Celtic Faces Running Australia.' Australian Human Rights Commission (AHRC), *The Australian.* Available at https://www.theaustralian.com.au/nation/politics/too-many-angloceltic-faces-running-australia-ahrc/news-story/e01d0475e36fef1ebd-40dd2625a17679 (accessed on 25 September 2019).
Bartlett, S. 2017, January. 'Cuban Medical Internationalism: Fidel Castro's Legacy Lives On.' Issue 4479/17. Penang Island: Third World Network.
Cammaerts, B., B. DeCillia, J. Magalhaes and C. Jienez-Martinez. 2016. *Journalistic Representation of Jeremy Corbyn in the British Press: From Watchdog to Attackdog.* London: London School of Economics. Available at https://www.lse.ac.uk/media@lse/research/pdf/JeremyCorbyn/Cobyn-Report-FINAL.pdf (accessed on 24 May 2019).
Chanda, N. 2014. 10 February. 'The Omnipresent Craft: Graft.' *Straits Times.*
Channel News Asia. 2016, 16 December. 'Thailand Passes Controversial Cyber-Crimes Law.' *CNA News.* Available at http://www.channelnewsasia.com/news/asiapacific/thailand-passes-controversial-cyber-crime-law/3372796.html (accessed on 24 May 2019).
Cheong, Yip Seng. 2015, 26 March. 'Under Lee Kuan Ywe, the Press Was Only as Free as It Need to be to Serve Singapore.' *South China Morning Post.*

Available at http://www.scmp.com/comment/insight-opinion/article/1747889/under-lee-kuan-yew-press-was-only-free-it-needed-be-serve (accessed on 24 May 2019).

Chomsky, Noam. 1991. 'Manipulating People: The Role of the Media Is Serving Power.' *Third World Resurgence*: 12.

Cockburn, P. 2013. 'Diary: Four Wars'. *London Review of Books*, 35(19): 38–39. Available at https://www.lrb.co.uk/v35/n19/patrick-cockburn/diary (accessed on 19 September 2019).

Cohen, B. 1963. The Press and Foreign Policy. New York, NY: Harcourt.

DePalma, A. 2016, 26 November. 'Fidel Castro, the Cuban Revolutionary Who Defied US, Dies at 90.' *New York Times*. Available at https://www.nytimes.com/2016/11/26/world/americas/fidel-castro-dies.html (accessed on 19 Sept 2019).

Dixit, K. 1997. *Dateline Earth: Journalism as if the Planet Mattered*. Manila: IPS.

Doward, J. 2017, 14 January. 'The Dark Side of Britain's Gold Rush: How Corruption Crept into Our Suburbs.' *The Guardian*. Available at https://www.theguardian.com/uk-news/2017/jan/14/corrupt-money-crept-britain-property-kleptocrats (accessed on 24 May 2019).

Florentino-Hofileña, C. 2004. *News for Sale: The Corruption and Commercialization of the Philippines Media*. Manila: Philippines Centre for Investigative Journalism.

Frau-Meigs et al. (2012). *From NWICO To WSIS 30 Years Of Communication Geopolitics: Actors and Flows, Structures and Divides*. UK/USA: Intellect.

Galtung, J. and R. C. Vicent. 1992. *Global Glasnost: Towards a New World Information and Communication Order?* New York, NY: Hampton Press.

George, C. ed. 2008. *Free Media Free Markets: Reflections on the Political Economy of the Press in Asia*. Singapore: Nanyang Link, AMIC.

———. 2014. *Sustaining Independent Journalism: Learning from Asia's Best*. Singapore: Asian Journalism Forum, NTU.

Goodman, M. 2017, 1 July. 'Why the Media Has Broken Down in the Age of Trump.' Opinion, *New York Times*. Available at http://nypost.com/2017/07/01/why-the-media-has-broken-down-in-the-age-of-trump/ (accessed on 24 May 2019).

Gauhar, A. 1979, July. 'Free Flow of Information: Myths and Shibboleths.' *Third World Quarterly* 1(3): 53–77.

———. 1984. '*Editorial: Putting the World on Notice*.' London: Third World Publications.

Gill, L. 2017, 27 November. 'Meghan Markle "Won't Be Allowed to be Black Princess" by Royal Family.' *Newsweek*. Available at https://www.newsweek.com/meghan-markle-will-be-told-royal-teachers-hide-her-biracial-identity-wont-be-723737 (accessed on 24 May 2019).

Grynbaum, M. M. 2017, 17 February. 'Trump Calls the News Media the "Enemy of the American People".' *New York Times*. Available at https://www.nytimes.

com/2017/02/17/business/trump-calls-the-news-media-the-enemy-of-the-people.html (accessed on 24 May 2019).

Gunaratne, S. A., M. Pearson and S. Senarath. 2015. *Mindful Journalism and News Ethics in the Digital Era*. New York, NY: Routledge.

Hall, J. 2016, 17 April. 'The Influencer Marketing Gold Rush Is Coming: Are You Prepared?' *Forbes*. Available at https://www.forbes.com/sites/johnhall/2016/04/17/the-influencer-marketing-gold-rush-is-coming-are-you-prepared/#229289834fb4 (accessed on 19 September 2019)

Hart, William. 2012. *Vipassana Meditation: The Art of Living*. Maharashtra, India: Vipassana Research Institute.

Herbert, J. 2005, December. 'East Meets West: Refocusing Communication and Journalism Education.' *Asia-Pacific Media Educator* 16: 33–39.

Herman, Edward and Noam Chomsky. 1988. *Manufacturing Consent: The Political Economy of the Mass Media*. New York, NY: Pantheon Books.

Herman, Edward and Robert McChesney. 1997. *Global Media: The New Missionaries of Global Capitalism*. London: Continuum.

Herman, E. 2003. *The Propaganda Model: A Retrospective, Against All Reason*, Vol. 1. Available at http://human-nature.com/reason/01/herman.html (accessed on 24 May 2019).

Hermawan, A. 2006, 23 July. 'Journalists Start against "Envelop Journalism".' *The Jakarta Post*.

Hickel, J. 2017, 14 January. 'Aid in Reverse: How Poor Countries Develop Rich Countries.' *The Guardian*. Available at https://www.theguardian.com/global-development-professionals-network/2017/jan/14/aid-in-reverse-how-poor-countries-develop-rich-countries (accessed on 24 May 2019).

Hobsbawm, J. 2003, 17 November. 'Why Journalism Needs PR.' *The Guardian*. Available at https://www.theguardian.com/media/2003/nov/17/mondaymediasection3 (accessed on 19 September 2019).

Husband, C. 1994. *A Richer Vision: The Development of Ethnic Minority Media in Western Democracies*. Paris/London: UNESCO/John Libby.

Irving, C. 2014. 'Its Time for Faith in Proper Stories.' *British Journalism Review* 25 (2). Available at http://journals.sagepub.com/doi/pdf/10.1177/0956474814538180 (accessed on 24 May 2019).

Kahn, J. 2007, 26 June. 'Murdoch's Dealings in China: It's Business, and It's Personal.' *New York Times*. Available at https://www.nytimes.com/2007/06/26/world/asia/26murdoch.html (accessed on 24 May 2019).

Khor, M. 2012. *Drone Strikes Have a Human Rights Dimension* (Third World Features 3847/12). Penang Island: Third World Network.

Klein, Naomi. 2017. *NO Is Not Enough: Defeating the New Shock Politics*. London: Allen Lane-Penguin.

Lloyd, J. and L. Toogood. 2015. *Journalism and PR: News Media and Public Relations in the Digital Age*. London: Reuters.

MacBride, S. ed. 1980. *Many Voices One World*. Paris: UNESCO.

Mair, V. H. 1994. 'Buddhism and the Rise of Written Vernacular in East Asia: The Making of National Languages.' *Journal of Asian Studies* 53 (3): 707–751.
Mankekar, D. R. 1979. *Media and the Third World*. New Delhi: Indian Institute of Mass Communication.
Masterton, M. ed. 1996. *Asian Values in Journalism*. Nanyang Link: AMIC.
McChesney, R. 1997. *Corporate Media and the Threat to Democracy, The Open Media Pamphlet Series*. New York, NY: Seven Stories Press.
McChesney, R. and E. Herman. 1998. *Global Media: Missionaries of Global Capitalism*. New York, NY: Continuum Books.
McCombs, M. E. and D. L. Shaw. 1972. 'The Agenda-Setting Function of Mass Media.' *Public Opinion Quarterly* 36 (Summer): 176–187.
McQuail, D. 2000. 'Some Reflections on Western Bias of Media Theory.' *Asian Journal of Communication* 10 (2): 1–12.
Meyssan, T. 2011, 20 August. 'War Propaganda: Libya and the End of Western Illusion.' *Global Research*. Available at https://www.globalresearch.ca/war-propaganda-libya-and-the-end-of-western-illusions/26084 (accessed on 24 May 2019).
Misra, S. G. 2000. *Democracy in India*. New Delhi: Sanbun Publishers.
Mishra, P. (2012). *From the Ruins of the Empire: Revolt Against the West and Remaking of Asia*. UK: Penguin.
Mitra-Jha, S. 2017, August. *Big Pharma, IP Wars and Profit over People* (4561/17). Penang Island: Third World Network.
Monbiot, G. 2016, *How Did We Get into This Mess?* Verso.
Morgon, J. 2012, 12 November. 'Buddhism's Diamond Sutra: Extraordinary Discovery of the World's Oldest Book.' *Huffington Post*. Available at http://www.huffingtonpost.com/joyce-morgan/diamond-sutra-buddhas-hidden-book_b_1859164.html (accessed on 28 May 2019).
Muzaffar, C. 2008. *Hegemony, Justice, Peace*. Kuala Lumpur: Arah Publications.
Nagara, B. 2015, 13 September. 'Invasion Have Effects.' *The Star*. Available at https://www.thestar.com.my/opinion/columnists/behind-the-headlines/2015/09/13/invasions-have-effects/ (accessed on 19 September 2019)
Ng, G. 2014, 16 February. 'China's Rich Migrating in Droves.' *Straits Times*, Singapore: 20.
Nordenstreng, K. 1997. 'Beyond the Fourth Theories of the Press.' In *Media and Politics in Transition: Cultural Identity in the Age of Globalisation*, 97–110. Born: ACCO.
Oeffner, A. 2005. *The Role of Inter Press Service in the International Mediascape: The Case of IPS Reporting on the 2005 World Social Forum* (Master's Thesis). Hamburg: Diplomica Verlag Gmbh. Available at https://books.google.co.th/books?id=MAjrDAAAQBAJ&printsec=frontcover&dq=inauthor:%22Anna lena+Oeffner%22&hl=en&sa=X&ved=0ahUKEwiQ5s_t597WAhULxbwK HXrWCrUQ6AEIJDAA#v=onepage&q&f=false (accessed on 20 June 2019).

Ostry, J. D, P. Loungani and D. Furceri. 2016, June. 'Neo-liberalism Oversold?' Finance and Development. Washington, DC: IMF. https://www.imf.org/external/pubs/ft/fandd/2016/06/pdf/ostry.pdf (accessed on 20 June 2019).

Quinn, S. 2013. *Asia's Media Innovators Volume 3: Crowdsourcing in Asian Journalism*. Jalan Besar: Konrad-Adenauer-Stiftung.

Payutto, P. A. 1992. *Buddhist Economics: A Middle Way for the Market Place*. Bangkok, Thailand: Buddhadhamma Foundation.

Pinter, Harold. 2005. *The Noble Lecture: Art, Truth and Politics*. Penang: Citizens International.

Profita, H. 2006, 31 March. 'Outside Voices: Samuel Freedman on the Difference Between the Ametuer and the Pro.' *CBC News*. Available at http://www.cbsnews.com/news/outside-voices-samuel-freedman-on-the-difference-between-the-amateur-and-the-pro/ (accessed on 20 June 2019).

Puntarigvivat, T. 2013. *Thai Buddhist Social Theory*. Bangkok: World Buddhist University.

Rajakarunanayake, L. 2010, 30 December. 'The East Path of Falsehood against Sri Lanka.' *Daily News*.

Raman, Anuradha. 2015, 23 March. 'Wrecking News.' *Outlook*. Available at http://www.outlookindia.com/magazine/story/wrecking-news/293690 (accessed on 20 June 2019).

Randall, D. 2011. *The Universal Journalist*, 4th ed. London: Pluto Books.

Roy, Arundhati. 2004. *The Ordinary Person's Guide to Empire*. London: Flemingo.

Sachs, J. 2012. *The Price of Civilization*. London: Vintage Books.

Sadouskaya-Komlach, Maryia. 2018, 9 February. 'Fake News in Visegrad: Overused and Underestimated.' *Green European Journal*. Available at https://www.greeneuropeanjournal.eu/fake-news-in-visegrad-overused-and-underestimated/ (accessed on 20 June 2019).

Seneviratne, K. 1998, 7 January. 'Currency Problem and the Media.' *New Straits Times*, Malaysia: 11.

———. 2003, 24 February. 'Need for Diverse Media Coverage.' *The Star*, Malaysia.

———. 2005. 'Devastating Silence: Why Is the Asian Tsunami Big News, But Not the Destruction of Fallujah?' *Aliran Monthly* 25 (11). Available at https://aliran.com/archives/monthly/2005b/11e.html (accessed on 20 June 2019).

———. 2012, December. 'Peoples' Movements or Dollar Chasing Democracy Vendors.' *Gateway*. Available at https://kalingasen.wordpress.com/2016/01/25/civil-society-peoples-movements-or-dollar-chasing-democracy-vendors/ (accessed on 20 June 2019).

Seneviratne, K. and Y. L. Hwee. eds. 2011. *Balancing Civil Rights and National Security: Impact of Anti-Terror Laws on Media and Civil Liberties in Europe and Asia*. Nanyang Link: EU Centre–AMIC.

Shafer, J. 2008, 13 February. 'The Political Re-education of Rupert Murdoch.' *Slate*. Available at http://www.slate.com/articles/news_and_politics/

press_box/2008/02/the_political_reeducation_of_rupert_murdoch.html (accessed on 20 June 2019).
Shipman, A. 2002. *The Globalization Myth*. London: Icon Books.
Siebert, F. S., T. Peterson and W. Schramm. 1956. *Four Theories of the Press*. Champaign, IL: University of Illinois Press.
Singh, U. B. 1998. *Administrative System in India: Vedic Age to 1947*. New Delhi: APH Publishing.
Somavia, Juan. 1980, 11 February. 'Can We Understand to Each Other?' *Newsweek*, p. 8.
South Centre. 2018, 19 July. 'The Contribution of Development, Including Poverty Reduction, in Promoting and Protecting Human Rights', No. 222. *SouthNews*. Available at https://www.southcentre.int/wp-content/uploads/2018/08/201807_The-South-Centre-Monthly-3.pdf (accessed on 10 June 2019).
Sparrows, J. 2017, 6 March. 'The Stench of the Iraq War Lingers Behind Today's Preoccupation with Fake News.' *The Guardian*. Available at https://www.theguardian.com/commentisfree/2017/mar/06/the-stench-of-the-iraq-war-lingers-behind-todays-preoccupation-with-fake-news (accessed on 20 June 2019).
Stableford, D. 2017, 29 June. 'Reporter Who Exploded at Sarah Huckabee Sanders During White House Briefing: "We Can't Take the Bullying Anymore".' *Washington*. Available at https://www.economist.com/international/2016/06/04/dont-be-so-offensive (accessed on 19 September 2019).
Tang, E. 2000, May. 'Sucidal Farm Policy'. Available at https://kalingasen.wordpress.com/2016/01/21/sri-lanka-suicidal-farm-policy/ (accessed on 25 September 2019).
Terra Viva. 1994. Conference daily published by IPS. 6 September. Cairo: IPS.
Thakurta, P.G and Reddy, K.S. 2010, 6 August. 'Paid News': The Buried Report. *Outlook*, India. Available at https://www.outlookindia.com/website/story/paid-news-the-buried-report/266542 (accessed on 19 September 2019).
The Economist. 2016a, 4 June. 'The Muzzle Grows Tighter.' Available at https://www.economist.com/international/2016/06/04/the-muzzle-grows-tighter (accessed on 20 June 2019).
———. 2016b, 4 June. 'Muted by Machetes.' *The Economist*, London. Available at https://www-economist-com.login.bibproxy.whu.edu/international/2016/06/04/muted-by-machetes (accessed on 19 September 2019).
———. 2016c. 'Don't Be So Offensive.' *The Economist*, London. Available at https://www.economist.com/international/2016/06/04/dont-be-so-offensive (accessed on 19 September 2019).
———. 2016d, 4 June. 'Under Attack.' *The Economist*, London. Available at https://www.economist.com/leaders/2016/06/04/under-attack (accessed on 19 September 2019).
The Telegraph. 2017, 16 March. 'What Is Fake News? Its Origins and How It Grew.' The Telegraph, London. Available at https://grassrootjournalist.

org/2017/06/17/what-is-fake-news-its-origins-and-how-it-grew-in-2016/ (accessed on 19 September 2019).

Thussu, D. 2007a. *News as Entertainment: The Rise of Global Infotainment.* London: SAGE Publications.

———. 2007b. 'The "Murdochization" of News: The Case of Star TV in India.' *Media Culture and Society* 29 (4): 593–611.

Time. 1997, 22 September. 'George Soros: He's Spending Millions to Save the World—And Getting Blamed for Wrecking Asia's Currencies.' *Time*, New York.

Vittachi, Tarzie. 1980, 11 February. 'Are Journalists News Vultures?' *Newsweek*, p. 8.

Wong, K. 2015. *Investments and ISDS in the TPP, Third World Resurgence* (Nov./Dec., No. 303–304, p. 16–23), Third World Network. Available at https://www.twn.my/title2/resurgence/2015/303-304/cover02.htm (accessed on 20 June 2019).

Xiaoge, Xu. 2005. *Demystifying Asian Values in Journalism.* New Industrial Rd: Marshall Cavendish.

Index

911 scuttling
   Global Justice Movement, 176
active pharmaceutical ingredients
   (API), 199
advertorial advertisement, 215–17
AID/WATCH, 191
Aleppo, 116
   Amnesty International (AI), 118
   BBC Moscow, 116
   ISIL, 115
   liberation, 120
   mainstream media, 118
   Media Lens, 117, 118
   Syrian city, 119
American communication text
   books, 28
American Media, 19
   autocarts language, 20
   Libertarian Media Function
   Theory, 21
   Trump, tweet, 19
Amnesty International (AI), 118
Anger Groups, 250
Anglo-American
   media, 121
   sanctions, 298
anti-Vietnam war movements, 62
Arab Spring, 247
   movement, 121
Arnab revolution
   news, panel discussion, 56–61
ASEAN Economic Community
   (AEC), 273
Asian Development Bank (ADB),
   286
Asian Media Summit in Bangkok, 88

Asian News Network (ANN), 237
Asian Tsunami of 2004, 112–14
Asia-Pacific Economic Cooperation
   (APEC), 178
Assange journalism, 67–71
Assassin Model of Censorship,
   150–51
Australia's Race Discrimination
   Commissioner Tim
   Soutphommasane, 12
Australian Broadcasting Corporation
   (ABC), 9, 223
Authoritarian Media Function
   Model, 4
   civil rights organisation, 6
   functions, 5

balancing civil rights and national
   security, 153–56
Bashar Al-Assad government, 298
Before Common Era (BCE), 273
Belt and Road Initiative (BRI), 274

Cheque Book Journalism (CBJ),
   217–20
civil rights, 62
coca-colonization, 311–13
commercialization and truth, 22
   media campaign, 23
Commitment to Reducing Inequality
   (CRI), 173
communication
   methodologies, 276
   technologies, 265
   theory
      balancing, 278

community news, 268–72
crisis in democracy, 64
cynical manipulation, 298

Daesh/Islamic State of Iraq and the Levant (ISIL), 115
Davos Class, 20–21
Delegitimizing, 226
  critical tone, 227
Department for International Development (DfID), 191
development rights
  model of Cuba and Castro Legacy, 139–46
disinformation, 256–58
Duterte's cybertroopers, 242–45

economically viable model, 303–306
envelopmental journalism, 214

fact-checkers, 110
fake news, 230–31, 252, 256–58
  claims, 237
  defined, 232–33
  origins, 234–35
  stifling democracy, 245–47
  stories
    The 21st Century, 250
filters, 31
Four Theories of the Press, 29
free media, 28, 62
Freedom of Expression (FOE), 146–49
  Blasphemy Laws and threat, 150–51

G20 Summit
  Argentinian capital, 83
  China daily, 83
  global media, 95–96
  Hiroshima and Pearl Harbour, 96–99
  interpretation
    Cairo and Baghdad 1994, 89–95

New York Times, 84
news values, 86–89
subjectivity, 86–89
  Cairo and Baghdad 1994, 89–95
Global Financial Integrity (GFI), 193
Global Media
  The New Missionaries of Global Capitalism, 207
globalized corruption, 182–84
glorious past, 13
Gross National Happiness (GNH) Index, 302

hope fading
  Beacon, 258–60
human rights, 126
  covenants
    UDHR, 135–36
  discourse, fundamental flaw, 127–30
  poverty reduction before, 138–39

imminent attack on Benghazi, 252–54
imperialism
  defined, 300
Indian Television News
  tabloidization, 55–56
Influencer Marketing (IM), 121
  ISIS armoury, 124–25
  journalism, 220–22
  video clip, 121
Intellectual Property (IP), 195
Inter Press Service (IPS), 202–204
  news agency, 88
Intercontinental Ballistic Missile (ICBM), 51
International Covenant on Civil and Political Rights (ICCPR), 137–38
International Criminal Court (ICC), 157
International Fact Checking network (IFCN), 111

International Media (IM)
  Mugabe, Zimbabwe, 130–35
  investor state dispute settlement
    (ISDS), 198
Iraq's weapons
  mass destruction, 252–54
journalism
  role, 49
  ICBM, 51
  Kim image, 52
  Korean dilemma, 52
  mass communication
    courses, 50
  peace in Korean peninsula, 52
  Singapore Summit, 50
  train jounalist, 53

Knowledge Ecology International
  (KEI), 199

labour migration, 285
laundering corrupt money
  west, 184–89
leaders
  Two-Thirds World, 108
liberalism dangers, 85–86
Liberation Tigers of Tamil Eelam
  (LTTE), 109
libertarian and cultural freedom
  model, 9
  ABC, 9
  Australia's Race Discrimination
    Commissioner Tim
    Soutphommasane, 12
  caste, issues, 14
  MCR, 10
  Ministry of Foreign Affairs, 11
  sensation, 15
  SLBC radio network, 10
Libertarian Media Function Theory,
  21, 22, 53
  features, 2
  practicalities, 2

roots, 28
strenghts, 2
Lippman's theory, 31

MacBride Report
  challenging international news
    norms, 78–83
Mahaveli Community Radio (MCR),
  10
mainstream media (MSM), 108
Malaysiakini, 239–42
manufacturing consent
  The Political Economy of the Mass
    Media, 30
mass communication, 276–78
Medecins Sans Frontiers (MSF), 196,
  199
  report, 197
media Delegitimizing
  attacks, 227
  lack of voice, 227
  ridicule, 227
  scron, 227
media genres, 265
media in crisis
  Chi, 18
  Murdoch's dealings, analysis, 18
  Western media values, 18
  world's biggest democracy, 24–27
media ownership
  concentration, 54
Mekong–Ganga Cooperation
  (MGC), 272
mindful journalism, 280, 291–92,
  287
mining taxes and development,
  181–82
Ministry of Foreign Affairs, 11
Mosul
  Amnesty International (AI), 118
  BBC Moscow, 116
  ISIL, 115
  mainstream media, 118
  Media Lens, 117, 118

neoliberalism
  backlash, 177–79
  economics, globalization, 173–76
  IMF policy, 179–81
  media, 21

New World Information and
    Communication Order
    (NWICO), 76–78
news filters
  advertising filter, 35–37
  arms manufacturers sponsor, 34–35
  flak filter, 38–39
  ownership filter, 32–33
  sourcing filter, 37–38
news vultures, 74–76
Nobel Peace prize
  Liu Xiaobo, 99–102
non-news producer, 209–10
North American Free Trade
    Agreement (NAFTA), 198

paid news phenomenon, 210–13
Panama Papers, 182–84
people-centric journalism, 297
Pew Research Centre Journalism
    Project, 22
Philippines Centre for Investigative
    Journalism (PCIJ), 65, 215
political leaders, 302
Press Foundation of Asia (PFA), 264
pro-China leanings, 73
pro-democracy activist, 62
propaganda (PR)
  blitz, 44
  demonising dissent, 46
  dramatic new evidence, 45
  emotional tone and intensity, 45
  manufacturing consensus, 46
  timing and strange coincidences,
      47–48
  campaign, 28
Propaganda Model (PM)
  essential ingredients, 31
public relations journalism, 39–44

Radio Free Asia (RFA), 293
Ramon Magsaysay Prizes, 103
  Abdon Nababan (Indonesia), 2017,
      104
  Conchita Carpio Morales
      (Philippines), 2016, 104
  Kommaly Chanthavong (Laos),
      2015, 105
  Thodur Madabusi Krishna (India),
      2016, 104
  Tony Tay (Singapore), 2017, 104
  Yoshiaki Ishizawa (Japan), 2017, 104
Regional Comprehensive Economic
    Partnership (RCEP), 195
Responsibility To Protect (R2P), 164
revisiting agenda-setting theory,
    114–15
Rohingya propaganda, 254–56
Rupert Murdoch's News Corporation,
    54

Sainath Formula, 294–97
small is beautiful, 204
social inequality
  dimension, 206
social media
  Guerilla War, 224–25
Social Responsibility Theory of
    media, 6
  Arab Spring, 8
  origin, 7
Sri Lanka Broadcasting Corporation
    (SLBC) radio network, 10
strategic communication, 256–58
Structural Adjustment Programme
    (SAP), 286
structural violence, 285
sufficiency economics, 204, 302
sustainable development goals
    (SDGs), 290
  devastating typhoons in South
      Pacific, 291–92
  farmers suicides, 292
  slum dwellers, 293

The Ganga-Mekong cultural flows, 273
Trade-Related Aspects of Intellectual Property Rights (TRIPS), 197
Trans-Pacific Partnership (TPP), 195
Trump's Fake News Awards, 228–30

unintentional misleading, 29
United National Human Rights Council (UNHRC), 157, 302
United Nations Economic and Social Commission for Asia and the Pacific (UNESCAP), 274
United Nations Educational Scientific and Cultural Organisation (UNESCO)
 report, 73
Universal Declaration of Human Rights (UDHR), 135–36
US Agency for International Development (USAID), 191
US mainstream media, 63
US war crimes in Asia, 307–310

video clip, 121
 gas attack, 123
 strategy, 123
 Western mainstream media, 123
war crimes
 adversarial reporting
  threat to human rights, 168–71
 ICC, allegations against Africa, 157–60
 R2P
  war on Libya, 164–68
 UNHRC
  bias against Sri Lanka, 160–64

Web 2.0, 260–62
Western journalism tradition, 266
Western journalists, 73
Western liberal democracies, 107
Western media, 248, 297
White House Correspondents Association (WHCA), 258
WikiLeaks journalism, 67–71
World Economic Forum (WEF), 201
World Social Forum (WSF), 201, 202

Yellow Jackets movement, 249

About the Author

Kalinga Seneviratne is a journalist, professor, radio broadcaster, television documentary-maker, media analyst and international communications specialist. He is former Head of Research, Asian Media Information and Communication Centre (AMIC), Singapore. Dr Seneviratne is a former Lecturer in the Faculty of Communication Arts, Chulalongkorn University, Bangkok, and Wee Kim Wee School of Communication and Information at the Nanyang Technological University, Singapore. He is a media analyst with many years of experience in journalism. He was the Australia and South Pacific correspondent for the Inter Press Service (IPS) news agency from 1991 to 1997 and continued to write for it for many years after that from countries in Asia, Middle East, Africa and Latin America. He has been a member of IPS' 'TerraViva' reporting team at a number of major UN conferences in the 1990s. He is currently the Southeast Asian Director for Berlin-based IDN (In-Depth News) and also writes for the *South China Morning Post* in Hong Kong and *Straits Times* in Singapore. Dr Seneviratne holds a PhD in international communications from Macquarie University, Australia, and MA in sociology from the University of Technology Sydney. He has been an award-winning radio broadcaster in Sydney. He received the Media Peace Award (1987) from the UN Association of Australia for a series on the relationship between rich and poor countries and the Educational Award (1992) from the Community Broadcasting Association of Australia for his services to the Australian community radio sector. He has several published works to his credit. Dr Seneviratne has also taught development journalism and international communications at the Macquarie University, Sydney; University of Technology Sydney; Bangkok University, University of Central Asia, Kyrgyzstan, and Ngee Ann Polytechnic, Singapore. He is currently working in collaboration with a number of Asian communication scholars to reform journalism education in Asia by introducing mindful communication strategies drawn from Asian philosophical roots.